The Humanities in Transition from Postmodernism into the Digital Age

The Humanities in Transition explores how the basic components of the digital age will have an impact on the most trusted theories of humanists. Over the past two generations, humanists have come to take basic postmodern theories for granted whether on language, knowledge or time. Yet Michel Foucault, Jacques Derrida and similar philosophers developed their ideas when the impact of this digital world could barely be imagined. The digital world, built on algorithms and massive amounts of data, operates on radically different principles.

This volume analyzes these differences, demonstrating where an aging postmodernism cannot keep pace with today's technologies. The book first introduces the major influence postmodernism had on global thought before turning to algorithms, digital space, digital time, data visuals and the concept to digital forgeries. By taking a closer look at these themes, it establishes a platform to create more robust humanist theories for the third millennium. This book will appeal to graduate students and established scholars in the Digital Humanities who are looking for diverse and energetic theoretical approaches that can truly come to terms with the digital world.

Nigel A. Raab is professor of Russian history at Loyola Marymount University, Los Angeles, California.

Routledge Studies in Cultural History

Cultural Organizations, Networks and Mediators in Contemporary Ibero-America
Edited by Diana Roig-Sanz and Jaume Subirana

Soldiers and Their Horses
Sense, Sentimentality and the Soldier-Horse Relationship in The Great War
Jane Flynn

The Magic Lantern at Work
Witnessing, Persuading, Experiencing and Connecting
Edited by Martyn Jolly and Elisa deCourcy

Women Photographers of the Pacific World, 1857–1930
Anne Maxwell

How Books, Reading and Subscription Libraries Defined Colonial Clubland in the British Empire
Sterling Joseph Coleman, Jr.

Russia's French Connection
A History of the Lasting French Imprint on Russian Culture
Adam Coker

Transatlantic Encounters in History of Education
Translations and Trajectories from a German-American Perspective
Edited by Fanny Isensee, Andreas Oberdorf, and Daniel Töpper

The Humanities in Transition from Postmodernism into the Digital Age
Nigel A. Raab

For more information about this series, please visit: www.routledge.com/Routledge-Studies-in-Cultural-History/book-series/SE0367

The Humanities in Transition from Postmodernism into the Digital Age

Nigel A. Raab

NEW YORK AND LONDON

First published 2020
by Routledge
52 Vanderbilt Avenue, New York, NY 10017

and by Routledge
2 Park Square, Milton Park, Abingdon, Oxon, OX14 4RN

Routledge is an imprint of the Taylor & Francis Group, an informa business

© 2020 Taylor & Francis

The right of Nigel A. Raab to be identified as author of this work has been asserted in accordance with sections 77 and 78 of the Copyright, Designs and Patents Act 1988.

All rights reserved. No part of this book may be reprinted or reproduced or utilised in any form or by any electronic, mechanical, or other means, now known or hereafter invented, including photocopying and recording, or in any information storage or retrieval system, without permission in writing from the publishers.

Trademark notice: Product or corporate names may be trademarks or registered trademarks, and are used only for identification and explanation without intent to infringe.

Library of Congress Cataloging-in-Publication Data
Names: Raab, Nigel A., 1968– author.
Title: The humanities in transition from postmodernism into the
   digital age / Nigel A. Raab.
Description: New York : Routledge, 2020. | Series: Routledge studies
   in cultural history; vol 89 | Includes bibliographical references and
   index.
Identifiers: LCCN 2020015959 (print) | LCCN 2020015960 (ebook) |
   ISBN 9780367896799 (hardback) | ISBN 9781003020493 (ebook) |
   ISBN 9781000091465 (adobe pdf) | ISBN 9781000091472 (mobi) |
   ISBN 9781000091489 (epub)
Subjects: LCSH: Digital humanities. | Postmodernism. | Culture—
   Philosophy.
Classification: LCC AZ105 .R28 2020 (print) | LCC AZ105 (ebook) |
   DDC 001.30285—dc23
LC record available at https://lccn.loc.gov/2020015959
LC ebook record available at https://lccn.loc.gov/2020015960

ISBN: 978-0-367-89679-9 (hbk)
ISBN: 978-1-003-02049-3 (ebk)

Typeset in Sabon
by Apex CoVantage, LLC

To the city of Los Angeles, my city of inspiration

Contents

	Acknowledgments	viii
1	Introduction	1
2	The Achievement of Postmodernism	23
3	The End of the Linguistic Turn	43
4	The End of Theory in the Humanities	70
5	The Influence of Algorithms on Humanistic Thought	89
6	Digital Space	110
7	Digital Time	130
8	Data Visuals	147
9	Digital Forgeries	161
10	Conclusion	176
	Bibliography	190
	Index	200

Acknowledgments

The thanks for every book should really be longer than the book itself, but I will keep it short. A big thank you to Max Novick at the press for his guidance. Once again, I have to thank Alice Raab, who in another era would have been a master editor at a major publishing house. She turns clotted prose into something readable and saves me from all my bad intellectual habits. I also must thank the anonymous readers who did much of the same by forcing me to clean up shaky ideas and drop anchors where I started to drift. My dad, Tony, has always encouraged me to seek new thoughts and pursue my dreams. Carolyn Peter, my wife, is the sounding board for so many crazy schemes. She is the warm soul whose sensitivity fills every room of our house, and without her I would probably be little more than moss on a log.

Venice Beach, 2020

1 Introduction

Well over a generation ago, a movement arrived on the academic scene and spurred a series of energetic debates that engaged the brightest minds on both sides. In the aftermath of World War II, a younger generation was ready for a fundamental reassessment of the Western project. If the Nazis were a reflection of a Western value system born in the Enlightenment of the eighteenth century, then the system was corrupt at its core. In the words of philosophers and literati, the core was formed by a rational worldview that could be as stifling and repressive as Enlightenment thinkers had believed it to be liberating. Rationality was the heart of the death star and had to be destroyed.

Combatant metaphors serve well because any attempt to undermine rationality was quickly challenged by traditional scholars who were convinced that the Western tradition with its emphasis on objectivity and rationality had improved the lot of human beings on planet earth. These scholars mocked the idea that knowledge was relative, that the outcome of science was the result of mob rule in the laboratory, and that human rights were a cultural construct. This stubbornness drew battle lines that were fought on many fronts, and these serious battles continued for decades.

As this division spread into curricula in colleges around the world, the academic environment became polarized between postmodernists and their predecessors. Postmodernists rejected attempts to save the Western tradition and urged their students to denounce male hegemony, discourses of power, and modern imperialism on the basis of some form of relativism. Much like the Slavophiles and Westernizers in Russia in the 1840s, the two groups could no longer walk on the same side of the street. Allan Bloom equated the demotion of the works of great white men with the closing of the American mind, as he titled his book.[1] Turning in the opposite direction, postmodernists saw their mission as the opening of the American mind and continued to fight vigorously against scholars such as Bloom.

Back then, postmodernism was in its early adulthood and acted with an energy appropriate to its age. If we can pin its adolescence to the seminal works by Jacques Derrida and Michel Foucault in the 1960s, by the

2   Introduction

1980s it was a mature and widespread force that sought its own place in the sun. This was a well-deserved place, and with time, postmodernists no longer had to worry about being silenced. In the 1960s, to suggest that science was socially constructed was radical and ran up against massive criticism from outside the humanities. Nowadays, to say otherwise is to invite massive criticism from within the humanities. Postmodern ideas slowly entered the mainstream—checking a box marked gender rather than one marked sex comes to mind—and their vision was accepted, if reluctantly and with certain reservations, by the rest of the academy. Even if this was by no means a clear victory, shared space had been achieved.

But what happens to a movement once it achieves its main goals? In the 1920s, many suffragists were at a loss because now that women had the right to vote, they were not sure what to do. In the Soviet Union, dissident artists struggled with perestroika precisely because art designed to disrupt censorship laws lacked oxygen when the censorship laws were reduced or eliminated. Similarly, postmodernism lost much of its flair not because it was objectively wrong, but because it became commonplace. Instead of harnessing youthful energies, it became a tool for established scholars who were satisfied with a few pithy references to postmodern theories. If mention of the 'gaze' brought excitement and bewilderment in the 1970s, it has now become a cliché lacking vital signs. One need only look at the basic vocabulary in numerous current books. Readers will see frequent references to discourse, language, agency, social construction, cultural construction, and more. In fact, with the aging of postmodernism, some ideas have taken on the quality of a truth, the idea they were designed to oppose. References to social construction are presented as absolutes; to proclaim an event or a tradition as socially constructed is to proclaim a self-evident truth. In accepting the notion in such an unquestioning fashion, intellectuals are unwittingly reversing the direction of the postmodern impulse. The adolescent has aged and, like us all, struggles to cope in a new environment as trends change and innovations shift our thinking.

The most energetic and dynamic challenges come from the digital world. Scholars have been adapting to technological change for generations, but few could predict the sweeping impact of digital technologies. Whether in public life, in the scientific laboratory, or amongst humanists, the digital influence is never far away. In the most straightforward instances, it is a source of marvel because of the ease with which it makes information accessible; curious individuals can create web platforms and spread their ideas more broadly. In San Francisco, the Internet Archive has preserved massive amounts of web data, searchable and available for research projects. On the surface, all these innovations sound like practical tools that simply facilitate larger, more ambitious undertakings.

It is too convenient, however, to think of these digital technologies as mere instruments that assist the completion of ongoing projects. The digital milieu represents a caesura with older methods for any number of reasons. In fact, the digital world collides with many standard postmodern themes. Unfortunately, the collision of postmodern theory with the digital world has been presented as unproblematic, especially in volumes such as *Debates in the Digital Humanities* where one regularly comes across references to *discourses, epistemologies,* and *narratives* as if they function no differently in a digital environment.[2] In a similar spirit, David J. Bodenhamer writes, "the use of appropriately cast spatial technologies . . . promises to develop a unique postmodern scholarship."[3] Alternatively, scholars present digital research as a practical and straightforward empirical affair. In *Digitization in the Real World,* the editors note this is "a book written by practitioners for practitioners" on the process of digitization; it is not interested in the interpretive impact.[4] As a result, little attention has been paid to analytical contradictions in the following domains: the discord between Big Data's link to positivist methods of the nineteenth century and postmodernism's basic mistrust of quantification; how digital translation tools have challenged the concept of linguistic incommensurability; the tension between social time of the postmodernists and the universal time which exerts an enormous influence in the digital environment; and the rapid increase in data visuals at the expense of traditional text in humanist scholarship.

All too often the answer to the digital challenge is to look backwards, not forwards. Instead of thinking about how postmodern ideas have to be adjusted to digital realities, the same terms and vocabulary are introduced as a humanist counterthrust to the digital impulse. In her article *Humanistic Theory and Digital Scholarship*, Johanna Drucker recognizes the potential danger of the Digital Humanities and stresses that "if we are to assert the cultural authority of the humanities in a world whose fundamental medium is digital," theories from the humanities must have a critical purchase on digital platforms.[5] Although this could not be more true, she advocates the promotion of humanistic theories—poststructuralism, postcolonialism, and deconstruction—that were developed more than half a century ago. How can theories developed in the 1960s in a completely different historical environment stand as a bulwark against the excesses of the digital age?

Time and again, there is a reluctance to move on from standard themes and standard vocabularies, as if no matter what happens in the external world, the same postmodern premises can offer an adequate solution. In a commemorative edition of Derrida's *Of Grammatology*, Gayatri Chakravorty Spivak downplays the technological revolution. The "cybernetic and infometrics revolution" is dismissed because its revolutionaries "are using not a new discourse to fix the new inventions, but versions of the millennial ethnocentric and Europacentric ideology of the thinking of Europe." In brackets, she adds, "The World Wide Web works on psychologistic and positivistic reductions of the ideas of text, recovery, memory, access, and especially, interaction."[6] The comments are ironic because they appear in the 40th Anniversary edition and give the impression that nothing has changed since the first edition appeared in France. It is not enough to dismiss cybernetics and infometrics with tools that were developed in the middle of the twentieth century. Many of the celebrated aspects of postmodernism are ill-suited to a contemporary world so distant from Paris of the 1960s, where postmodernism first gained momentum.

The digital world is not incommensurable with postmodernism, but one cannot assume that postmodern ideas can operate timelessly in any environment; it as an inherent corollary to postmodernism that its natural force will erode. The accomplishments of postmodernism do not have to be denied, but the achievement must be met with critical eyes to see both where its energies are still vibrant and where the spirit has waned. The energies are best revealed by highlighting the brazen ventures whose lasting impact is not always self-evident. Within the ivory tower and out on the street, postmodern gestures are ubiquitous if often unrecognized, as so much of its accomplishments go unnoticed. There is no contradiction celebrating success as a lifetime achievement award, while recognizing that the recipient is no longer at the summit of her career. It becomes necessary to evaluate those aspects of the canon that demand more urgent change. In the spirit of the idea that every end is a new beginning, the postmodern predilection for language and theory deserves a more critical eye because these positions are nearing their end. The end of the linguistic turn and the end of theory may ring overly dramatic, yet these two crutches of the postmodern generation need a deeper evaluation because they simply cannot exist in the same way in the digital environment.

Digital developments have presented humanists with convenient tools which are shifting basic methodologies and, as a consequence even if yet unspoken, are nibbling away at the underlying premises of postmodernism. For example, the algorithm is a common buzzword, almost an invective at this point, but little effort has been made to examine how basic decision-making processes within an algorithm impact humanist theories. Since humanists have actually started to employ algorithms, the basic principles have to be contextualized relative to older conceptual models. Similarly, the relevance of Big Data requires elucidation in a multifaceted manner. From its basic principles to its modification of concepts of space and time to its visualization in any number of forms, Big Data must be better positioned vis-à-vis postmodernism because to simply accept Big Data is to undermine postmodernism altogether. Conversely, to reject it in favor of a naïve allegiance to postmodernism is to live in an age other than our own. A closer look creates a more congenial atmosphere for the two even if one partner is definitely the elder statesperson. In addition to these digital concerns, the discussion is rounded out with words on digital forgeries. Because postmodernism was so concerned with blurring the boundaries between fact and fiction, forgery is an exemplary test case that has yet to receive the philosophical attention it merits: what is a digital forgery, and does it have the same authorial and epistemological connotations of art forgeries that have been the subject of such fascination over the years? The subject of forgery, complex in the simplest of times, confirms the old saw that there is always more work to be done. All these issues need elaboration, but the path to clarity must begin by understanding the postmodern achievement, tracing its waning powers, and then examining what happens in the digital age.

Stripped of much of its tedious jargon, postmodernism was at heart a celebration of human diversity and the complex qualities of life: the qualities that fill us with emotion, make us see many colors where previously we saw only one, and distinguish between the sounds in our environments. In this sense it took its lead from Nietzsche, who was truly of the earth, explored all our inner instincts, and situated humans in a world of plants, animals, and diverse geographical terrain. It took a relativistic interpretation from Nietzsche to argue that truths were social constructs, the mind a convenient fiction, and the world a home to fluctuating values.

Practically and indirectly, postmodernism opened the way to accepting cultural achievements. Bypassing Mozart and Beethoven as the standards of excellence, Westerners reluctantly came to realize that other cultures had rather complex musical schemes that produced enjoyable sounds. Instead of viewing African artistic production as magical native crafts, as Picasso did at the ethnographic museum at the Palais du Trocadéro in the early twentieth century, philosophers of a postmodern persuasion argued that *crafts* was a derogatory term that denied these cultures an artistic aesthetic.[7] On the street level, this meant that postmodernism was instrumental in moving non-European artistic creation from museums of natural history to *bona fide* art museums. Although this took decades, eventually this process would be promoted by individuals who had no direct connection to postmodernism. To repurpose words of Isaiah Berlin intended for positivists, the postmodernists had done their work so well, they no longer needed to be mentioned.[8]

A similar phenomenon lies with the simple shift from sex to gender—a simple shift that took an enormous amount of intellectual energy but is now something that, far from being locked into a theoretical ivory tower, has an accessible public moment every time someone fills out a form. And it is more than filling out forms. The word 'gender' as mentioned earlier incorporates options and diversity that were more limited when an applicant filled the rectangle marked 'sex' with either male or female. That box became a window through which one could see oneself in many ways—homosexual, heterosexual, transgendered, and anything in between. Identity is by no means a solved problem, but when that window is opened, a breeze of broad acceptance fills the room.

The study of science also underwent change and was a significant battleground because it represented the most protected bastion of objectivity. On the heels of Thomas Kuhn's *Structure of Scientific Revolutions*, postmodernists pressured scholars to look for subjectivity in science.[9] If James Conant had presented his readers with objective sketches of measurement devices, a generation later Steven Shapin and Simon Schaffer looked at how the seventeenth-century air-pump was situated in religious and political representations.[10] Using extensive references to Foucault, they argued that science was as much about discursive acts as it was about laboratory experiments. To be sure, many of these arguments were overdrawn and too many historians flogged the discourse of science, but science is now analyzed more holistically.

The net is being cast widely, and maybe too much credit is being given to postmodernism. One can come to respect other cultures and value their achievements without dipping into relativism and rather arcane theories of language (Johanna Drucker gives the mistaken impression that poststructuralism and its kin are the only prisms through which to glimpse the aesthetic life).[11] Because Mozart's operas were rejected as a universal standard, some circles forgot about Mozart altogether. When this happened, we can sympathize with Allan Bloom and his talk about the closing of the American mind; a narrow approach to theoretical innovation closed many minds.

Postmodern arguments were designed to invite controversy, but in the main, more avenues were opened than closed. Although it took decades, fields of research broadened out as philosophers promoted a world without a center, a world of pluralistic inquiry. The central focus was the dynamic possibilities of human expression. The emphasis was on the qualitative and not quantitative aspects of human life, whether as studied by the historian or by the philosopher or by the literary critic. Historians, for example, left quantitative research to quantitative disciplines. This pleased humanists because in a technological century, they no longer had to justify themselves against the hard sciences (since they gained a degree of self-confidence having debunked the objectivity of science). This was great news at the end of the second millennium.

Although the achievements deserve acquaintance, shortcomings are of more consequence when studying transitions because they show the position of postmodernism as it was about to bump up against digital realities. This is an opportunity not to argue that the original was wrong but that the original idea lost its compass as the energies waned. This is particularly true with respect to the linguistic turn and the philosophy of language. The philosophy of language predates postmodernism by a number of generations, and it is no exaggeration to suggest that the twentieth century was the century of the philosophy of language. Leonard Bernstein argued that music was language, Christian Metz maintained that film was a language, and Arthur Danto posited that an artwork was akin to a text. Ultimately, it became the cause célèbre of postmodernists and therefore warrants closer attention so the role of language in a digital environment will be understood in the largest context possible.

The postmodern approach was to take the philosophy of language and employ it in the service of relativism. It began with the premise that all knowledge was mediated through language (a premise that is nowadays often forgotten) and built a number of outcomes from that position. In its pithiest form, the linguistic turn is expressed in Derrida's popular slogan: there is no *hors texte*; nothing exists outside of language. Thereafter, studies put linguistic usage on center stage. It gave the impetus to seminal works such as Hayden White's *Metahistory*.[12]

Those in favor of the linguistic turn were not arguing that language was important, for that has been clear ever since the Bible asserted God gave humans the word. Nor, in the spirit of Johann Gottfried Herder, were they taking the origins of language from God and placing it in the hands of humans.[13] Rather, they were arguing that the primary factor in the formation of knowledge was language, and therefore they gave language the primary epistemological role; language became more than *primus inter pares*. This role had previously been dominated by theological or metaphysical ponderings. With this step taken, it was another short step to argue two principal positions. First, knowledge was a social construction dependent upon linguistic conventions of individual communities. Second, to control language was to exercise power. This last version relates to the link Foucault made with discourse and power that inspired humanists up and down the line.

Soon variants of these ideas became commonplace, though they were all based on postmodern assumptions. Hayden White contended that the structure of historians' prose could be compared with the structure of fictional prose, thus suggesting that this stylistic fiction was more central than the objective facts historians wanted to present to their readers. The blurring of the lines between historical fact and fiction was a key postmodern strategy. Other scholars argued that totalitarian states were successful because they managed to control the language or build a new civilization with a few well-placed expressions. Over the years, language gained a hegemonic position, shoving alternatives to the periphery. Linguistic usage, however, has become a much more data-driven affair, upsetting notions of discourse that thrived in a purely humanistic world. As databases become more available, humanists will be tempted to employ the methodologies of cognitive linguists who have been collecting language samples for years.

To be sure, the linguistic turn was instrumental in destabilizing objectivity. Along the way, however, it employed linguistic ideas selectively and pushed numerous alternatives to the side. In reviewing the literature of the 1980s and 1990s, one cannot avoid the impression that analytic philosophers and cognitive linguists were conveniently ignored. In worst cases, these philosophers were used indiscriminately to do no more than drive home the same point over and over again. Random invocations of Ludwig Wittgenstein, a philosopher of language in the British analytic tradition, litter the landscape. Wittgenstein's language game, a prominent concept in Shapin and Schaffer's seminal work on the history of science, has suffered more than its fair share of abuse. It is deeply unfortunate that Wittgenstein employed the term *game* because it has become associated with the loose play, the playfulness of the postmodernist, rather than the complex rule-oriented system of the analytical philosopher. Over and over again, the expression is invoked to mean that two sides were doing different things (playing different games), though no linguistic evidence or linguistic rules are presented to substantiate the claim. How can one know the boundary between two language games if both sides are speaking English?

Rarely, if ever, are such questions addressed. In the process, linguistic rules, grammatical forms, verb tenses, or other complexities find no place in the discussion. The dominant form is to focus on select words and draw conclusions from there, though words represent a tiny fraction of the complete structure of language. In the heyday of the linguistic turn, such methods could be excused because they were part of the excitement of a young movement. Now, however, these are signs that the time has come to move on.

The concept of distant reading is symbolic of emerging challenges to a twentieth-century understanding of the linguistic turn. In a book of the same title, Franco Moretti has taken aim at the common postmodern practice of close textual analysis.[14] Instead of dissecting the multiple valences of a single word, Moretti established a digital laboratory that canvasses the appearances of words in thousands upon thousands of written texts; Moretti's laboratory could offer a literary interpretation without anyone on the team actually having read the novel or all the novels in the sample. The approach differs dramatically from Derrida, who looked for multiple traces in each word. Nor does it resemble a Geertzian thick-or-thin description, as the digital approach has a method of its own. Although distant reading is both a real and metaphorical confrontation with the linguistic turn, it does not fully flesh out those increasingly unacceptable components of the linguistic turn.

In particular, the dynamic elements of the linguistic turn have dissipated over time. The original philosophical puzzles that intrigued Wittgenstein and his followers are now gathering dust, as linguistic analysis is being equated with basic linguistic usage. Scholars make assertions about the language of specific cultures or societal groups to point out that these people used language and meant something by it. Hardly the most fascinating idea. They rarely pay attention to grammatical forms or philosophically re-evaluate the relationship between language, the external world, and our own biological composition. Most such suggestions are met with resistance and the reassertion of sweeping claims about the social construction of language.

In his early work, the *Tractatus-logico-philosophicus*, Wittgenstein wrote about the limits of language, a theme that sounds familiar to postmodernism. He recognized that language had limits, but these were not the limits of experience since something operated on the other side of language.[15] One of his central points was that certain things, such as spirituality, existed outside the trivial contours of linguistic usage. In this vein, all sorts of experiences—sound, touch, odor, vision—have nothing to do with language at all, nor need they be translated into some form of language. If we begin to recognize this, though many historians of the senses still adhere to discursive methodologies, this silent admission will open new doors and admit changes into the applicability of postmodern ideas.

This plea to end the linguistic turn is not asking to end the study of language. It seeks only to attenuate the dominance of language. Language should be neither the omnipresent arbiter nor the holistic umbrella under which all studies find themselves; then it falls in the hegemonic trap of philosophy before it. The inquisitive mind will want alternatives and a means to visit those parts of the world whose existence begins before language and ends outside of it. Moreover, tools such as Google Translate have changed the rules dramatically and have effectively eliminated linguistic incommensurability. To recognize this shifting terrain, one has to look at how the linguistic turn has been unsettled. By examining the original euphoria that accompanied it, one gets a better sense for its sweeping impact and the blind devotion it encouraged. It then sets a foundational position to see clearly where the digital age forces a divergent path upon us.

In its application, the linguistic turn was surrounded by a nimbus of theory. Not all authors understood the theories, but they happily and often carelessly referred to theoretical slogans such as the *hors texte*. This came about because a fascination with language was tied to postmodernism's association with theory. Over the centuries, disputes have regularly pitted scholars against each other, but only postmodernists were involved in a dispute called the theory wars.

As the theory wars were such an intense part of postmodern identity, talk of the end of theory must sound like heresy. While the idea was conceptually impossible for a combatant of the 1980s to grasp, 'the end of theory' has become an increasingly popular word sequence that pops up in unexpected places. In 2008, Chris Anderson published an article with the phrase in the title.[16] He argued that the traditional method of scientific theory-making had lost its effectiveness. Since algorithms analyzed data without a real-world understanding of that data and could still present identifiable and meaningful trends, the older methods no longer had any function. Data processors could independently identify trends and actively provide solutions to problems. Not everyone has agreed with this controversial proposition, but it nevertheless demonstrates that scientists will have to shift their perceptions of theory.[17]

Theory in a scientific milieu differs from theory in a humanistic milieu, but Anderson's assertion should not be ignored. Humanists successfully showed that scientists were not immune to social forces and thus humanists will not be immune to scientific forces. Research which involves databases has become so common amongst humanists, they too will be subject to the same pressures as scientists. Of course, the end of theory would come as quite a blow, especially for scholars such as Quentin Skinner who wrote about the "Return of Grand Theory."[18] For theory to return in the 1980s only to then disappear a generation later represents quite a conundrum. Yet there can be no doubt that the presence of data in the humanities will change the theories we choose and the manner in which we understand what a theory is.

As Skinner's title suggests, the process being considered is one of departures, returns, and arrivals. As such, the transition must be considered in a broad historical time frame, for an expression such as the return of grand theory suggests theory had its moment, was replaced by something, and then reemerged. If we accept that chain of events, then the potential end of theory represents another moment of departure. These ups and downs require historical perspective, because if it was acceptable for Skinner to write about the return of theory, then something akin to the end of theory might equally be considered the return of something else.

For this reason, the number one suspect for a return is positivism, a movement most postmodern theories were designed to reject. Yet the surge of modern data production has many commonalities with Comtean positivism—collect data on human activities upon which to make sweeping claims (the potential resurgence of positivism has already been noted in a variety of circles). Auguste Comte emphatically rejected the abstraction of theologians and metaphysicists before him, so he represents a movement against the abstract theories so popular amongst postmodernists. Postmodernists were neither theologians nor metaphysicists, but they promoted abstract theories that did not require mass data.

Comte was not fundamentally against theory, as he did search for general laws, but he was against abstract theorizing. To fully contextualize Comte's version, the road from his positivism to today's world of Big Data needs to be traced insofar as it pertains to conceptual theories. On the one hand, Comte's positivism, in whatever mutated form, had a massive impact until the 1950s. On the other hand, almost immediately after he introduced his ideas in the 1830s and 1840s, voices were heard calling for more abstract theorizing and less of a dependency on naïve factuality. If Comte's positivism stressed a deep empirical bias, thinkers such as Wilhelm Dilthey pushed for more abstraction. Soon thereafter, the European intellectual world took theorizing to its limits as more and more abstract impulses guided intellectual and artistic creation. Theorizing was detaching itself from realism and advocating new constellations. Martin Heidegger was deeply troubled by shifts in theory, and the postmodernists later built on this trend in the middle of the twentieth century. The postmodern upswell came precisely at that time when philosophers were ready to declare the death of positivism. It took a hundred years, but fact-based proclivities were finally replaced by abstract theorizing.

It is this historical process that needs to be examined because it puts the contemporary pressure on theory into context. Moreover, it opens a space to discuss how the arrival of data will invite more positivist trends. Even if we accept that the original positivism has worn thin, emerging strands of a positivist approach are a corollary to the current theoretical transformation: not in the *urform* Comte desired (few self-proclaimed academic positivists followed him anyway), but in a form that shows greater respect for well-ordered facts, facts researchers have come to depend upon in the digital age. This theoretical rupture thus becomes a singular moment to re-evaluate conceptual schemes when the return of grand data is nudging aside the return of grand theory.

Once this historical and theoretical excursus has exposed initial problems for postmodernism in the digital age, one can put the conversation on a digital footing and investigate applications in the digital world. The foremost candidate in this regard is the algorithm, because the algorithm produces a massive amount of directed data. Chris Anderson wrote, "statistical algorithms find patterns where science cannot."[19] The power of the algorithm has become well known, almost legendary, and it has emerged as a dominant player. Rather than dissecting the algorithm to reveal its mathematical nuts and bolts, one must take a closer look at the algorithm in a manner the humanist can understand.

The reluctance of humanists to dig into mathematics is no surprise, and one does not necessarily need to heed a call to code. Nevertheless, more effort is required to see how the nature of algorithmic decision-making runs up against the postmodern canon. Postmodernists railed against binary decision-making, yet this underlies fundamental algorithmic commands; an algorithm cannot function without logical commands that depend on binary operations. The output of the algorithm does not have to create a binary, but all the decisions that result in that output do. How can one deny binaries while depending upon them?

Algorithms as active tools in the humanities have been around for a relatively short time, but they have already been evaluated. In what is to be expected, humanists have pointed out that Google algorithms, far from representing objective mathematics, can have socially disturbing outputs. In *Algorithms of Oppression*, Safiya Noble has shown troubling racist and gendered outcomes that are often unknown to the producers of the algorithms.[20] These important analyses are, however, embedded in a postmodern language and focus on the empirical output of the algorithm. Noble writes of the gendered discourse these algorithms produce, a sentence that might well have appeared in a postmodern work of the mid-1980s. The producer of data is new, but the analysis follows a familiar road. The thornier question about the theoretical impact of the algorithm on discourse theory is left aside for what might be considered more pressing practical matters. Noble's work directly addresses a grave contemporary concern, but it still treats the algorithm as a black box with a disconcerting output. When we probe into that black box, unexpected discoveries will shift conceptual frameworks and reveal new dilemmas.[21]

Alternatively, the algorithm can be situated in a variety of helpful contexts that make a logical phenomenon of structural interest to humanists. For example, every algorithm has a feedback loop that returns a past answer into a future decision. This immediately suggests a complex attitude to time within the calculation. More directly, the feedback loop can be compared to Derrida's notion of the trace, an idea that involves a lingering past presence in the future of an object; no object is pure unto itself. The two concepts may come from different worlds, but the parallels will reveal similarities. A determined postmodernist will simply want to harness the feedback loop to Derrida's idea, to subordinate it to the trace, but that would obscure changes that Derrida could not have foreseen.

Algorithms also present a unique opportunity to think about the layers of language. Programming code has often been designated as a language, so the reference immediately positions it next to comfortable theoretical friends. In resisting the temptation to gamble on weathered clichés, the analysis looks at the layered quality of programming code and the barrier that separates the internal code from its translated expression in the external world. These layers operate simultaneously yet perform different functions and express basic linguistic qualities, such as time, in different ways. An exercise attuned to the particular linguistic qualities of algorithms again attenuates the omnipresence of the linguistic turn.

Algorithms are not the only producers of data, but they increasingly play that role. It therefore makes sense to examine the producer of data before looking at the data itself. Once the algorithm has been explained in a humanistic manner, attention can turn to the data and individual instances of this massive data production. In 2010, then Google CEO Eric Schmidt told his audience in Lake Tahoe, California, that "from the dawn of civilization to 2003, five exabytes were created. The same amount was created in the last two days."[22] The claim is wishy washy but makes the point that Big Data is upon us, and, as an extension of the idea, increasingly so in the work of humanists. A historian today can avoid Big Data, but a generation from now scholars will be studying individuals whose decisions were guided by the data of algorithms. In the future, scholars will be studying past generations who themselves read digitally—born digital readers. Historians and archivists will also have to do their best to preserve the databases stored in private and public collections around the world. Philosophers will be no less immune because moral decisions become increasingly steered by data trends.

Big Data is a popular term but is not always well defined, being even more metaphorical than Moretti's distant reading. The term first surfaced in the 1990s and came to embody data accumulation in the digital age.[23] Despite the quantitative adjective, Big Data is not a mere measurement but an attitude; one does not just cross a numeric threshold to enter into the world of Big Data. Since it is considered a qualitative term, its definition has been more difficult to pin down as scientists and humanists have tried to give it an adequate description. Its technological side has been defined with reference to the three Vs: volume, variety, and velocity. The three Vs suggest that sophisticated technological hardware and software are at play when processing Big Data. As the technologies for processing Big Data have gained in sophistication, the definition has been refined over and over again; the three Vs have become five.

Many of these definitions require a technological understanding, but Big Data does not always have to be presented in technical detail. It can be more simply referred to as data which is too big for a normal computing device to handle. This definition is loose, but it can be lightly modified to fit the parameters of its usage in the pages that follow. Big Data is large enough to force humanists to interact in a radically innovative way with their source material; their normal procedures are inadequate to the task. It implies an unfamiliar interaction with knowledge whose importance far outweighs the size of the data itself. For the humanist, the presence of Big Data alters space, time, and even the way we view things.

The first of three chapters involving Big Data explores our understanding of digital space, since it can be said that a database occupies no space at all. To be sure, data is stored on physical servers that absorb intense amounts of energy, but the stored data is unlike the physical objects that were always at the heart of most empirical studies. In an odd way, space gets transformed when it enters a database. For example, Foucault's panopticon depended on a real-world spatial positioning, one in which sightlines traveled through space. In contrast, the Digital Panopticon project, a database of nineteenth-century English prisoners, has eliminated that space altogether. Instead, it has parsed and divided all the prisoners who no longer resemble physical or dimensional objects. They can be reconstituted based on specific characteristics, but they cannot leave the database with the same spatial characteristics with which they entered. The Wayback Machine from the Internet Archive also has a strange relationship with space because it stores digitally born websites. The stored websites may represent objects outside the digital world, but the websites themselves never had a third dimension, and the Wayback Machine pays no attention to this third dimension.

These spatial oddities ultimately impact an understanding of facts and knowledge. What is the nature of a digital fact if an original object gets dismantled, stored as a fragment in a database, and then can be reconstituted in any number of ways? What space does this fact occupy if it occupies any space at all? Similarly, what happens to local knowledge in this environment? These questions expose the notion that a massive flood of information has peculiarities that require elucidation. The nature of facticity will change immensely. Since these enormous databases are essentially an intermediary of experience, one might say they contain no facts at all. Yet from the other perspective, these are some of the most reliable facts scholars have ever had. These twin poles highlight a problem and demand that the facticity of Big Data be given a little more attention; the facts can then be linked with the act of digital knowing.

One should not be fooled into believing that Big Data will become a totalitarian experience, eliminating conventional experiential sources altogether. Sources that persist in traditional dimensions, what might be called Little Data, will continue to intersect and impact Big Data. How will humanists integrate the quantities of digital facts with all the traditional sources that won't go away? Of course, there is always the risk that Little Data will be treated as a lesser breed, but its position has to be anchored in the world of Big Data to make sure humanists continue to appreciate the widest array of experiences.

From the outset, it should be clear that the discussion is about the conceptual impact of large databases and not just the Digital Humanities. A large component of the Digital Humanities deals with distribution, publication, and preservation, complex technical problems in their own right. What happens to data if it is preserved on outmoded technology? How can one create public portals to best interact with materials that have been painstakingly digitized?[24] These questions give birth to intricate projects that involve archivists, curators, library scientists, computer programmers, and others. Map collections, entire bodies of national literature, and archival documents have found their way onto websites, and the Internet Archive scours the web every day to preserve three-dimensional and digitally born materials. Many of these projects embody a primeval empirical urge, and though this urge, at its base positivistic, is worthy of contemplation, it remains but a stop on the longer journey that follows.

More philosophical issues, such as the emergence of an entity called digital time, will also be looked at. The connection between digital technologies and time may seem obscure but only because no attention has been paid to it. More often than not, the result of data crunching is presented in a timeless manner. Distant reading, for example, is almost entirely a spatial phenomenon. Yet the modern production of data has a critical time component. On the surface, the emergence of digital time confirms a Heideggerian critique—the present, *das 'jetzt,'* the *nunc* was becoming smaller and smaller because in sports, with its tenths of seconds, and in physics, with its millionths of seconds, the present was being reduced to the tiniest of fractions; and rather than gaining anything, humans in a technological age were losing time.[25] Big Data has continued this trend and is as guilty as Heidegger suggests.

Time in the digital age is, however, much more complex and, like language, has to be understood in a longer sequence to grasp how the loss of the present is incidental to other factors that impact a postmodern depiction of time. At the end of the nineteenth century, intellectuals were dissatisfied with a Newtonian conception that put time on a rigid and immutable axis. Einstein's name easily comes to mind, as his theory of relativity situated time in a system of coordinates tied to the observer. Einstein's theory, though it is often presented otherwise, had no absolute connection with humans per se. The 'observer' was an occupier of certain coordinates rather than a flesh-and-blood human being with social and cultural proclivities that might impact his or her position in time; the story of the clocks at the train station only has meaning for someone who knows how to read an analog clock (not something to take for granted in a digital age).

Despite Einstein's indifference, other scholars sought to humanize time and give time a subjective quality. Henri Bergson in *Duration and Simultaneity* argued that each consciousness experienced duration on its own terms.[26] While the philosophical idea of consciousness would be foreign to most postmodern thought, Bergson created a gap into which subjectivity could flow. Years later, Norbert Elias built on these premises, while pushing them in a different direction. Elias, who was more concerned with the social and disdainful of consciousness, argued that time was little more than a relationship.[27] This social relationship had been its primary function until Galileo locked up time in his laboratory and used it as a raw measurement tool absent of any social function. All these trends encouraged twentieth-century postmodern thinkers to promote the endless subjectivity, whether individual or communal, of time.

Digital time in a world of Big Data could slip easily into this talk. It is not a function of the universe nor of the pulse of a quartz. Rather, it has conventional qualities determined by the individuals and organizations that regulate it. It would thereafter not be difficult to make claims about the high priests of the digital world and how they control time. Yet the repetition of this trope would inflict a substantial intellectual loss and shed no light on the fascinating nooks and crannies of digital time.

As an introduction, one can look at the centralizing function of digital time, a process of which Elias was aware within the context of the Industrial Revolution. Digital time has spread a uniform clock throughout the globe and created an identical time grid that localizes the farmer in Nebraska and the restaurateur in Inner Mongolia. It is not that they use the same timing system (the 24-hour clock), but that their times are identical. The centralizing and universalizing tendency of digital time is much closer to Kantian idealism than postmodern relativism. Lived experience follows an unspoken temporal imperative, and most contemporary research falls within this grid.

More intriguing aspects can be added. Consider the words that are regularly pulled from their initial textual setting and placed in databases. This practice is common amongst scholars who want to chart word usage over time, but most of these studies don't consider the temporal environment in which these terms existed. The original word was situated in a time environment determined by verb tenses and other sentence structures. All these time tags vanish when the word is placed in a database. Not only does the first time vanish, but the term is now surrounded by the time tags of the digital grid. Its original sense of time becomes fragmented by the digital order. Is there even such a thing as an original time in the digital milieu? How can the time embedded in Latin hexameter be preserved, or how is it altered, once these words enter a database? What would happen to Walter Benjamin's flâneur and the rhythms of that walker if he was drawn too deeply into the digital time frame? Fluid steps would surely become fragments. Similarly, will the ring of a grandfather clock be mere noise because it has no role in the digital world?

Time in this context has undergone enormous changes since the start of the twentieth century: fragmentation, relocation, re-adoption, and mutation from one digital application to the next make it an elusive character to follow. Readers of Proust's *In Search of Lost Time* know how artful time can be, and time is no less crafty today. Yet the parameters of digital time have a novel quality, such that this quality must be brought to light.

Not surprisingly, the advent of Big Data forces a rethinking of mysteries that have occupied philosophers since humans began to philosophize. Time belongs in the category of the mysterious, and so does the notion that seeing is believing. This last proverb expresses a direct link between the sense data received in the eyeball and its registration in the mind. In the worldview of the empiricist, most commonly associated with John Locke, we can only know and trust the information that arrives to us through the five senses, such as the sense data the eyeball perceives. If we begin with a tabula rasa, then the sense data fills our brains with ever increasing information from which we can learn. A chapter on data visuals explores this more closely.

Criticisms of Lockean empiricism began already with David Hume and Immanuel Kant, indicating the sense data approach had critics well before postmodernism. With their skeptical views, postmodernists naturally kept their distance from any neutral acquisition of knowledge but were, in particular, concerned to undermine the status of vision.[28] Vision was so closely tied to observation and observation was so closely tied to the scientific method—therefore, the status of vision had to be dismantled. Moreover, vision was associated with truth and objectivity—photographs don't lie, because they record a moment in time.

Postmodernists therefore found creative ways to denounce vision. Three brief examples from three visual media—painting, photography, and film—make this point. At the start of *The Order of Things*, Foucault fascinated readers with his discussion on Velazquez's *Las Meninas*.[29] He developed the idea of a 'gaze.' The gaze did not collect objective knowledge, as the classic eyeball was supposed to do, but surveilled a situation to exert influence or establish subtle control. The gaze was much more than the physical act of seeing; the gaze was wrapped in a series of social codes. In *Chambre claire*, Roland Barthes looked beyond the sense data and wrote about the stadium, the cultural connotations clear in each photograph, and the punctum, which unbalances or abstracts the stadium and has an unregulated quality.[30] On film, Christian Metz argued against a "cult of the 'visual'" that bordered "upon the irrational."[31] He preferred more discursive definitions of the visual.

The visual landscape has changed dramatically since these works were written. When Foucault wrote about the gaze, Americans were already watching massive amounts of television, but the learned community was still by and large textual. Moreover, even for television watchers, the intensely visual component of their day was over once the television was turned off. With the Internet and YouTube, so much more time is spent absorbing moving imagery; this global phenomenon is fascinating insofar as the preference for the visual tells us something about our biological selves. In the future, the learners who become professionals will have done so on a visual diet and will have a different attitude toward visuals. In a society filled with so many visual learners, the visual pessimism will lose its attraction.

Come what may, the continued production of quantified data will change much of this because the visual representation of data content has become such an integral component of visual experience. The nature of a database or Big Data is such that it must be displayed in a visually sophisticated manner. As such the presentation of knowledge is experiencing a visual revolution. Not long ago, visuals were the domain of art historians, but that has changed. Any humanist who chooses to use Big Data has to decide how to display it and thus select a mode of graphic expression; this step is unavoidable. The selection of a graphical mode of representation is not identical with eyewitnessing a crime scene, but the expanding presence of data and our interactions with it are not completely separate from the situations that agonized postmodern theorists. If a scholar is perfectly content to present factual data in a graph, how could that scholar simultaneously succumb to arguments about a gaze, since you cannot neatly 'gaze' at these graphs?

Historians used graphs in the past, but they tended to be rudimentary ones with simple X-Y axes and a single slanted line that indicated growth or decline. This tradition has little space in the world of Big Data because of the variables that need to be presented and the dynamic interactive manners being developed to convey information in digital projects such as those being developed with the support of Stanford University Press. The practice then is much closer to what Edward Tufte has been studying over the past few decades, his favorite example being Charles Joseph Minard's statistical visualization of Napoleon's retreat from Russia.[32] The trajectory present in Tufte's world introduces a likely future for the humanities, a future that must be understood now.

Visuals are already appearing in publications, offering a twist to Peter Burke's appeal for more visual material.[33] The visuals are not traditional images but specially designed representations of knowledge that elicit intrigues. For example, viewers are becoming accustomed to seeing millions of bits of information aggregated into a few straight lines—individual items remain essentially invisible, but the lines vividly present conclusions at a general level. This might be considered distant viewing, a cousin to Moretti's concept. The selection of colors also becomes critical and opens doors to rethinking the social significance of these tones. The publication of knowledge in these instances reveals itself in a manner foreign to traditional textual forms.

The emerging abundance of data visuals has inherent complexities because it straddles two sides of a debate. On the one hand, these visuals are based on bits of strictly regulated and logically generated information. Few scholars evince grave epistemological concern about relying on such data. On the other hand, the best means to present the data has an aesthetic and artistic component that could overshadow the data itself. Unlike the rudimentary charts and line graphs of yesteryear or even the monochrome graphs on early computers, the dynamic possibilities of visuals, seen on a daily basis in publications such as the *New York Times*, add a layer of analysis. Soon the dominance of these visuals will further erode the authority of the linguistic turn.

Data visuals then are yet another realm where complacency and familiarity are unwelcome. For those who have worked with data visuals for decades, the discussion on visuals may be of less interest. Textual scholars will find much more to ponder since the same rules don't apply when reading a text as when looking at a graph. In fact, new skills are already being honed to cope with graphical representation. Tufte's promotion of objective truths in visual representations is a throwback to the days before postmodernism, but there are better alternatives to his stance than to rely on another throwback, postmodern anti-ocularism. If there is a middle ground, only further exploration will reveal it.

After three chapters focused on large data sets, the discussion moves on to the last and perhaps most intriguing issue, that of digital forgeries. The question of forgeries is multipronged. First, the notion of a forgery ties into the insecurities of the emerging digital universe. Fake news has already become a common expression, abetted by the Internet, social media, and the glut of data production. The website of the Foreign Ministry of the Russian Federation identifies what it considers fake news with a digital red stamp. Fake news and other elements in the post-truth world are not forgeries per se, but they demonstrate the need for extreme caution when looking at or listening to digital information. They suggest that a little more probing will reveal forgeries familiar to readers from more traditional times.

Forgeries have been a big part of postmodern thought because they link with efforts to undermine authorship and authenticity. When a forger creates a perfect copy of a Picasso, painting being a traditional realm for forgeries, how can one assert single authorship if one cannot identify who the author is? The postmodernist strategy was to seize upon the little window of doubt that opens when one cannot be certain that one is looking at an original. There are no objective standards to judge its status, and therefore what should be easy to determine as the fact of the matter becomes a matter of convention. The next step is to route the forgery through the linguistic turn and make the forgery (or original) answer only to discursive evidence. This intellectual trajectory is hardly surprising and therefore worth investigating once it arrives in a digital environment.

Traditional forgeries are not that difficult to conjure. We talk about forged signatures, forged letters, and, in famous cases, forged works of art. In the 1930s, Han van Meegeren fooled the art world with his forgeries of Johannes Vermeer. Digital forgeries are more problematic because they defy straightforward categorization. One can forge a digital signature, but what would it look like to forge a digital artwork? Could one forge a digital correspondence or add an e-mail to an existing correspondence? Could one completely forge a massive database and place it in some dark corner of the web with the hope that a naïve researcher will seize upon it two decades down the road? With all these dizzying questions, the parameters of digital forgery are not even clear.

Nevertheless, opening a discussion on digital forgeries sets up possibilities. The first task is to define digital forgeries relative to traditional ones and develop an instinct for identifying novelty over tradition. Once this has been established, the discussion can move onto more philosophical ground because outside of auction houses, forgery quickly becomes a philosophical issue. Rudolf Arnheim and Nelson Goodman provided their thoughts on forgery in the heart of the postmodern period.[34] Carlo Ginzburg, a microhistorian fascinated by small traces, looked at forgeries from a more empirical perspective.[35] Juxtaposing their insights with digital possibilities indicates, if only lightly, how to proceed with digital forgeries. Thereafter, the discussion turns to the process of identifying forgeries. This process was critical for Ginzburg, who insisted on visual identification and reminded his readers of Sherlock Holmes's magnifying glass, perhaps a precursor to the digital zoom function. Identifying digital forgeries is altogether different, however; the zoom function has only a few commonalities with a magnifying glass. Once again, identification will depend upon characteristics that lie below the surface. Much like art connoisseurs rely on chemical analyses to date painting materials, analysts will consult with computer programmers to get at the digital layer that lies below the forgery itself. This process brings logic and binaries back into the world of the humanist, but in a mystifying way that requires some form of revelation. Digital forgeries are often contiguous with postmodern experience, but one must note where they go their separate ways.

All the previous comments should not give the mistaken impression postmodernists were blind to technological developments; on the contrary, they belong to a long line of discontents. From the physical destruction of the Luddites in the nineteenth century or Heideggerian nostalgia for undammed rivers in the German Middle Ages, postmodernists have their antecedents. For postmodernists, regimes of technology became a stock phrase with which to criticize modern times. Nor can it be said that the postmodernists' technological pessimism precedes the modern computer as could be said of Heidegger's. In the early 1990s, Gilles Deleuze associated computers with social control and excited his followers with new ways to denounce what others saw as progress.[36]

These postmodern technological critiques were done from a distance before humanistic scholarship was fully immersed in the technological world, before Digital Humanities became the cutting edge of research (and sharp edges are designed to be divisive). In the 1970s, it was still possible to remain aloof from or indifferent to technologies and to treat technology as discursive rather than personally invasive. Nowadays scholars are enmeshed in them in deeper and deeper ways. At a casual level, scholars interact with them when shopping groceries, buying shoes, or having Netflix or Amazon suggest additional viewing pleasures. Professionally, algorithms and their fruit have embedded themselves in the methodologies of so many disciplines, it has become impossible to avoid them.

A well-paved path is preferred by those with thin soles, but it does not make much sense to repurpose these older critiques for every new technological development; can we imagine regurgitating these phrases on technologies that lie fifty or a hundred years in the future? Surely they will run out of gas at some point. If we don't do otherwise, and this is the main point, we will be dealing with ideas that have taken on the air of truths. The only subsequent step from there leads to stagnation. When so many new adventures lie ahead, why seek the security of old friends? We will find ourselves like the narrator at the end of Proust's *A La Recherche*, who enters a salon only to see how all his friends have aged; it takes him a while to realize that he has grayed as well.

Evidently, this transition has to be grappled with and accepted in the world of humanist research. Acceptance, however, does not imply capitulation if capitulation is to be understood as a complete transition to quantitative analysis. It does imply taking a strenuous look at how to preserve the irregular, emotional, aesthetic, humane, and qualitative aspects of the humanist tradition without assuming that nothing has really changed over the last fifty years. Methods will adapt dramatically and, as a consequence, reconsiderations of the postmodern canon will become the norm. This is not a rejection of this canon but an awareness that the time has come to move on. What follows takes us forward, and even if some basic avenues will be laid, it is still too early to tell where we will land. But this uncertainty, such a charmed word amongst postmodernists, has to be welcomed for what it might bring.

Notes

1. Allan Bloom, *The Closing of the American Mind* (New York: Simon and Schuster, 1988).
2. Matthew K. Gold and Lauren F. Klein, eds., *Debates in the Digital Humanities 2016* (Minneapolis and London: University of Minnesota Press, 2016). Lara Putnam writes about a "discipline's epistemology." See Lara Putnam, "The Transnational and the Text-Searchable: Digitized Sources and the Shadows They Cast," *American Historical Review* 121 (April 2016): 379.
3. David J. Bodenhamer, "The Spatial Humanities: Space, Time and Place in the New Digital Age," in *History in the Digital Age*, ed. Toni Weller (London and New York: Routledge, 2013), 34.
4. Kwong Bor Ng, Jason Kucsma, and Metropolitan New York Library Council, eds., *Digitization in the Real World: Lessons Learned From Small and Medium-Sized Digitization Projects* (New York: Metropolitan New York Library Council, 2010), xi.
5. Johanna Drucker, "Humanistic Theory and Digital Scholarship," in *Debates in the Digital Humanities* (Minneapolis: University of Minnesota Press, 2012), 86.
6. Gayatri Chakravorty Spivak, "Afterword," in *Of Grammatology*, edited by Jacques Derrida (Baltimore: Johns Hopkins University Press, 2016).
7. Arthur C. Danto, *After the End of Art: Contemporary Art and the Pale of History*, The A.W. Mellon Lectures in the Fine Arts 1995 (Princeton, NJ: Princeton University Press, 1997), 111.
8. Isaiah Berlin, *Historical Inevitability*, Auguste Comte Memorial Trust Lecture 1 (London: Oxford University Press, 1954).
9. Thomas Kuhn, *The Structure of Scientific Revolutions* (Chicago: University of Chicago Press, 1962).
10. James Bryant Conant, *On Understanding Science: An Historical Approach* (New Haven: Yale University Press; London: G. Cumberlege, Oxford University Press, 1947); Steven Shapin and Simon Schaffer, *Leviathan and the Air-Pump: Hobbes, Boyle, and the Experimental Life* (Princeton, NJ: Princeton University Press, 1989).
11. Drucker, "Humanistic Theory and Digital Scholarship."
12. Hayden V. White, *Metahistory: The Historical Imagination in Nineteenth-Century Europe* (Baltimore: Johns Hopkins University Press, 1973).
13. Johann Gottfried Herder, *Abhandlung über den Ursprung der Sprache* (Stuttgart: Reclam, 1969).
14. Franco Moretti, *Distant Reading* (London: Verso, 2013).
15. Ludwig Wittgenstein, *Tractatus Logico-philosophicus* (London and New York: Routledge & Paul, 1961). The *Philosophical Investigations* does not bound experience with language at all.
16. Chris Anderson, "The End of Theory: The Data Deluge Makes the Scientific Method Obsolete," *WIRED*, accessed April 24, 2018, www.wired.com/2008/06/pb-theory/.

22 Introduction

17. For a dissenting view, see the introduction in Michael N. Jones, ed., *Big Data in Cognitive Science* (New York, NY: Routledge, 2017). See also Patrik Svensson and David Theo Goldberg, eds., *Between Humanities and the Digital* (Cambridge, MA: The MIT Press, 2015).
18. Quentin Skinner, ed., *The Return of Grand Theory in the Human Sciences* (Cambridge and New York: Cambridge University Press, 1990).
19. Anderson, "The End of Theory."
20. Safiya Umoja Noble, *Algorithms of Oppression: How Search Engines Reinforce Racism* (New York: New York University Press, 2018).
21. On the algorithm as a black box, see Frank Pasquale, *The Black Box Society: The Secret Algorithms That Control Money and Information* (Cambridge, MA and London: Harvard University Press, 2015).
22. "Eric Schmidt: Every 2 Days We Create as Much Information as We Did Up to 2003," *TechCrunch* (blog), accessed September 25, 2019, http://social.techcrunch.com/2010/08/04/schmidt-data/.
23. Steve Lohr, "The Origins of 'Big Data': An Etymological Detective Story," *Bits Blog* (blog), February 1, 2013, https://bits.blogs.nytimes.com/2013/02/01/the-origins-of-big-data-an-etymological-detective-story/.
24. Roy Rosenzweig, *Clio Wired: The Future of the Past in the Digital Age* (New York: Columbia University Press, 2011). These issues have been discussed for at least twenty years. See John H. Whaley, Jr., "Digitizing History," *The American Archivist* 57, no. 4 (Fall 1994): 660–72. Most recently, see Ian Milligan, *History in the Age of Abundance? How the Web Is Transforming Historical Research* (Montreal and Kingston: McGill-Queen's University Press, 2019).
25. Martin Heidegger, *Was heisst Denken?* (Frankfurt am Main: Vittorio Klostermann, 2002), 104.
26. Henri Bergson, *Duration and Simultaneity: With Reference to Einstein's Theory* (Indianapolis: Bobbs-Merrill, 1965).
27. Norbert Elias, *Time: An Essay* (Oxford: B. Blackwell, 1992).
28. See Martin Jay, *Downcast Eyes: The Denigration of Vision in Twentieth-Century French Thought* (Berkeley: University of California Press, 1993).
29. Michel Foucault, *Les mots et les choses: Une archéologie des sciences humaines* (Paris: Gallimard, 1990).
30. Roland Barthes, *La chambre claire: Note sur la photographie* (Paris: Cahiers du cinéma, 1980).
31. Christian Metz, *Language and Cinema*, vol. 26 (The Hague: Mouton, 1974), 34.
32. Edward R. Tufte, *Beautiful Evidence* (Cheshire, CT: Graphics Press, 2006).
33. Peter Burke, *Eyewitnessing: The Uses of Images as Historical Evidence*, Picturing History Series (Ithaca, NY: Cornell University Press, 2001).
34. Their essays appear in Denis Dutton, ed., *The Forger's Art: Forgery and the Philosophy of Art* (Berkeley: University of California Press, 1983).
35. Carlo Ginzburg, "Clues: Roots of an Evidential Paradigm," in *Clues, Myths, and the Historical Method* (Baltimore: Johns Hopkins University Press, 1989).
36. Gilles Deleuze, "Postscript on the Societies of Control," *October* 59 (1992): 3–7.

2 The Achievement of Postmodernism

Sometime in the late 1950s and early 1960s, certain intellectual energies converged in Paris to give the world postmodernism. What began as an isolated intellectual movement in a few obscure books gathered momentum, crossed the Atlantic, and spread throughout the United States, where it challenged basic assumptions at all the elite universities. As the foundation of these theories would have it, no two postmodernists were alike; yet common themes and accustomed challenges kept surfacing regardless of the angle from which they came. Rationality, objective truths and a mind that mirrored nature had to be sacrificed to the new ideal. The pillars of Western civilization were not to be carved with classic inscriptions from Antiquity but hammered into smithereens. In their place came relativism, subjectivity, and a deep mistrust of Eurocentric worldviews. These ideas were constructed upon a skeptical philosophical premise and then spread across disciplines and eventually into daily life. In light of Foucault's devastating analysis of the rationality that informed nineteenth-century institutions for the insane, scholars in the medical profession started to rethink basic premises.[1]

These attacks on established norms did not go unnoticed. Many historians, for example, mocked the claim that facts were social constructs. Instead, they adhered to the more solid vision of facts that E.H. Carr had presented to them in the early 1960s; it was a duty, not a virtue, of the historian to get the facts right, and thus there were right facts.[2] Noam Chomsky debated Foucault and John Searle locked linguistic horns with Jacques Derrida. More virulently, political and moral philosophers decried the wildness of these ideas. If scholars were comfortable denouncing signal achievements of the Western tradition, such as the immutable legal premises that supported parliaments, what could we expect to replace them? So much work had been done to overcome authoritarian regimes that removing the safeguards would allow society to slip back into older habits. An author such as Francis Fukuyama in *The End of History* could see no future for postmodern relativism in the world of political philosophy; the Western standard was the standard.[3]

Supporters of sacred institutions such as marriage linked postmodern philosophy with the dissolution of the traditional family and a descent into societal chaos. They would not accept assurances that the family was a historical construct and could go as easily as it came. Strong objections appeared in almost every field and in extensive public debates.

Despite the strength of this opposition, postmodernism made its way into the fabric of everyday life, the true barometer of any philosophical theory. Victory is probably too emotional a word now that the dust has settled, but many postmodern theories have been successfully translated into social behavior. As postmodernism articulated the harrowed plight of those on the margins, it gave many a reason to celebrate. Even if few citizens who look upon gay pride parades with admiration see postmodern smiles in the faces of those marchers, postmodernism was instrumental in accelerating acceptance of homosexuality. Critiques of scientific objectivity undermined the assertion that homosexuality was a clinical condition. Critiques that emphasized the moral relativity of laws emphasized that anti-gay legislation was a societal feature and not the manifestation of a godly morality. Postmodernism certainly had assistance because scholars had already railed against imperialism and the lack of women's rights but did so without the sweeping philosophical underpinnings that made postmodernism so effective. It became a host for so many other movements and injected them with the added energy they needed.

With these thoughts, postmodernism must be explored in a way that is more than a searing philosophical critique or an expression of blind support; those two worldviews can be witnessed in other venues. Instead of exposing old wounds by reliving intricate debates about the merits of philosophical principles, time is better spent acquiring a general sense of its vitality. By limiting the discussion to basic and accessible philosophical principles, its impact in a scholarly environment as well as its value in real-world situations will sit at the forefront of memory. Postmodernists were justifiably criticized for opaque treatises and writing filled with repetitive jargon. This inclination towards murkiness should not obscure how postmodern ideas impacted everyday life though, like the gay pride parade example, would not be recognized as such. In establishing this brief overview of the postmodern achievement, it serves well to include examples with a common touch, that is, moments where postmodernism escaped the academy and made a difference in the tiniest of circumstances.

This chapter might well be considered an obituary. In the heyday of postmodernism, detractors would have welcomed a short and less-than-sweet obituary or an opportunity to witness the movement being buried deep in the forest. By contrast, a proper obituary is not good riddance but a reminder of accomplishments, dreams left unfulfilled, and imperfections in an otherwise glorious life. An obituary is a memorandum to friends about what they already know but have let slip from their minds.

It is also a testament to the flow of time, a ritualistic passing of the torch, for nothing is eternal.

Once the basic philosophical premises of postmodernism have been outlined, it will become clear how scholars employed it to undermine the classic notion of the rational citizen. Objections to objectivity also underlined the attack on the Enlightenment—here we can investigate how science became subjectified as scholars looked at the social practices of famous scientists and undermined naïve attitudes to scientific progress. This debate is still ongoing, but we are much more sensitive to the social issues surrounding science. Finally, the nexus between knowledge and power, an outcome of an inevitable subjectivity, requires attention to present its societal impact. These investigations are designed to give a general sense of the movement and how it echoed throughout the world, before switching to a lengthier discussion of the digital environment. It establishes a warm touchstone for future discussions and a point of reference when these ideas crop up later on.

Since postmodernism attacked the eighteenth century at all levels, reason is as good a place to start as any. The Enlightenment was subject to withering criticism precisely because it had universal and global pretensions based upon reason. In the eighteenth century, Voltaire believed he was writing rational tracts for everyone, and the Declaration of the Rights of Man, issued at the outset of the French Revolution in 1789, embodied universality. Rationality gained momentum over the course of the Enlightenment and remained the standard bearer until after World War II.

While this had long been seen as a fundamental achievement because it struck a blow to feudal social categories, postmodernists argued that it simply masked other ongoing aspirations to power. Postmodernists rejected the Cartesian view of a rational subject that lorded its status over the external world. Michel Foucault spurned the idea that a universal human nature existed. Instead the subject and its historical development were embedded in an intricate social environment. As Foucault wrote in *The Order of Things*, "the 'I think' does not . . . lead to the evident truth of the 'I am.'" The 'I am' is intertwined with a social setting and the "discovery of life, work, and language."[4] There is, as is so often the case with postmodernism, a more than faint echo of Nietzsche, who rejected the *cogito ergo sum* in favor of *vivo ergo cogito*.

By degrading the role of rationality, paths opened up. First, as the early works of Foucault indicate, the abuse of rationality could be confronted head on. His history of madness demonstrated how the rise of rationality created boundaries where there had been none before. The heightened status of the rational necessarily implied the demotion of anything that had a hint of the irrational. The insane were incarcerated in an institutional setting, where the treatment of these prisoners was a cruel as it had ever been. They became the objects of scientific inquiry and tools of the Enlightenment laboratory rather than individuals in their own right.

This example is commonplace because the work sparked a flurry of intellectual activity. Historians criticized it intensely because they accused the author of playing loose with the facts, a heresy for historians. But these empirical objections did not stick in the greater scheme of things; most scholars were not concerned with a few factual infelicities. Instead, the study fostered and furthered a general suspicion that rationality could be easily criticized from any number of perspectives. The history of madness launched more works on madness. Of no less significance, it encouraged feminist scholars who wanted to undermine the nineteenth-century stereotype of women being irrational, a convenient designator which when placed on binary terms made men rational by default. It essentially swept the philosophical grounds from under this idea.

The demotion of rationality eventually could be experienced by going to the movies. In 2003, the Norwegian director, Bent Hamer, released the film *Kitchen Stories*.[5] Set in postwar Sweden, a scientific institute wanted to measure exactly how many feet a housewife walked in her kitchen to help them rationalize the design of kitchens. As a twist, a team of fieldworkers were sent to northern Norway to observe the habits of bachelors in their kitchens. To ensure a more objective process, the observer sat in a high chair—mimicking and mocking the alleged bird's-eye view of the objective philosopher—at a distance from the subject. From this lofty height, the fieldworker could map movement without bias. Of course, the objectivity was bound to fail, as a romance developed between the observer and the lonely northern bachelor. This was not a Hollywood blockbuster, but it captured postmodern themes, poked fun at the hopelessness of rationality, and presented them in a touching manner outside the academic environment.

Rationality has an ephemeral, a materialistic character that served the interests of philosophers who, like the man in the highchair, envisioned themselves above the dirtiness of everyday life. Yet philosophy as an academic discipline also had its position shift within the academy. Traditionally, philosophers were satisfied with their pursuit of universal truths; they pursued the timeless aspects of human existence. If rationality, however, was a social and not a mental phenomenon, then the philosophical understanding of rationality required a social component, and philosophers had to pay more attention to the historical circumstances in which intellectual ideas came to life. In this regard, the American pragmatist, Richard Rorty, was unambiguous in his desire to return philosophy to the social fray. In *Philosophy and the Mirror of Nature*, he explained how philosophy became a foundational discipline by the end of the nineteenth century, enabling "philosophy professors to see themselves as presiding over a tribunal of pure reason able to determine whether other disciplines were staying within the legal limits . . . of their subject matters."[6] Rorty believed this was a mistaken worldview and thus brought together his own cohort of philosophers to place philosophy in context—side by side and not above other humanists.[7] Ian Hacking, who explored the historical development of probability, would be a classic example of a Foucault-inspired philosopher who was deeply committed to historical context.[8]

A corollary to the attack on the universal rationality of the Enlightenment is the decentralization of knowledge or, as the title to a German collection of Rorty's essays suggests, *A Culture Without a Center*.[9] Romantics already challenged the universalism of the Enlightenment at the start of the nineteenth century as they sought to revive local and folk culture as an antidote to a universal ethos. Yet the Romantics were much less concerned with epistemological issues such as the acquisition of knowledge. Postmodernists, who denied the rational acquisition of knowledge, argued that not only were cultural practices different but each society existed within its own knowledge network, a network that did not need to correspond with any other. Marshall Sahlins's *Islands of History*, which looks at the islanders in the Pacific Ocean, fits this pattern.[10] As his fellow anthropologist Claude Lévi-Strauss liked to have a little play in his titles, so did Sahlins. The islands are not mere physical protrusions above the water level in the Pacific, but a metaphor for the uniqueness of knowledge systems in individual settings. France could be an island of history even if geographers would never think of France as an island.

Sahlins was not a postmodernist per se, but his island metaphor captured the spirit of postmodernism. His affiliation with anthropology also testified to the interdisciplinary nature of the movement. Another anthropologist with a philosopher's training became a key reference point in overcoming universalist aspirations. Clifford Geertz advocated local culture and urged his colleagues to stop transforming village life into a categorical imperative for all; village life was just that, village life.[11]

A key component to Enlightenment thought was the assumption that it involved everyone; eventually, the project would impact all of humanity even if non-Europeans and non-Americans had yet to travel a great distance on this path. While this reflected a desire to portray a Western tradition worthy of emulation, detractors had other thoughts. Those who saw no reason to measure their own lives against a Western standard saw this as insulting. Thus postcolonial scholars from around the world embraced critiques of the Enlightenment as they sought to reinvigorate their own cultural heritage after centuries of imperialism. Not everyone rejected the Enlightenment unconditionally, but an opening had been forged.

Identifying the evils of imperialism was not unique to postmodernists, but more than lamenting past invasions, the movement found a way to give local (or any classically underrated) culture its own voice. Intellectually, this spawned hundreds of studies demonstrating the ingenuity of local knowledge around the world. For example, instead of assuming that Europeans were the innovators from whom other cultures should inevitably borrow, scholars demonstrated that Europeans learned from local medicinal practices and incorporated, if uncredited, this knowledge from their extensive travels.

In *Provincializing Europe*, another playful title, Dipash Chakrabarty carefully navigates the universals of the Enlightenment without letting those values "define the project."[12] Chakrabarty wanted to look at "pasts" and not a single past—the plural noun being a key postmodern strategy since postmodernists had a remarkable fondness for putting an 's' at the end of English words. If the past is plural, so is the future—the futures "make it impossible to sum up a present through any totalizing principle." The futures resist "the objectifying procedures of history writing."[13] This boldness encouraged scholars to write truly local histories rather than histories of European imperialists in foreign lands; histories which inevitably marginalized local accomplishments as they were transfixed by Western technologies both institutional and scientific.

In a more philosophical manner, Gayatri Spivak opened similar doors when in 1988 she raised the question: can the subaltern speak?[14] Spivak is completely committed to postmodern discursive techniques, thus the selection of *speak* rather than *think*; *can the subaltern think?* would have been an imperialist projection emerging from Enlightenment rationality. The postmodern idiom makes her analysis a little opaque to outsiders, but it is an attempt to amplify the voices of those marginalized by the imperialists; it seeks to recognize that specific local stories have remained untold because of the *episteme* of imperialism. Not surprisingly, Spivak paid careful attention to the ritual practice of wife-burning or *sati* in India. In the spirit of the Enlightenment, the British overseers banned the practice in the early nineteenth century based on universal principles. The step seems non-problematic, but Spivak wants her readers, not listeners, to know that complex traces are being set aside if we leave it at that.

Specifically, the role of women is complicated because it lies somewhere between the imperialist universalisms of the British and the entrenched cultural habits of the Hindu population: "As one goes down the grotesquely mistranscribed names of these women, the sacrificed widows, in the police reports included in the records of the East India Company, one cannot put together a 'voice.'"[15] Locating that voice is excruciatingly difficult. One could accept British claims about the barbarity of the practice, but that would be equated with imperialist disdain for local culture, as the mistranscribed names suggest. To give the women a voice, however, is to accept that they might have actively sought to express their free will through the ritual sacrifice. The tension is clearly apparent in Spivak's formulation: "Obviously, I am not advocating the killing of widows."[16] The local is not perfect, either, but somewhere between the local and the universal lies a space where these voices can be heard.

Any number of other factors complicate the situation, but each step of the complication opens more space for the marginalized. Spivak has to include her own origins in the story to assert that she is part of that history but cannot be completely involved in that history. As she writes, "I turn to Indian material because . . . that accident of birth and education has provided me with a *sense* of the historical canvas."[17] Hers is not the only accident because the fate of the subaltern women is itself an accident caught "Between patriarchy and Development," a position that continues to define subaltern women.[18] The accident is no accident because it represents a specific postmodern strategy to imbue all situations with contingency and overwhelm the simplicity of imperialist claims. In Spivak's case, it is done to problematize the position of women in India over the last two hundred years.

Positively, this led to a shift in attitude. Instead of assuming the rest of the world was hopelessly backwards, it became common to demonstrate that Westerners (even if they only reluctantly admitted it) learned from sea voyages and rather than imposing their values on foreigners, incorporated foreign techniques—of medicine, of science—from what they came across. In March 2018, the Getty Museum in Los Angeles opened an exhibition displaying works of Rembrandt that he based on Mughal originals. Because of the vast shipping interests of the Dutch, Rembrandt had access to cultural products from India. He took advantage of the opportunity to examine the paintings of Mughal artists and then drew sketches based on these Mughal pieces. In addition to this visual inspiration, Rembrandt also liked to paint on paper with a Japanese provenance. Traffic thus went in many directions, unlike in the Enlightenment story where everyone—at a different pace—was headed in the same direction.

It would be misleading to suggest that condemnations of imperialism were possible only with the tools of postmodernism. Before the Russian Revolution, Vladimir Lenin exposed the exploitative relationship between capitalism and imperialism; Lenin was no relativist. Despite a Soviet desire to see originality with every stroke of his pen, Lenin was building upon well-established censures from Western Europe. Thus a common message emerged from both sides. The postmodernism position, however, attacked imperialism without assuming the birth of a universal society of commonly shared values. Imperialism could be eliminated without sacrificing local identity; everyone could have the chains removed without joining a cosmopolitan society. As the world grapples with globalization and the postcolonial trauma that refuses to go away, these points remain relevant.

A more common variant of this theme relates to music and shifting listening habits in society. Not so long ago, classical music was upheld as the pinnacle of sonic achievement and therefore reflected the universal standard towards which we should all strive. The standard narrative would assert that Georg Friedrich Handel, who lived during the Enlightenment, found the secret to many universal chords, thus composers after him continued to do the same. Since European and American cities had opera houses and symphony halls, these societies determined the standard of excellence. Other musical forms were marginalized and though they were not accused of irrationalism, they were not taken seriously. Nowadays, in the wake of all these critiques of the Enlightenment, the musical scene has become more accepting. A music professor can teach Japanese drums or Gamelan tunes from Bali without having to explain why Mozart is not on the syllabus. Performing arts centers regularly feature global music. This tolerance has been evident for at least the last twenty years, and the tolerance should be seen as overcoming the imperialist tendencies of the Enlightenment.

A problem emerged with the promotion of local or incommensurable islands of knowledge. The emphasis on the local seemingly eliminated all standards; as everyone had different aural tendencies, anyone could claim to be listening to beautiful music—a fundamental denunciation of the Kantian aesthetic. Staid members of the humanities feared the ensuing havoc and a literal demolition of everything that was cherished because the ability to distinguish and discern, the ability to recognize high or low culture, was eliminated; the daughter's love of Cyndi Lauper was of no less cultural significance than the father's appreciation of Verdi. The expression of this fear was repeated over and over again, whether in published sources or in passing conversations amongst scholars. But as much as one side feared the lack of a standard, the other side embraced it. The mayhem it induced opened the doors for all kinds of music to be played in the concert hall, letting in all sorts of tonal diversity.

This angered many traditionalists (who were not musical elitists), worried that any piece of junk could be considered music. But this did not really come to pass as music critics could embrace a variety of styles and still impose their own rigorous cultural standards—there was good reggae, better than bad classical, and good classical better than bad jazz. The same holds outside the realm of music as well. Culturally, French cuisine may have suffered as gourmets were encouraged to treat their palates to Asian goodies that lay outside the canon. This did not mean that the distinction between the gourmet and the gourmand was lost; it meant a greater appreciation for a wider world of accomplishments that had been lost when the yardstick had been determined by Western chefs and philosophers. Museum curators may no longer hold to a Kantian standard of beauty, but beautiful exhibitions persist. The slippery slope, the bane of philosophers, never gained real traction. Society found its way along a road with lots of commercial pop music but did not lose sight of unique musicians who developed their own forms of creativity that didn't align with any universal idea.

Hubris accompanies these assertions because they place the emphasis of social change on complex academic theories, when academic theories are a part and not the whole of change. Throughout the entire postmodern period, Western society was in upheaval; protest movements from 1968 onwards had a deep impact on social norms and on the thinking of philosophers in Paris, New York, Berkeley, and beyond. Gay rights, civil rights, and women's rights were a product of the same postwar discontent as postmodernism. Yet even if we choose to demote theoretical influences, postmodernism offered a crux to overcome the universalism of the Enlightenment, a set of ideas that had long since stood in the way.

The Enlightenment borrowed heavily from Newtonian scientific discoveries in the seventeenth and early eighteenth centuries, so it was only natural for postmodernists to put science and technology in their crosshairs. When postmodernists wrote about technologies, it had a much broader definition because the usage was intended to cast suspicion on a wide range of rational activities. A narrower discussion of science, the most objective of all pursuits, suffices because it indicates how postmodernists shifted the study of science even if they could not cause airplanes to fall out of the sky.

Postmodernists first had help from various skeptical philosophers. Thomas Kuhn, who can hardly be considered a postmodernist, published *The Structure of Scientific Revolutions* in 1962 and launched a battle pitting the defenders of objective science against those who only promoted subjectivity and relativism. Kuhn was accused of suggesting that science was little more than mob rule, yet he simply provided the intellectual community with the clearest statement of ideas that had been swirling around for a while.[19] He established an environment that allowed postmodernists to push his ideas further towards a less comfortable intellectual precipice. Historians and philosophers of science could combine a reading of Foucault, who was not directly concerned with science, with a reading of Kuhn and draw more extreme conclusions.[20] In the most outrageous cases, scientists were depicted as doing little more than satisfying subjective pleasures as they tried to advance their careers. The idea of local knowledge was being applied in a scientific context: no one scientific system worked better than any other.

The thrust of postmodernism encouraged a refreshing look at science, regardless of the degree to which one submitted to subjectivity. Whereas older scientific explanations focused on the progressive improvement of elements such as measuring instruments, the next generation of historians and anthropologists examined the social context that produced such items. In a history of science from the 1940s, James Conant looked at how scientists improved measuring techniques for specific phenomena, demonstrating how subsequent generations of inventors improved upon accuracy.[21] The imagery Conant offered his readers was telling because it focused on the mechanics of the devices, and therefore he was satisfied with modern sketches to help his readers understand the processes. The underlying assumption was that the process itself was timeless. Only towards the end of a section on measurement did he explore how science prospered in different religious settings, but even here the religious beliefs did not undermine the objectivity of the science. Lest one be inclined to dismiss Conant as a remnant of a bygone age, Thomas Kuhn credits him for inspiring his interest in the history of science.[22]

Years later, a seminal historical and postmodern work on science came from Steven Shapin and Simon Schaffer, who studied seventeenth-century British science.[23] The book began with references to Foucault and was only peripherally interested in the physical intricacies of science; instead it focused on how the social standing of the participating scientists influenced the acceptance of the respective scientific theories. Shapin and Schaffer carefully mentioned the venues in which the science was presented, the social class or estate of those in the audience, and the visual props that were used to promote the scientific discovery, the discovery being the presence of a vacuum. The visuals were not devoted to instrumentation, as one might expect in Conant or even Kuhn, but chosen to demonstrate the emblematic significance of the air-pump when it was situated in social settings. One image showed a woman in the vicinity of the air-pump, thus giving the air-pump a social significance outside of its usefulness. This approach spurred a flood of scientific histories that practically ignored the instruments and focused on elements such as the emotions of the scientists and how scientists crafted languages that had a greater impact than the object of study itself.[24]

Of no less importance was the revival of alchemy. In medieval Europe, alchemists played a controversial role with their experiments and with their visits at royal courts. They became legendary for their magical efforts to transform metals into gold; thus they could be of assistance to a mining industry in need of alloys. When the Scientific Revolution gathered momentum in the seventeenth century, the "magical" alchemists were easy targets; in an emerging era of reason and rationality, who needed superstitious science?[25] Hence, until postmodernism gained a footing, alchemists were portrayed as wizards practicing something, but not laboratory science.

The mood which postmodernism created allowed a more pluralistic approach, and soon it became fashionable to talk about Isaac Newton, the paragon of objective science, and his interest in alchemy. It wasn't that Newton's alchemical interests were unknown—in 1946, John Maynard Keynes called Newton the "last of the magicians"—but his alchemy was not taken seriously as a science or understood as a preliminary to other discoveries. Nowadays, the links are easily accepted. William Newman writes about the "obviously alchemical character" of Newton's *Of Natures Obvious Laws & Processes in Vegetation*.[26] Based on a review of experimental notebooks, Newton relied upon the works of Johannes de Monte Snyders and Eirenaeus Philalethes, "authors whom no sane person today would deny to be alchemists."[27] One can debate the extent to which alchemy influenced specific Newtonian conclusions, but it cannot be dismissed because alchemy does not fit tidy parameters of the Scientific Revolution and the Enlightenment.

This attitude did not have to come straight out of postmodernism, and the postmodern element is not always evident in a historian of science who promotes the alchemical interpretation. Nevertheless, its emphasis on decentralization, a focus on the margins, and interest in marginalized groups (here, the alchemists) was heard. Boundaries between historical epochs were dismantled, and scientists were viewed as more than laboratory automatons pursuing objective truths—their interests could veer off in numerous directions.

And sometimes postmodernism itself veered off the road. In 1996, the physicist Alan Sokal submitted an article to a postmodern journal—the ensuing episode became known as the Sokal hoax, and though it is now but a blip on the horizon, it warrants brief mention as it revealed unfortunate tendencies in the postmodern strain.[28] In particular, the willingness to accept a desired conclusion without paying attention to evidence. His article was full of scientific error which he had intentionally planted to expose the flaws of relativism in postmodern thought. The editors at *Social Text* never questioned the scientific content because the article argued that quantum gravity was a linguistic construct, which is precisely what they wanted to hear. Sokal wrote nonsense on purpose, but postmodernism must share some of the guilt because it encouraged well-intentioned but misguided scholars to publish nonsense of their own. Despite this hoax, Sokal did not prevent the flourishing of more sound postmodern ideas.

This was true also amongst a handful of scientists. Kenneth Hewitt, a physical geographer who worked in a traditional scientific environment, became an advocate of postmodern ideas in the early 1980s.[29] He researched the impact of natural disasters and slowly came to realize that natural disasters were not purely natural phenomena. He objected to an "agent-specific" approach in which the researcher focused entirely on the earthquake, hurricane, or flooding river and encouraged his colleagues to give agency, a postmodern expression, to the communities who had decided to live in disaster-prone environments and who were accustomed to a rhythm of life, which included regular disasters. They were not vulnerable citizens subject to the whims of nature but active participants in their own fates.

At the time, these words were radical in a scientific community obsessed with the physicality of our planet's bad moods. Seismologists, for example, put their efforts into prediction models rather than talking to villagers or Los Angelenos. The Richter scale is a perfect example of this tendency—it reports the absolute physical strength of an earthquake regardless of its impact on the human environment. The Richter scale can report a massive 7.0 earthquake in the middle of the ocean, though a relatively modest 5.0 earthquake in a city will cause much more damage to urban dwellers. For this reason, under the distant influence of relativist ideas, the Mercalli scale is experiencing a modest comeback. The Mercalli scale does not measure earth movement but quantifies the earthquake based on specific damage to settlements. Although it is much older than postmodernism, it is the postmodern scale par excellence. These shifts would not have been possible if the interests of scientists such as Hewitt had not taken a detour through the humanities.

Because of postmodernism's ability to inspire unexpected partners in meaningful ways, the Sokal hoax did not limit the spread of its principles; not everyone was obsessed with the nitty-gritty of its theoretical arguments. At times, general ideas were sufficient to implement change. Through the tangle of these complex theories, real progress (a word anathema to die-hard postmodern practitioners) was made. In a basic way, medicine has developed a more subjective quality in a manner that complements postmodernism. The MRI still has objective qualities, but the medical profession has incorporated the subjective views of patients, who are encouraged to perform self-analyses, in their diagnoses. The all-knowing doctor in a white coat now has assistants who share their subjective impulses with her. This attitude is a sea change from the 1950s, when patients were perceived as bodies to operate upon rather than as individuals with personal qualities. It has become common to read stories about the shortcomings of medical practice when social, political, and racist elements are allowed into the conversation.

The story of Henrietta Lacks is instructive. Henrietta Lacks (née Loretta Pleasant) was born in 1920 in Roanoke, Virginia, into poor circumstances. Her adult life effectively began at the age of fourteen when she gave birth to her first child. By 1941, she was married and working on a subsistence tobacco farm in Virginia. When the war with Japan intensified, a steel factory on the outskirts of Baltimore began to offer better work opportunities for African Americans. Lacks abandoned the farm and moved into the city. Soon thereafter, she complained of abnormal bleeding and went to the nearby Johns Hopkins Medical Center to seek a diagnosis. In 1951, the doctors determined she had cervical cancer, and she died the same year. It so happened, however, that Lacks visited a medical center where researchers were taking much deeper looks into the origins of this form of cancer. These doctors wanted to produce malignant cells—that is, 'immortal' cells—which could be used endlessly in subsequent experiments. As it turned out, Lacks had the perfect cells.

This African American woman provided the medical profession with her cancer cells but was never asked for permission nor compensated, despite the profits made by researchers. After her death in 1951, her identity, essentially disembodied, was reduced to the usefulness of these cancer cells, and no one addressed issues related to posthumous patient rights. A broad public is now willing to look away from the raw science and sympathize with the plight of an individual who, to use an earlier expression from Spivak, could not speak. Lacks was not mute, but she had no voice to take control of her body. Half a century after her death, she has become a public personality. In 2009, Rebecca Skloot wrote *The Immortal Life of Henrietta Lacks* to explore issues of class, race, and medical ethics that were being ignored as long as science was considered a pure endeavor. The book became the basis for a film starring Oprah Winfrey.[30]

The same point could be made by stating that these Eurocentric medical researchers in the 1950s had a specific type of knowledge and could therefore exert power over African Americans. This nexus between knowledge and power was a foundational issue for postmodernists. On the heels of Foucault, postmodernists took a premise from Francis Bacon at the start of the seventeenth century and flipped it on its head. When Bacon linked knowledge and power (*Scientia potestas est*), he had optimistic goals in mind. The acquisition of scientific knowledge could help European states modernize and improve the standing of its subjects and citizens. In contrast, postmodernists demonstrated the pernicious manner in which knowledge could discipline and punish citizens. Knowledge was capillary, meaning that it dripped and oozed its impact in slow yet socially lethal doses. Despite postmodernists who mistakenly invoke their apostolic leaders to argue something about raw power, the link between knowledge and power has little to do with raw power per se. The power–knowledge connection transformed the first term into an invisible quality, not quantity, that surfaced every time knowledge was invoked. When we read on the book cover of Dipesh Chakrabarty's *Provincializing Europe* that it is part of the Princeton Studies in Culture/Power/History, the power is qualitative.

Foucault spread these ideas with such verve, one should not be surprised that the original intent was sometimes lost. But Foucault did write: "It is not possible for power to be exercised without knowledge, it is impossible for knowledge not to engender power."[31] The intricate link between power and knowledge led to a search for "mechanisms of power" that had an impact far from the "histories of kings and generals."[32] The most famous example is the Panopticon, because it took aim at the acquisition of knowledge in a visual fashion; vision was supposed to be a matter of eyewitnessing, and a straightforward phenomenon at that. With the Panopticon, a nineteenth-century surveillance device to monitor the behavior of prisoners, power became invisible to those who endured its consequences. Thus the Panopticon, an actual 'innovation' in the prison system, became the symbol for the exercise of power through the acquisition of visual knowledge and encouraged associated, if not identical, thoughts. For example, schoolchildren sitting in rational rows of chairs were gazing not at their teacher but at each other, and thus monitoring each other's behavior. The pupils thus exercised power over each other even if they were not fully aware of the process. The Panopticon further became related to the 'gaze,' an idea Foucault explored at the start of *The Order of Things* with his discussion on Las Meninas. The mirror and the hidden view of the canvas undermined the transparency of vision. The gaze did not collect objective knowledge, as the classic eyeball was supposed to do, but surveilled a situation to exert influence or establish subtle control. A male gaze absorbing the contours of a woman was a form of control exacting submission. This could be any man and not just the king.

These capillary affects of power were critical to gender scholars who adopted the power–knowledge nexus to decry the world of male knowledge; the manner in which men acquired knowledge became a tool of submission. For example, Patricia Hill Collins posited that Black feminist thought can be viewed as "subjugated knowledge."[33] Power has not been used in this expression but the association is clear, and the assertion indicates how the subjugator can be almost anyone and not only white men. In an earlier essay, chronologically better suited to highlight the growing impact of postmodernism, Collins explored the marginalization of African women in the academic setting. She indicated how "dichotomous oppositional difference" impacted "hierarchical relationships that mesh with political economies of domination and subordination," which affect the production and evaluation of knowledge.[34] Foucault is not mentioned specifically but the postmodern themes are all there, even if one has to be cautious about evaluating an individual author's commitment to specific aspects of postmodernism.

An interesting variation of this theme appears in Isabel Wilkerson's *The Warmth of Other Suns*, a history of African Americans fleeing the Deep South.[35] A popular work, it does not show any direct interest in power–knowledge debates but it introduces an idea of a closely related spirit and embodies the postmodern concern to overturn Enlightenment thought. Wilkerson writes that an invisible hand, a hand of oppression, thwarted black efforts every time they strove to live a normal middle-class life. Adam Smith's invisible hand, from the middle of the eighteenth century, was capitalism's way of boosting the standard of living. Wilkerson inverts the idea to suggest that blacks were hamstrung by the *knowledge* of white oppression; the white southerners did not even have to act to prevent blacks from succeeding because the system encouraged a form of power that was unseen yet incredibly effective.

Patricia Hill Collins's academic reference to the dichotomous oppositional difference is a rephrasing of what might be the most popular postmodern trope—the binary opposition. Binaries in all their forms were contested because they oversimplified reality and created a means of opposition through which a majority could persecute a minority in this either/or equation: either you were a heterosexual, or you were not; either you were a European, or you were not; either the fact was true, or it was not. Identifying these binaries and then eliminating them became the key to pluralist discourse. A key inspiration came from Derrida, who introduced his readers to the presence of absence. The presence of absence argues that opposing sides cannot be isolated; there persists a little bit of both in each. It simply means that there is little bit of homosexuality in every heterosexual and a little heterosexuality in every homosexual. This unsettled hegemonic claims because it eliminated the axis around which these issues were supposed to revolve.

Historically, scholars had looked at European revolutions to observe the pains of a binary world. In the French Revolution, Maximilien Robespierre invoked his terror to eliminate his opponents. A follower of Jean-Jacques Rousseau and committed to universal values, Robespierre could not compromise with alternatives. Hence the clergy, representatives of an anti-rational and superstitious worldview, had to be eliminated, and the terror was unleashed. Over a century later, the Bolsheviks followed a similar practice. The violent tactics of the Bolsheviks were not the survival mechanism of a small party but the application of a Marxist worldview built on Enlightenment principles; this *Weltanschauung* or *mirovozzrenie* was built on a binary that placed the working classes opposite the bourgeoisie (and the nobility and the clergy, in the Russian case). If the Civil War was not horrendous enough, the Stalinist terror took terror to a more horrifying level as the leadership of the Bolshevik party continued to see the world in binary terms.

These two examples represent the grand political stories and highlight dramatic and well-known cases. But postmodern binaries were not really about rulers and those who tried to oppose them. Binaries could be discovered in scientific laboratories, in the statutes of volunteer organizations, and in the attitudes of the colonizers to the colonized who insisted on treating the conquered as the Other. Othering, a familiar concept in the canon, defined an us/them relationship that emerged around the globe as a result of imperialism. To parade the most common example, the British in the nineteenth century saw themselves as independent of the Indians and happily ignored how Indian culture, through imported textiles and foods, had a deep impact on their own habits. The binary prevented them from experiencing a true exchange in a conscious fashion; it wished away appropriations from the Other.

Theoretically, the elimination of binaries eliminates Othering even if the problem persists on the ground. An excellent contemporary and subtle example is the push for transgender rights and the particularly thorny question of bathroom usage: before the dawn of postmodernism, citizens had a choice between two binary oppositions presented as objective biological facts. You walk towards one of two doors and disappear behind one of them; airports, stations, and stadiums have been designed this way for decades. Yet those footsteps have been the subject of prolonged academic and social debates tied with efforts to overcome a binary opposition that forced individuals to select between two norms, men or women. Because gender is a social category, it is much more flexible, even if the choices themselves have not changed. Clearly, these ideas still meet resistance, as the court battles and news reports suggest, but the conversation has been transformed over the course of a generation; the ability to even discuss transgender rights is a first step.

These comments suggest a philosophical approach to the problem, but they also inspire interdisciplinary cooperation. The moment the normative aspects of bathroom politics are raised, historians intuitively look to past examples. In the early ages of the European settlement of the American continent, outhouses were not gender specific, and each individual outhouse welcomed men, women, and transgendered individuals. Although one could not admit to being transgendered back then, one could certainly use the outhouse. Historians will then look back at housing arrangements in the Middle Ages to determine when it became customary to separate male and female toilets, which social classes promoted this behavior, and whether it was linked to civilizing trends such as the Enlightenment or the Industrial Revolution.

In an immediate context, the attack on binary oppositions has become more complex because the digital world depends upon binary assumptions to create the pluralism of the Internet. The digital universe is premised on the idea that, when broken down, life can be described as a series of 1s and 0s. When Heidegger criticized technologies, he did so in an environment with analog radio signals; the 1s and the 0s played almost no role in technology. Today, however, these binaries are the key to success, and anyone who now listens to music listens to the sum of these 1s and 0s. The music is sampled and the reproduction will be good enough for the ear so that the gaps between the 1s and the 0s are imperceptible. These binaries are an essential foundation in the third millennium, whether in music or in the way that algorithms make decisions. They are not as self-evident as the bathroom example, but they cannot be wished away as a technological Other. Later chapters will look at this paradox more closely.

The focus on binary oppositions has other identifiable weaknesses. The search for these pairs became so popular it became a self-fulfilling proposition. Contrasts that had always been loose and nebulous had to be built up and solidified so they could be labeled as binary oppositions. The scholar then, and not the historical or social actor, became the creator of the binary opposition. In the history of academic work, this had precedents. Researchers in the late nineteenth century became fixated on identifying microbes because they believed glory came to those who could locate a microbe and create a universal cure; these researchers overlooked the concept of viruses, and the quest for microbes entered the annals of history, not contemporary research.[36]

This reflected an intellectual aging process and the standardization of older ideas. Thus as postmodernism has aged, many of its ideas have become commonplace and to a degree risk stagnating. Ironically, we might invoke the method of Hayden White. If we remember, White argued that narrative structures informed the writing of historians. Now, equally prominent narrative structures can be identified amongst adherents of postmodernism. Postmodernists would accept the rhythmic ascription, but the structure is more repetitive and acts like a template for rote learners. Readers will quickly realize when a postmodern analysis is following a certain script. When an author urges attention upon a discourse, writes about knowledges, or simply takes aim at the Enlightenment, the reader cannot avoid a sense of déjà vu.

This evinces an odd feature of postmodernism. It was designed to overturn standard hierarchies and give marginalized groups access to power structures. Yet it has come to be associated with an elite cohort of practitioners who have mastered the narrative structure. Consequently, the movement was notorious for presenting obtuse papers that few could understand (hence the Sokal hoax). The academic literature became packed with foggy writing to which no one would want to return. In fact, some authors must flinch when they reread what they wrote a generation ago—the experience must be similar to the adult who looks back at a hairstyle in a high school photograph. Fortunately, this theoretical posturing can be ignored without diminishing the impact of postmodernism; let it be considered an innocent case of overenthusiasm.

While striking a postmodern pose should not be of such great concern anymore, relying on these theses lacks the flair of doing the same activity three decades ago; today's proponents of Einstein's theory of relativity are not considered pathbreakers. Surprisingly, postmodernism appears in robust and traditional form even amongst the digital humanists. To advocate the insertion of humanistic concerns in the digital world, Johanna Drucker *tout court* equates the humanities with postmodernism (and unwittingly sidelines scholars who did not subscribe to the postmodern project). She employs benchmark postmodern positions to demonstrate the humanities' incompatibility with digital techniques. In reaction to Google Maps, she makes the time-worn assertion that "All maps are constructions."[37] Her article questions the rigidity of the time-space axis and notes that in the humanities, "time is as frequently noted in relativistic terms as in absolute ones."[38] Furthermore, "almost all current information visualization is anathema to humanistic thought, antipathetic to its aims and values."[39] Her example embodies both contemporary anxieties and the false sense of security that depends on postmodernism to be a bulwark against digital realities.

All Drucker's points are well taken, but one cannot help but wonder if methods developed in the 1950s and 1960s can offer resistance to the evolving power of the digital world. To be sure, Google Maps has its ideological problems, but it has emerged as such a transcendent force across all international boundaries that it runs roughshod over postmodern notions of incommensurability and local knowledge. Google Translate may be an imperfect tool, but it has also confronted incommensurability as it finds creative ways to build more than bridges between islands. Instead of countering Google Maps or Google Translate by reverting to a fading postmodern critique, constructive energy should be spent examining how the humanities can create space within the digital world. This accepts the assumption that the digital world will metamorphose the parameters of traditional debates, but it simultaneously develops tools to prevent digitization from overwhelming the humanist, Drucker's stated goal.

Drucker's assertions respect the postmodern achievement that has been outlined in this discussion, but they don't establish a path forward. Instead, they embody the naïve assumption that no environment is too foreign for the postmodern canon; that postmodernism can jump from island to island without any need to adapt to local circumstances. This reflects too much faith in a set of ideas. The justification for this is not far at hand because the sweeping success of postmodernism, as presented here, has given it an impenetrable aura. The aura is so blinding that one no longer notices when the paint is peeling and a renovation is required.

This is particularly true of language and discourse, a topic that has so far been left untouched although it was the pivot of almost all postmodern ideas. The digital age has drastically altered linguistic practice and theory because translating has dispensed with dictionaries and works with an entirely new set of principles. "Of Grammatology" makes no sense to an algorithm that has no interest or feeling for grammatical rules; it would simply not understand the fuss. Yet these digital translators have become the single most powerful tools for effective communication. They quickly diminish the impact of discursive claims because they are not bounded by a textbook or a dictionary with a limited set of words. The alphabetization of the dictionary has lost its meaning. Necessarily, so many standard language claims have to be reconsidered.

This can be done only by looking at the linguistic turn in a historical context and demonstrate the appeal of language to postmodernists and analytic philosophers alike. To get a toehold on these concepts is to realize how forcefully language obsessed thinkers of the twentieth century. The narrative then ceases to be one of achievement and becomes one of obsession, a fixation that has resisted adaptation to the digital environment. Therefore, a discussion that canvasses this twentieth-century obsession has to end with digital alternatives for the twenty-first century.

Notes

1. Shirley Lindenbaum and Margaret M. Lock, eds., *Knowledge, Power, and Practice: The Anthropology of Medicine and Everyday Life*, Comparative Studies of Health Systems and Medical Care (Berkeley: University of California Press, 1993).
2. Edward Hallett Carr, *What Is History?* (New York: Vintage Books, 1961), 10–11.

3. Francis Fukuyama, *The End of History and the Last Man* (New York: Free Press, 1992).
4. Michel Foucault, *The Order of Things: An Archaeology of the Human Sciences* (New York: Vintage Books, 1970), 324–5.
5. Bent Hamer, *Kitchen Stories* (2003).
6. Richard Rorty, *Philosophy and the Mirror of Nature* (Princeton, NJ: Princeton University Press, 1980), 139.
7. Richard Rorty, Jerome B. Schneewind, and Quentin Skinner, eds., *Philosophy in History: Essays on the Historiography of Philosophy* (Cambridge [Cambridgeshire] and New York: Cambridge University Press, 1984).
8. Ian Hacking, *The Emergence of Probability: A Philosophical Study of Early Ideas About Probability, Induction and Statistical Inference*, 2nd ed. (Cambridge and New York: Cambridge University Press, 2006).
9. Richard Rorty, *Eine Kultur ohne Zentrum : Vier Philosophische Essays und ein Vorwort* (Stuttgart: Reclam, 1993).
10. Marshall Sahlins, *Islands of History* (Chicago: University of Chicago Press, 1985).
11. On his philosophical background, see Clifford Geertz, *Available Light: Anthropological Reflections on Philosophical Topics* (Princeton, NJ: Princeton University Press, 2000).
12. Dipesh Chakrabarty, *Provincializing Europe: Postcolonial Thought and Historical Difference* (Princeton, NJ: Princeton University Press, 2000), 250.
13. Chakrabarty, *Provincializing Europe*, 251.
14. Gayatri Chakravorty Spivak, "Can the Subaltern Speak?" in *Marxism and the Interpretation of Culture*, ed. Cary Nelson and Lawrence Grossberg (Urbana: University of Illinois Press, 1988), 279–313.
15. Spivak, "Can the Subaltern Speak?" 297.
16. Spivak, "Can the Subaltern Speak?" 301.
17. Spivak, "Can the Subaltern Speak?" 281. In a recent version, Spivak writes, "I have some accident-of-birth facility there."
18. Gayatri Chakravorty Spivak, "Can the Subaltern Speak?" in *Can the Subaltern Speak? Reflections on the History of an Idea*, ed. Rosalind C. Morris (New York: Columbia University Press, 2010), 56.
19. For more details on the project, see Peter Novick, *That Noble Dream: The "Objectivity Question" and the American Historical Profession* (Cambridge: Cambridge University Press, 1988), 526–35.
20. Foucault had interests in medicine but was less focused on physics, chemistry, math, and similar scientific fields. See Michel Foucault, *The Birth of the Clinic: An Archaeology of Medical Perception* (New York: Pantheon Books, 1973).
21. James Bryant Conant, *On Understanding Science: An Historical Approach*, The Terry Lectures (New Haven and London: Yale University Press, 1947).
22. See the preface to Kuhn, *The Structure of Scientific Revolutions*.
23. Shapin and Schaffer, *Leviathan and the Air-Pump*.
24. Jessica Riskin, *Science in the Age of Sensibility: The Sentimental Empiricists of the French Enlightenment* (Chicago: University of Chicago Press, 2002).
25. William E. Burns, *The Scientific Revolution in Global Perspective* (New York: Oxford University Press, 2016), 18, 35–6.
26. William Newman, "A Preliminary Reassessment of Newton's Alchemy," in *Cambridge Companion to Newton* (Cambridge: Cambridge University Press, 2016), 455–6.
27. Newman, "A Preliminary Reassessment of Newton's Alchemy," 463.
28. Alan D. Sokal, ed., *The Sokal Hoax: The Sham That Shook the Academy* (Lincoln: University of Nebraska Press, 2000).

29. Kenneth Hewitt, "Excluded Perspectives in the Social Construction of Disaster," in *What Is a Disaster? Perspectives on the Question*, ed. E. L. Quarantelli (London and New York: Routledge, 1998), 75–92.
30. Rebecca Skloot, *The Immortal Life of Henrietta Lacks* (New York: Crown Publishers, 2010). The information on Lacks comes from this volume.
31. Michel Foucault and Colin Gordon, *Power/Knowledge: Selected Interviews and Other Writings, 1972–1977*, 1st American ed. (New York: Pantheon Books, 1980), 51.
32. Foucault and Gordon, *Power/Knowledge*, 51.
33. Patricia Hill Collins, *Black Feminist Thought: Knowledge, Consciousness, and the Politics of Empowerment* (New York: Routledge, 2000), 251–72.
34. Patricia Hill Collins, "Learning From the Outsider Within: The Sociological Significance of Black Feminist Thought," *Social Problems* 33, no. 6 (1986): S14–S32, https://doi.org/10.2307/800672.
35. Isabel Wilkerson, *The Warmth of Other Suns: The Epic Story of America's Great Migration* (New York: Random House, 2010).
36. Paul De Kruif, *Microbe Hunters* (San Diego: Harcourt, Inc, 1996).
37. Drucker, "Humanistic Theory and Digital Scholarship," 90.
38. Drucker, "Humanistic Theory and Digital Scholarship," 92–3.
39. Drucker, "Humanistic Theory and Digital Scholarship," 86.

3 The End of the Linguistic Turn

Johann Gottfried Herder in his *Abhandlung über den Ursprung der Sprache* from 1772 had already taken language out of the hands of God, but it took at least another hundred years before the arrival of modern forms of linguistic analysis.[1] Gottlob Frege wrote his linguistic masterpiece only at the end of the nineteenth century.[2] By the time of the Great War, it became increasingly common for philosophers to place their main focus on language. Wittgenstein published his *Tractatus* in 1921, and the 1920s gave birth to the Vienna Circle, a group of philosophers known as the logical positivists who were determined to develop a unique metalanguage. As Richard Rorty notes, analytic philosophy came to regard the philosophy of language as 'first-philosophy' and the discipline "which exhibits the 'foundations of knowledge.'"[3] As time progressed, more and more philosophers threw their weight behind language. John Austin had his ordinary language philosophy, W.V.O. Quine had gavagai and radical translation, Jürgen Habermas had his ideal speech situations, Derrida had his *hors texte*, Reinhart Koselleck had his *Begriffsgeschichte*, Hans Blumenberg had his metaphors, Foucault had his discourse, John Searle had his speech acts, Noam Chomsky had his universal grammar, and the list goes on and on. The movement was so strong, it swept traditional rationalists and empiricists right out of the way. If the eighteenth century was the century of rational thought, the twentieth century belonged to language.

No movement likes to be without a name, and soon it was christened the Linguistic Turn; at the end of the 1960s, Rorty edited a volume with this title.[4] The Linguistic Turn did not refer to everyone who studied language because it was more focused on those who positioned language in a social context. For example, Chomsky had already suggested the existence of a universal grammar, but this theory was at odds with the spirit of Rorty's work. The turn, a bend and not a right angle, was supposed to help scholars overcome truths and question the facticity of phenomena. Slogans such as 'there is no hors texte' or *Bedeutung ist Gebrauch* (meaning is use) became the most common academic currencies. Soon one could read that the words of scientists were more significant than whatever they saw with their telescopes and how social groups invented brand new languages and thus brand new worlds. This practice persisted for at least half a century.

Unfortunately, however, the linguistic turn has not been without its problems. For example, all too often, it appears holistically. Even without referencing Derrida's slogan, authors gave the impression that no experiences lie outside of language. Like an earlier generation insisted that all decisions can be reduced to rationality, a position still popular amongst game theorists, the last three generations saw language structuring all thought and were disinclined to limit the influence of language. In the humanities, the issue is exacerbated by an unwillingness to expand interests to philosophers of language outside the postmodern circle. It is therefore essential to outline the development and parameters of the linguistic turn before delving into the digital universe. By taking a closer philosophical look at the application of the linguistic turn over the last fifty years, one cultivates a better sense both for the work it did and for the chinks in its armor. It will take a while to survey this development, but it has the advantage of refreshing our minds, understanding where the linguistic turn came from and how it came to be applied in surprising ways. It reveals weaknesses and weary aspects that don't seem to be so effective anymore. When they are placed in greater focus, it is easier to see why postmodern ideas are especially vulnerable in the digital world. How will digital technologies with their practical and logical programming languages shift assumptions about the incommensurability of languages? What added layers are attached to a world of digital languages?

A more general analysis is needed, an analysis that showcases the persistent arguments of Foucault and Derrida without overlooking the alternatives that were always at hand but rarely grabbed. It occasions a closer look at the non-linguistic components of Wittgenstein's thought, such as more constructive comments about the language game, as well as other ways to think about a world without language. The last task may seem patently obvious, but one should not forget the thousands upon thousands of scholars who insisted upon routing their analyses of almost anything through a view of language developed in the 1960s. In this spirit, one has to revive the actual senses—hearing, smell, touch—so they are not merely appendices to their representation in language. Throughout the discussion, the impact of the digital world is never far away, showing how these technological innovations will accelerate the end of the linguistic turn.

In the 1960s, the linguistic turn crystallized around Derrida and Foucault because they developed key slogans that could jump easily from discipline to discipline. Derrida denied the existence of an *hors texte*, commonly even if controversially understood to mean that our knowledge of the world was limited by the languages we employ. Foucault continually referred to a discourse of power and linked the control of language with power in general. Thus a historian could as easily write about the discourse of power as the sociologist or even, by the 1990s, the economist. Of the two, Derrida had a better eye for the mechanics of language and therefore found a home amongst scholars of literary criticism; Foucault was more interested in language as an everyday rather than grammatical phenomenon, thus his search for discourse could be considered part of a common language platform attractive to the social sensitivity of the historian.

Derrida had been a close reader of Martin Heidegger, whose own writings were dense with linguistic play. The abundance of German prefixes gave Heidegger an opportunity to mix and match prefixes *à discrétion*. Heidegger took the German word for difference (*Unterschied*) and added a hyphen to make it Unter-schied.[5] Derrida built on this play and toyed with a similar word, merging the French for defer and differ to get *différance*, this concept became fundamental to the reception of his philosophy of language.[6] The term eliminated a strict difference (or binary opposition) between entities because these entities defer to each other and therefore contain a little bit of each other within themselves. The pithy term undermines notions of purity and objectivity, shifting attention to a definition of meaning based on relationships. This theory promoted philosophy as the fluctuating and often flummoxing relationship between linguistic terms. This represented the maximal understanding of the linguistic turn and embodied the refusal to accept the existence of an *hors texte*.

Many authors struggled to find a way to merge such extreme claims with more effective analyses that recognized an empirical reality. Gabrielle Spiegel represents the interesting case of someone who recognized the perils of the maximalist approach but still adhered to the basic parameters of that approach. She portrays one of her essays as an attempt to combine the linguistic turn with "an insistence on the still viable notion of empirical research as the foundation of historical scholarship."[7] Her ideas, however, give language the dominant position:

> It acknowledges that "reality," "context," "social structure," and the like appear to present historians only through past texts that are interpretively reconstituted and that history as the object of our knowledge is, inevitably, absent and knowable only through textually mediated representations.[8]

These lines are fascinating because they evince the enormous centripetal force of the linguistic turn. Spiegel was fully aware of its potential limitations and yet could not escape its orbit.

One sees this with her reference to the word text because its meaning appropriately wavers between a text as a physical object and as texte, as suggested by the *hors texte*, a linguistic expression that carries epistemological significance. At times, the reference is to a medieval document which contains words and sentences that have to be understood in a social setting. This meaning has a slight element, but only slight, of the positivism that Spiegel did not admire.[9] In contrast, text also appears as something more grand that implicates the acquisition of knowledge; here it is synonymous with Derrida's usage. Both meanings share traces with each other and keep each other in equilibrium. The example demonstrates how difficult it was to evade the study of language as the single largest performative force.

Dominick LaCapra, a historian of France, was fully invested in the linguistic philosophy of the postmodernists but recognized that "when excess . . . is fixated on, there is a marked inclination to overdose on the antidote."[10] The excess was a strict reliance on Derrida, the antidote was an objection to binary oppositions, and the overdose was the fascination with these seductive linguistic technologies. Despite these concerns, LaCapra was promoting an interdisciplinary methodology that depended upon linguistic analysis and critical theory. It did not deviate from this path; it only suggested that sometimes the historian had to pull back from fiction a little and remain true to a less narrative version of events; somewhere through the thicket of linguistic theory, facts were still discernible. LaCapra wrote these comments in 2000, shortly after the peak of linguistic theory, so they contain a little bit of the fatigue that came from witnessing the blind use of methods.

These authors indirectly acknowledged that the *hors texte* was a perilous idea to begin with. Some philosophers criticized its absolutist tendencies, whereas others such as Ludwig Wittgenstein would have denied it altogether had he still been amongst the living. In less philosophical circles, the idea was more readily integrated, either because the consequences were not fully pondered or because of an awkward interdisciplinary exchange. The risk for the historian was that of getting trapped between a philosophical and a factual claim. It is one thing to philosophically support the *hors texte*; it is another to argue that someone from the past was confined by the language they used. How could a historian determine the linguistic boundaries of an individual from the past? A historian could identify word preferences and shifting usages, but the boundary is elusive because no correlation exists between the sentences someone actually uses and the unspoken sentences they would otherwise have the ability to have said. The *hors texte* also makes it difficult to evaluate the non-linguistic experiences of historical actors or variances amongst those who listened to the wilderness, bird songs or songlines, but only rarely spoke.

Derrida's was the world of philosophers and literary critics, whereas Foucault was more concerned with history and politics—real power and real control. In *The Order of Things*, Foucault does discuss a few Indic phonemes as Ursounds, a passing observation on a much longer journey.[11] The broad public qualities of his linguistic analysis link Foucault more closely with discourses formed to create convenient forms of knowledge and exert power. Discourse became inherently combative and the measure of the world.[12] As a corollary, if power relations are embedded in discourse, then the most effective way to mount a subversive attack is through discourse itself; this process has been referred to as taking control of the language. A homosexual discourse can challenge the hegemonic role of a heterosexual discourse by taking control of a once-derogatory term such as *queer* and turn the term against the oppressor. Foucault's presentation of language rarely gets dissected by analytic philosophers of language precisely because it is better suited to more confrontational attacks in the public sphere.

The method has been significant but not without confusion, because no one has ever denied the key role of language in a social setting. Throughout the ages, rhetoric and the meticulous crafting of speeches has been of great concern. Cicero authored careful language well before Foucault came along. Many cases exist in which language has been designed to express power—in the speeches of politicians or in the sloganeering of the Bolsheviks after the revolution of 1917. With the thousands of references to discourse, however, it has become almost impossible to distinguish classical rhetorical strategies from more contemporary discursive ones in political and historical writing. To be sure, Foucault's method allows one to look at language at all levels of society. His assertions were tied to claims about knowledge, adding an epistemological edge absent in traditional rhetoric. Yet this distinction is often lost or ignored given the pure enthusiasm for the linguistic turn.

Part of the confusion stems from eliding two close concepts—using language to control a situation such as Cicero would have aspired to, and controlling a language as postmodernists often posit. The first instance is reminiscent of raw power and political might, and the second more subtle. Despite the subtlety, however, it can also run up against problems when treated holistically or applied with maximum force. Irregularities arise in empirical situations when controlling the language is linked with controlling the thoughts or the minds of constituents. No doubt, the medical association develops a specific terminology, and the state can prescribe a specific grammar in its schools (note that the Russian Empire banning Ukrainian in the middle of the nineteenth century is not subtle enough to enter into Foucault's analytic world), but language with all its verbs, tenses, and possibilities for negation appears too large to control; especially, when the grand structure of language offers speakers so much to choose from. What are the limits, not of language, but of linguistic control when language does not even need a subversive intellectual underground to create new forms of expression. Unfortunately, authors of a maximalist interpretation of the linguistic turn overlook these possibilities and, paradoxically, oversimplify the structure of language in order to argue that someone has gained control of the language. In fact, many references to discourse take language as a self-evident entity and are much less interested in its inner organs or expansive capabilities. They remain satisfied to do an external autopsy and thus make claims about control that a more substantive understanding of language would not support.

All too often, claims about language ignore the philosophically meaningless idea that language is a dominant means of expression amongst humans. One has to be able distinguish those cases in which the linguistic turn does real theoretical work from those in which it does none. In most applications of the linguistic turn, the actual reliance on language is minor and doesn't really affect the linguistic apparatus as a whole. Studies have been made on shifting word usage and the distribution of slogans, but these are all, after Wittgenstein, moves made within the same language game.[13] Creating a neologism does not create a new language, nor do minor orthographic changes, such as eliminating the hard sign after a consonant as the Bolsheviks did in Russia, or decapitalizing personal pronouns as the Germans recently did in their new *Rechtschreibung*. We should study the impact of any linguistic change, however minor, but resist the temptation to place it in a grand philosophical scheme.

These problems are widespread but not universal, and thus it would be unfair to leave the discussion with these loose threads. One of the most sophisticated applications comes from the early 1970s in the form of Hayden White's seminal *Metahistory*. Seminal not because it launched the linguistic turn or even became a reference work for philosophers of language, but because it effectively expanded the relativist claims of language into the heavily positivist domain of the historian; it made the linguistic turn an interdisciplinary phenomenon. Without the atomistic approach that studies words as the fundamental linguistic element, White examined the style of nineteenth-century European historians to make the point that their writing followed literary conventions; and writing had a poetic component: therefore, how objective could it be? Thus the reader encounters a rather unique theoretical style from White himself. The opening chapter refers to the "Poetics of History" and the "formal verbal structures" of the historians as it embarks on a search for inaugural and transitional "motifs" to decipher the "emplotment" that guided the historians' explanations.[14] White's was a maximalist projection of the linguistic turn because it was easily associated with the assertion that any writing, no matter how factual it may seem, was hopelessly mired in its own subjectivity.

It is much less common to come across minimalist projections of the linguistic turn because it fit so well with the relativist theses of postmodernism. Rare are the researchers who argue that a nineteenth-century writer 'at times' drifted into the poetic mode but otherwise wrote in good old factual prose. Seldom does one find works on scientists suggesting that some of their terminology reflected the social construction of phenomena whereas other terms really did describe the way the world operates. Mixed methodologies have little place in the canon.

The extent of the linguistic influence emerges in even greater clarity when seen through a philosophy of music and a philosophy of art. It indicates the power of the linguistic turn and the alternatives that were marginalized because of the persuasive character of postmodernism. In 1973, Leonard Bernstein gave a series of lectures at Harvard University during which he argued that music has a universal language; he went to great pains to map musical notation to grammatical structures. The famous conductor and composer couldn't resist the attraction to link music to language. He did it under the intellectual tutelage of Noam Chomsky.

Since Bernstein's inspiration came from Chomsky, an opponent of Foucault's relativism, he accepted the existence of an underlying universal grammar and wanted to discover the composer's equivalent. How, then, can one translate musical sounds into grammar? First, the word has to be linked with music. Therefore, Bernstein argued that "if it is literally true that In the Beginning Was The Word, then it must have been a *sung* word."[15] Language and song have become more complicated since then, but the careful researcher can reveal an "innate musical-grammatical competence which we may all possess universally."[16] It therefore makes sense to look for the grammatical components of language in musical notation. In bold font, Bernstein created a chart that mapped equivalents: a musical phrase is a linguistic word, and a musical movement mirrored a sentence in language.[17] Although this is hardly a popular approach to music, readers should appreciate Bernstein's willingness to risk opprobrium by presenting a table of equivalencies. Most proponents of discourse analysis would shy away from such a risky step because it allows the reader to directly question the analogies when more vague references to the power of language do no such thing. The chart is part of an age during which language was the center of all things, since it seems farfetched that musical composition could be reduced to grammatical forms.

Most recently, the study of music is being paired with digital technologies and a recognition that structural parallels exist between music and the digital world. A German commentator recently noted that even the first academics who asked *Quid est musica?* looked to the "bits and bytes of individual tones."[18] Although the project has the same atomistic ambitions as Bernstein, who wanted to find a match with words, it has no interest in language per se. The interdisciplinary partnership is being made with mathematics, a more traditional partner, and digital technologists. Interestingly, it foreshadows other digital approaches that would be equally foreign to Bernstein.

In 1981, Arthur Danto wrote a philosophy of art comparing art to texts. Danto had already experimented with narratives in an earlier work, so he had a long history with languages.[19] In the *Transfiguration of the*

Commonplace, Danto asserted that "works of art are logically of the right sort to be bracketed with words." And "artworks as a class contrast with real things in just the way in which words do."[20] No table of equivalencies exists as in Bernstein's scheme, so the sentence was demoted and has less importance than the word. The mechanics of the linguistic situation are left by and large unexplained. Instead, linguistic concerns are expressed with more speculative questions that capture the spirit of the 1980s: "is there a 'grammar' of pictures which can be a touchstone for standard or deviant pictures?"[21] This is the exact same question Bernstein asked about music, though Danto refrained from answering with any grammatical references (Danto does leave the door open that the picture might come before or exist independently of the language).

The quotation marks positioned around the word grammar are not insignificant. On the surface, they associate Danto's ideas with a wider research community and could be left at that. They also suggest uncertainty. What is he referring to when he writes of a grammar? Is he looking to find the imperfect in Picasso and the perfect in Matisse, or to take that as a step to discovering that the Black Square was in the dative? What temporal components of language have analogous features in art? These possibilities seem absurd, but only because we don't expect his reference to relate to grammatical rules. Rather, his reference to grammar is to something amorphous and less distinct; it is at odds with Bernstein's serious attitude towards grammar. The vagueness can be useful at times, but it also tends towards the conclusion that it really has nothing to do with language at all. If the structure and composition of language are completely unimportant, why make a reference to grammar?

Bernstein notwithstanding, most humanists preferred the *hors texte* and discursive analyses because they lacked a scientific veneer. By and large, Chomsky's ideas never found the ear of philosophers, historians, or literary scholars. The same can be said of cognitive linguistics, although many of their conclusions would be familiar in a postmodern framework. In part, they were neglected because they assigned language a secondary role; language was a means to another end. This approach, accessibly summarized in Steven Pinker's *Stuff of Thought*, argued that the human brain essentially created a language to reflect its desires.[22] Our grammatical expressions are the function of cerebral requirements. These assertions were based on a scientific method with data collection that existed outside a social context (i.e. comparing the dative in different language groups). It therefore pushed the study of language in a more scientific direction and with its emphasis on data, foreshadowed aspects of the digital age. In incredibly intricate ways, these researchers parsed, pulled, and paraded every 'aspect' of language. It made interesting claims about language that do not appear in the humanities—thus both the findings and the methods are of interest, especially since they have the closest link to contemporary digital scholarship. A few thoughts on language and time and the associated methodology are warranted a quick look.

The expression of time in language is so incredibly complex that it has remained beyond the purview of all except those who specifically study it. For example, most historians ignore it completely and do no more than study the words used by past humans. Stephen Kotkin coined the expression *Speaking Bolshevik* to characterize the propaganda strategies of the young communist regime, but the *speaking* makes no effort to analyze how the Bolsheviks manipulated verb tenses to their advantage (despite the Russian language having critical distinctions between the perfect and the imperfect tenses).[23] Chakrabarty has commented on colonial practices associated with the word *labour* as a noun but not as a verb with shifting tenses.[24] It is telling how these analyses cling to a temporally static version of language that cannot begin to foreshadow digital inroads into language.

A cognitive linguist, however, casts time in numerous ways. First, the expression of time in language is inexact. If we want an exact expression of time, we need numerals because verbs won't perform this function. Second, verb tenses tend to work with reference points and are thus related to the position in time of the speaker. Steven Pinker provides the sentence: "Francesca had already written the fateful letter [event being located] when the count knocked on the door [reference event in the past]."[25] The expression has no exact time; time is based relative to the actions of the count. Surprisingly, the lack of exactitude, a pillar of postmodernism, never caught on.

But how does this linguist arrive at conclusions? Many examples are culled from stock phrases in English or across a multitude of languages. The word butterfly, a neat little curiosity, is different in English, French (papillon), and German (Schmetterling). This difference inspires the collector to create a list of the word butterfly in all European languages to discover that it is always different (even if there are lurking phonetic similarities). The art of collection goes hand in hand with analysis, a key component to research in the humanities. The methods are therefore not so different from those of the modern literary scholar or historian, though they are more closely tied to a scientific community. Thus the more familiar humanists are with cognitive linguistics, the better positioned they will be to anticipate the influence of empirical methods based on Big Data. Humanists can maintain a love for the study of language, though the basics will differ from those principles embodied by the linguistic turn.

Tracking down expressions in texts is old hat, but contemporary digital methods make the method more practical for humanists, as the recent phenomenon of *distant reading* suggests.[26] Historical and literary documents can be canvassed for tense changes, aspect uses, spatial references, and more. An expression such as Speaking Bolshevik won't refer to minor (effectively infinitesimal) changes in a home language but will have a more intricate awareness of language, a thrust, and a charge that is sorely lacking. Then both the mechanics of language and the social context can work together. This might be one way to save parts of the linguistic turn in the context of emerging digital technologies.

Furthermore, much of cognitive linguistics is designed to show how the brain wants to see the world; it does not claim that the brain sees the world only through language. Hence it also suggests that as much as language bounds certain experiences, others are not filtered through language at all. The acceptance of this statement moves the discussion towards the importance of the senses, such as hearing and touch, that have no relation with language whatsoever. This last thought brings to mind Ludwig Wittgenstein's suggestion that some senses, perfectly real, lie beyond language, a concept that collides with reductionist theses which still insist on passing all our senses through a discursive gatekeeper. Treating the senses as senses demonstrates the limits of the linguistic turn by emphasizing those experiences that must be considered free of the 'grammar' of which Danto wrote. Although an extralinguistic reality may seem self-evident, scholars of the senses still have a hard time liberating themselves from a discursive worldview. Martin Jay speculates on the birth of new "discursive traditions" and, when commenting on the complexity of the senses, writes that they "require all the resources of language to communicate their power."[27] Ironically, a closer look at Wittgenstein wrestles the discussion free from a dependency on language before turning specifically to the senses.

As Bernstein and the cognitive linguists suggest, not everyone looked to postmodernists for linguistic inspiration. In the flurry of excitement, Parisian philosophers were clearly the first choice, but Wittgenstein managed to enjoy widespread influence beyond his home base in analytic philosophy. His analytic perspective and background in mathematics put him outside the postmodern circle per se, but he shared its emphasis on a language that was not fixed by God or grammatical rules. His claims from the Tractatus in the 1910s about the limits of language have been linked with Derrida's denial of an *hors texte*.[28] Although Wittgenstein proposed a limit to language, he recognized the existence of something beyond language that language was powerless to describe; language did not circumscribe knowledge, emotion, or existence. Decades later the less rigid analytic formulation of the *Philosophical Investigations* gave it some prominence amongst non-philosophers. Shapin and Schaffer treat Foucault and Wittgenstein interchangeably as they, like scores of others, invoke the language game to socialize language and its usage. Their adoption of this analytic philosopher reveals a highly selective process—one either directly referenced a postmodernist or transformed an outlier and aligned him with postmodernism.

Despite the wider distribution of his later ideas, the discussion must begin with the *Tractatus*, a mathematically inclined text that sought to link logic with the structure of language (rather than the other way around, linking a grammatical structure to music). Although the *Tractatus* was deeply influential amongst members of the Vienna Circle in the 1920s, the logical structure has had an alienating impact on readers without a mathematical background. This feature notwithstanding, two well-rounded phrases will be looked at more closely because they frequently appear in the writing of humanists in defense of the linguistic turn. In contrast, here they set a transitional tone for non-linguistic experiences.

The first phrase appears in 5.6, where Wittgenstein wrote that "*the limits of my language* mean the limits of my world" (emphasis in original). At the end of the *Tractatus*, Wittgenstein offers another spark for the linguistic turn, a spark that has been quoted over and over: "what we cannot speak about we must pass over in silence." These two assertions gave more fodder to those who saw language as the key to understanding human existence. It has a dramatic moment that suggests we are lost without language; that even the mysticism of a language-less world is no compensation. But most instances make a wrong assumption about silence, as if the limit and especially the silence denoted the absence rather than the presence of something else. What could then be implied by silence which arises when we do not speak?

It permits a bold step away from language and a closer inspection of the senses. Making the senses independent of discursive techniques also makes them more independent of digital analysis; the moment the senses are presented as a discourse, they will quickly be routed through digital technologies because digital technologies can parse language with such ease. As a first step into the senses, silence is refreshing because it maintains its independence from the linguistic turn and also shows humanists a style of analysis resistant to Big Data.

Wittgenstein's formulation establishes another world of experience. The silence, *das Schweigen*, appears to be cutting us off from something, though that something is ill-defined.[29] Silence, however, is a much more complicated phenomenon than the one presented in the *Tractatus*. Philosophers of the senses, particularly of sound, would be less concerned because they would quickly recognize alternatives—the silence actually opens up worlds of experience rather than shuts them down. The Christmas carol "Silent Night" (*Stille Nacht*) embodies a different type of silence (*Schweigen*) than appears in Wittgenstein's comment but captures the spirit of his views. The carol implies a religious, historical, and emotional silence that transcends the words of the carol.

R. Murray Schafer, who spent a lifetime studying soundscapes, was much less interested in language than sound. He imbued silence with a lived complexity that transcends language and has no real limits until we impose ourselves on it. In this sonic worldview, silence is a sound because it requires the act of listening and an awareness of acoustic space. Silence is not the aural equivalent of a vacuum, an empty nothingness, but the presence of a unique aural environment. Silence is not completely without noise; it makes a strong appeal to our ears and does not preclude the activity of other senses. In Schafer's words, *Temples of Silence* are "the quiet environments where sounds are more conspicuous by their scarcity."[30] Paradoxically, where there is silence, there is sound.

The emphasis on reception in the form of listening is important; the ear has a muscle which can be flexed. In contrast, *Schweigen* does not take listening into consideration; as if the absence of the production of language means critical other senses are handicapped as well. Maybe Wittgenstein should have written, *Stimmlos* (voiceless) rather than *Schweigen*, though the German *Schweigen* is more closely related to 'not speaking' than to listening and thus more conducive to a book on language. By neglecting listening, it emerges as a philosophy without sound.

Fortunately, we do listen, and listening is particularly important with respect to natural sound. In a modern age, we have become particularly adept at tuning out sounds (maybe this non-listening is *Schweigen*), but in a natural environment, listening to is more important than speaking to. Schafer takes the example of the Russian steppe from an Anton Chekhov novella in which the author (as a fictional character) travels across Ukraine. The sound of the wagon accompanies the travelers along the entire journey and the sound injects "their speech the way clothes dictate behavior: comments are choppy, thoughts desultory and observations haphazard."[31] A more haunting example from a Russian short story comes from Ivan Turgenev's *Sportsman's Sketches* (*Zapiski okhotnika*). "The Clatter of Wheels" (*Stuchit!*) is the story of a nobleman and his servant who take a trip across the countryside in the middle of the night. Although they are silent in speech, they suddenly hear a faint noise in the darkness—the light rattling of wagon wheels, a sound linked to the presence of midnight marauders. Kilometers and kilometers of acoustic space are filled with fear the moment the main characters recognize the sound. In the night, the steppes were alive with other sounds, but the travelers filtered out, what was to them, the socially most meaningful sound. The night was quiet, socially silent if you will, but not without sound.

Turgenev's travelers were focused on a particular sound, but we should not think of acoustic space as a uniform space. In the same way that postmodernists denied singular truths in favor of pluralistic outcomes, acoustic space represents a pluralistic environment. In the *Battle Between Carnival and Lent* (1559), Peter Brueghel composed an inanimate painting that abounded with different sounds. Schafer draws the sound from the painting, demonstrating the absence of bells and the presence of a lute player and a woman "with a friction drum."[32] The entire painting is a "scene with as many acoustic centres as there are activities."[33] A soundscape without a center can be compared to Richard Rorty's culture without a center.

For all this, Schafer is not indifferent to the structure of language. His emphasis turns away from the ears and moves to the mouth as a physical producer of meaningful sounds. The words that emerge from the mouth are critical, but the experience is not configured holistically. In an Egyptian creation myth, "the eye follows the voice as the instrument by which the creative act is assessed."[34] The All-Lord speaks as Khepri and asserts that "Many were the beings which came forth from my mouth."[35]

The mouth also uttered specific words. In the Khadogya-Upanishad, the Om is an attempt to condense the whole of creation into a single aural syllable. As we repeat the same symbol, we move from consciousness to pre-consciousness, meditating on phenomena around us. The Om and its repetition are deeply associated with the act of breathing, a key to life itself. While it may seem as if the focus is drifting towards Indian philosophy, the drift is towards a comment made by Nietzsche. In his classic statement on S*chein* becoming *Sein*, he said *esse*, the Latin *to be*, once meant little more than to breathe and only later developed into an essence.[36] Yet the breath exerted to express the Om was already a unifying essence—*Sein* was already *Sein*, and not the grammatical *sein* learned by a young Nietzsche at Schulpforta in the 1850s. The Om reminds us that simple sounds have dramatic meanings.

This modest excursus was triggered by the last line in the *Tractatus*. The digression added a layer to emphasize that silence, not a normal component of the linguistic turn, has its own intricacies that can be pondered. Wittgenstein, however, did not stick with the *Tractatus*. As his admirers amongst the logical positivists dissected its ordered aphorisms, he embraced the idea that the importance of language lay not with its logical structures—meaning was use, regardless of any inherent logic. In a new series of aphorisms (this time with a simplified numbering system), Wittgenstein fueled debates about common language and social discourse and transcended the boundaries that hemmed in analytic philosophers. The *Philosophical Investigations* therefore undid earlier assumptions.

The most common approach is to mine the *Philosophical Investigations* for the pithy aphorisms that hint towards a social function. As a novel pursuit, the following pages understand the *Philosophical Investigations* as a metaphor for something larger than language. This takes into consideration the fact that many of the challenges in the book are not about language. For example, instead of considering what an excursus on chess tells us about language, the more fruitful approach is to see how the aphorisms speak to games, such as chess, that have no inherent connection to language at all. It also bears mentioning that it is a rather quiet text with a subdued soundscape. The silence of the *Tractatus* has therefore been maintained.

The *Philosophical Investigations* is not absence of utterances. As expected, the most common act is for someone to 'say something.' Orders are given, the imaginary interlocutor challenges the philosopher with statements in standard quotations and, famously, cries of pain demonstrate that no obscure thought process, no Enlightenment mind if you will, lingers behind the scream. But in this example, one of the most cited, the stress lies on the grammatical word *pain* and not the aural environment the declaration of pain produces; a scream quickly transcends the concept of a word, yet it has no volume because Wittgenstein is making a point about thinking. Even the language games, the most widely abused concept, transpire without a peep; the crowd does not roar in these games.

Language games suggest that language is a shifting corpus; one could not label an object with a word and be done with it. Critically, the language game is rule-based. Wittgenstein's first formal example of a rule-based game is chess, a contest that normally requires no speech whatsoever; a chess game has no necessary words, nor do rules suggest a pattern for word usage.[37] Most frequently, the rules have been ignored and humanists have focused on the term *game* because it seems to imply jostling, playfulness, and fun. A scholar influenced by Derrida's playfulness can easily convince herself that she has found a common theme in the language games. Yet placing the language game within the sphere of postmodern mischievousness distracts from the rules without which a language game cannot exist; amusement is not a necessary quality of a language game, but rules are. Rules are instrumental in fixing parameters, but they do not fix outcomes. No two hockey games are alike even if both are played according to the exact same rules.

With respect to earlier themes, the language games have no sonic component. Chess, for example, has a unique aural environment. Except for the ticking of a clock, one would expect silence and little verbal communication between participants. Wittgenstein includes fewer intellectual pursuits, but they are all equally quiet in their presentation. He discusses ball games, card games, and games of combat to demonstrate how rules overlap but are not identical. He entreats his interlocutor to "think not, rather look" to pull the discussion away from a substratum of rational thought.[38] Consequently, when he urges to look at a ball hitting a wall, the ball makes no noise whatsoever because looking is not listening; yet the sound of the ball has a significance that has nothing to do with language. Wittgenstein was not willing it away by not paying attention to it.

The examples just outlined are non-linguistic. Wittgenstein was not making the claim that a board game can be reduced to linguistic parameters as Leonard Bernstein claimed that music had a universal grammar. The board game and the ball throwing persist as non-linguistic phenomena in the world, although they are conveniently used to describe linguistic processes. Nor do the rules have to be expressed in a known language. The primary purpose with the games was to push away from a logical language. This shifts the intent of Wittgenstein's analysis in light of the dominance of the linguistic turn. In the current climate, the language games can be used to push away from the linguistic turn without resurrecting the logical language Wittgenstein sought to deny. Accepting this strategy also means that the language game can easily be adapted to a non-discursive digital universe.

These points may be trivial without the appropriate intellectual context, but they rarely appear when one takes a closer look at the reception of Wittgenstein in non-philosophical circles. Analytic philosophers have focused on what it means to follow a rule in these language games, whereas historians and sociologists have employed the expression with less concern for its mechanics. These last two groups, more focused on playfulness than rule-based rigor, have been content to portray almost any situation in which two sides have a disagreement as evidence of competing language games (and subsequently of epistemological incommensurability). This is the strategy in Shapin and Schaffer's work on seventeenth-century science; they do not attempt to explain why a disagreement between Thomas Hobbes and Robert Boyle represents separate games rather than competing positions from within the same game, as we would expect from two teams in a soccer game. These views rely far too much on naïve assumptions about the linguistic turn and ascribe a dominance to language it does not even have in the Wittgensteinian system. These scholars also invoke the language game with the understanding that language games always involve linguistic situations when the original examples suggest otherwise.

Since the postmodern view of language is designed to highlight competing worldviews and thus establish epistemological islands that operate on their own terms, discourse theory is often confrontational. Thus if Foucault had designed the concept of the language game, underlying the concept would be the idea that games are played to be won. It therefore seems only natural that Hobbes should be portrayed in a fundamental contest against Boyle. In contrast, the Wittgenstein games are about engaging in rule-based behavior and have little or nothing to do with winning, though some of the games have implicit winners. When the confrontational aspect is removed, it becomes easier to understand why two historical characters can disagree within the same language game—it is not a clash to the finish.

The comments on the *Tractatus* and the *Philosophical Investigations* are more about the fragilities of the linguistic turn than about reinterpreting Wittgenstein. These works have too often been put to service to advance a position they don't represent. Against common expectations, they never circle the wagons around language but give language a limited but respectful role. It would be ridiculous to claim Wittgenstein had no interest in language, but it is equally ridiculous to claim his attention did not extend beyond language. The language game, for example, is a metaphor for something much larger than language. Unfortunately, the idea was oversimplified during the prime of the linguistic turn. Scholars were so intent on promoting language, they lost track of the rules, and when they lost track of the rules, they simply couldn't see how the language games were about anything other than language.

Similarly, the low volume in Wittgenstein's work shifted attention away from the senses. Wittgenstein, however, has all sorts of examples where the senses are more important than language. Of course, the linguistic turn was specifically designed to challenge the sense data of the empiricists, so it was quite convenient, perhaps even intentional, to pass over all the purely sensual aspects of Wittgenstein's writings. The senses and what they told us about human experience were an unintended casualty because they lost their independence and became subordinate to language claims, as the position of Martin Jay suggests. In sum, much of what has been outlined can be condensed into the notion that the senses have been ignored. To regain the senses, one has to look beyond linguistic analysis.

Ignoring the senses is not a recent phenomenon. In his time, Galileo launched a scientific revolution, but one with a disdain for the senses. His ambition was to examine "figures, numbers, and movements but not smell, nor tastes, nor sounds."[39] Research with a scientific inclination embraced these words for centuries. But even the philosophy of language, the key contemporary means to defy Galileo, did not do better with smells, tastes, or sounds, despite its contempt for the sciences. In *Unterwegs zur Sprache*, Heidegger asks "What is stillness?" but the stillness has neither sound nor silence because these aspects get quickly appropriated by teasing aphorisms about the stilling of stillness and the restlessness of rest.[40] The potentialities get reduced to toying with language.

Even well-natured attempts to specifically focus on the senses cannot free themselves from a linguistic stranglehold. For example, scholars have started to write about a "sensory turn," piggybacking on the terminology of the linguistic turn. As a result, historians have explored such fascinating episodes as the Great Stink of London in 1858.[41] But caution is required. It helps to repeat verbatim Martin Jay's words from a 'senseless' article: he writes that the senses "require all the resources of language to communicate their power."[42] Once again, we are left with the feeling that language has pulled rank on the senses. The comments are to be expected because they come from an article that respects the postmodern canon, mentions the Foucauldian archaeology, Derrida's "fart," and the regimes associated with the senses. The "sensory turn," then, is a bit of a misnomer because it emerges in a straight line from the linguistic turn.

In Galileo's remarks quoted earlier, he did omit vision, for vision was to become a pre-eminent tool in the Scientific Revolution and the

Enlightenment. The seventeenth and eighteenth centuries launched an ocularization that would be overcome only in the twentieth century. If seventeenth-century scientists elevated vision above all else, the French thinkers of the twentieth century "denigrated" it and decried, with salty tears, the link between objectivity and the truth. As Jay points out, the French thinkers were not promoting an end to vision and the birth of a blind society. They aspired to a plurality of visions and the "proliferation of models of visuality."[43] These models of visuality should, however, be able to exist without using language as a crux.

Any return to vision risks being characterized as an anachronism because of decades of work designed to undermine vision, whether as a penetrating gaze or as a flawed eyewitness. Yet even during the height of the linguistic turn, vision had its sophisticated caretakers. John Berger's *Ways of Seeing* was a seminal effort to complicate vision.[44] The plural noun in the title leaves no doubt. The cover of the book emphatically reminds the reader that "Seeing comes before words. The child looks and recognizes before it can speak." The format of the intellectual effort confirms this—it was a BBC television series first, and only thereafter did it become a book. In an age when television had yet to gain intellectual credibility, the order of creation is significant. Even in the book, certain chapters have images only. Berger makes it quite clear that words can quickly infect the understanding of visual imagery: "Reproduced paintings, like all information have to hold their own against all the other information being continually transmitted."[45] Words compete against words and images compete against images, but Berger expresses a deeper concern for those instances when words and imagery intersect; precisely because of the role being ascribed to language when he undertook this project.

Despite the massive influence of this book in art historical circles, the statements on seeing did not transcend the discipline as did linguistic expressions—Speaking Bolshevik has a ring that Seeing Bolshevik does not. And in the spirit of Galileo, Sniffing Bolshevik has no chance at all. (And how would the meaning of Reading Bolshevik differ again?) Perhaps imagery is closer to the heart of art historians, but when phrased broadly, *Ways of Seeing* sends a message that should appeal beyond the frame into other disciplines without raising the concern that a return to a naked empiricism is around the corner.

Light and lighting have a place in this worldview as well. Seeing is still related to the eye and therefore can still, despite all efforts, have an empirical feel, whereas light is that which surrounds and impacts the eye—a combination of seeing and light, like sound is related to listening. The lighted environment can have an unexpected impact on experience. Playing with shades stretches the discussion beyond well-worn metaphors of lightness and darkness (more closely tied to the image of the

Enlightenment) and adds more substance to the assertion that the senses, which have otherwise been underestimated or reduced to language, are significant.

Linguistic reduction always lurks around the corner and can be seen with respect to naming practices of colors, which have gained greater attention than the colors themselves. Crayola has rightly been forced to rename some of its colors, but the renaming does not change the color in its natural environment. At other times, the inability to provide an exact match between a physical color and a name has been taken as an opportunity to detach the label from the color and focus on the label. The well-ordered color palate at Sherwin-Williams might not replicate the natural environment, but it reveals the gentle transformation from one shade to the next as well as the abrupt discrepancies between shades that don't lie anywhere near each other; neither the names nor the shades have to be exact to respect the independence of the colors. As light changes and our position in the landscape shifts, so does the perception of the environment; language does not track these alterations.

Since the discussion is about shades and not primary colors, an example from Marcel Proust can lead us closer to our goal. The madeleine, that clichéd biscuit, has dominated discussion outside the circles of committed Proustians; its shade is not up for discussion. We should, however, remind ourselves that the taste of the cookie, and not the sight or the semantics, triggered the memories.[46] Fortunately, within the thousands of pages of his epic work, Proust has at least one scene where the lightest of shades makes the greatest of differences. In his last volume, *Time Regained*, the colors have faded as the years have passed. The narrator, once again in Paris, walks into the house of the Princess of Guermantes to attend a soirée. After reminiscing in the library for a while, he enters the main salon and immediately experiences the passage of time through a change in color, a subtle change in shade. Proust may not have given the color *white* a positive connotation, but the scenes depicting the narrator's encounter with old friends express time relative to the transformation of color in the room.

When the narrator slipped into the room, he did not immediately grasp why he had such trouble recognizing the host and the guests. The changes slowly dawned upon him as he noticed the prince's "barbe blanche" and a moustache of the same color.[47] D'Argencourt, an old rival, had made the transition from a salt-and-pepper beard to one of an "invraisemblable blancheur."[48] This was not a healthy white, one sometimes associated with a doctor's gown, but a palsied color. Proust refers to an "optic view of the years" to characterize the narrator's experiences with his friends, but it is more than the recording of optical stimulus. It is the non-verbal association of color with age and the shades of color that impact experience. The white and the grays don't just meet the eyes of the narrator, they fill the room.[49]

Historical lighting has not been ignored, either. Over the centuries, the light profile of inhabited areas has changed dramatically.[50] The presence or absence of light, even the selected control of daylight, impacted social behaviors—blinking neon signs are associated with night life. Nineteenth-century authorities introduced street lighting to reduce crime in more prominent quarters and push it to the margins of town, where less concern for law and order prevailed. In an economic sense, artificial lighting tempted consumers who were drawn to the attraction of window shopping. The presence of light had nothing to do with the familiar on-off toggle of a wall switch (the dimmer switch would be closer to the truth). Lights varied in color and shade could be refracted by thick uneven glass in shop windows. Whereas pure darkness casts no shadows, a weak light might reveal but the outline of an object, further inducing a range of behaviors. If a pedestrian were to scream, the shades, not words, were at the source of the cry.

All these examples assume an urban worldview. Berger's contested space of words and images occurs in urban museums (which not everyone visits) and capitalist advertising in magazines and billboards. The distribution of magazines, however, was not limited to urban areas—when George Kennan visited the Koraks in Siberia in the middle of the nineteenth century, a Korak brought him a page from Frank Leslie's *Illustrated Newspaper*. According to Kennan, the "poor Korak" had no idea the images represented women. In another village, an Orthodox peasant had placed an image of the American major general John Adams Dix in the corner of a room, where it could be worshipped as a saint.[51]

The odd usage transpires in a visual and multisensual environment unimpeded by language. It is true, as Heidegger claims, that "language is encountered everywhere [*Überall begegnet Sprache*]," but it does not mediate experience everywhere.[52] And though we "do speak when we are awake and we speak in our dreams," this phenomenon does not circumscribe experience. As Schafer makes clear, dreams have sound components, and memory can be stored in any part of the body and even preserved in objects that surround us. When the Korak took the paper in his hand, it was tactile, was illustrated, and made paper-crinkling sounds other than those from his familiar milieu.

Illustration, the bringing of light, does more than engage in a sparring match with linguistic interpretations. Contemporary developments show visual tendencies have come to dominate everyday experience. In this mode, the real revolutionary component of Berger's effort was that it originated in a television format, foreshadowing the video format of the digital age. Nowadays, the visual is increasingly encroaching upon what was once a purely textual world. Even in the deepest textual environments, such as a philosophy seminar, visual footage and similar aids are being introduced; modern philosophers cannot afford to ignore visuals as Wittgenstein did in the *Tractatus*. Reading nowadays rarely occurs without visual accompaniment, whether the visuals belong specifically to the text or are adjacent to text in another field of meaning, with advertisements that pop up in another window while reading a digital copy of a nineteenth-century treatise. The digital transmission of snapshots has replaced e-mail and writing as the dominant mode of communication; is this a newly learned social tendency, or a deep sub-conscious human desire that only recent technologies could bring forth from the depths? Had the iPhone been invented in 1900, we might suppose that the linguistic turn may never have occurred because the fascination with visual stimulus would have overwhelmed alternative interpretations.

The extent of the visual—the sheer inseparability of the textual from visually processed information—cannot be underestimated; instead of words infecting images, as Berger contemplated, visuals are infecting texts. The lonely reader of the 1970s could isolate herself in a library carrel and see little more than the mixed combinations of Latin letters that we recognize as words. As Peter Burke has shown, history journals of that period rarely published imagery.[53] Now technologically created visuals impact the most dedicated textual academic, whether on screens in the restaurant with the football game and CNN charts, or even at the modern library. Data visuals, which have their own chapter in this volume, are a key part of the visual revolution.

Strangely enough, a philosopher of history, R.G. Collingwood, comes to mind. Writing in the first half of the twentieth century, he propagated a notion of historical idealism, one in which the thinking powers of humans took precedence over the qualities of the 'real' world (he was a great defender of the separation between the *Natur-* and *Geisteswissenschaften*). Collingwood's idealism made a concrete demand of the historian—she had to place herself not in the shoes, but in the mind of historical actors and, in effect, rethink the situation. Obviously, as an offshoot of the philosophy of mind, this position has lost its appeal amongst historians, but the exercise can be repeated with the senses—what did it smell or taste like for them? Can we recreate those smelly situations like we can, at least according to Collingwood, recreate the thoughts of our ancestors? Are reenactment societies the preferred method once historians have overcome their fascination with the linguistic turn?

Collingwood's assertions require a brief explanation because many of them also apply to language. We could get into the thoughts of past ancestors only if we believed in unchanging rational qualities of the mind. Individual thoughts will naturally differ, but the structure that determines the operational character of those thoughts remains constant over time and across languages (translation is unproblematic for Collingwood). When we insist on the primacy of language, the same problem emerges. If we use language to describe those old smells and sounds and reduce their existence to linguistic forms, then we are ordering them within a transcendent grammatical structure much like Collingwood placed them in a transcendental thought structure. It cannot be forgotten that despite claims about the shifting nature of language, the grammatical structures remain almost identical over large swaths of time, and our efforts are limited to finessing the right word or expression (a flexibility that was no less available in Collingwood's system).[54]

What if the researcher, instead of placing his mind or language into that of an ancestor, placed his nose in his? Or his eyes in his? What would it mean to re-sensorize something? The nose has been caricatured in all its different forms for its visual contribution to aesthetics, but visual depictions of the nose rarely mention its prime function; we all know Gogol's satire *The Nose* but few of us can identify with what it smelled even if we have read the story. The same holds true for touch and sound yet an obligation exists to report on these sensations when making statements about them. As Wittgenstein wrote, "Zur unwägbaren Evidenz gehören die Feinheiten des Blicks, der Gebärde, des Tons."[55] The 'Feinheit,' or subtlety, refers to a discriminating skill, and this sense must be trained to recognize nuances.

Practically, Schafer suggests a problem when he relates his experience at an academic panel on sound; he marveled at the fact that the presenter made no effort to reproduce the pluralistic sounds of which he spoke and was happy to listen to the hum of his own voice. Academic quibbles won't amount to a substantial critique; but Schafer's point has an echo, and as Ovid's Echo so painfully learned, an echo is a plaintive anthem. Not all sounds or tastes have to be reproduced in their entirety in the *American Historical Review*, but at some point, something of this order must happen. It is disingenuous to write an article on the senses without reproducing any of those stimuli and then suggest the senses are bounded by the language in which the article was written.

Much of the work sketched here lies in the domain of history, and the senses have long since found proponents amongst historians, many of whom remain immune to the linguistic turn. French church bells as a status symbol and as a producer of noise have been well studied.[56] In a Soviet context, a historian has examined how the film director, Aleksei German Sr., lets odors ooze out of the silver screen. One scene shows the main character sniffing the putrid body of a dying Stalin.[57] The friends of Schafer have explored soundscapes throughout the world. In Germany and Austria, historians have drawn attention to the growth of anti-noise associations in the mushrooming urban environment.[58] These historical works draw various conclusions about social status, religious battles with secular authorities, the nature of totalitarianism, cultural trends, and more.

The senses are not merely a historical curiosity, for the greater concern should be the digital impact on the senses. The lived environment of the digital world is as physically small as the volume of data is large. Whether sound is packed into tiny headphones or a comprehensive viewing of videos is constrained to a tiny little screen, the digital world can compact experiences into the tiniest of experiential spaces. The archeologist who only a decade ago had to travel to Hami on the edge of the Gobi desert to examine archaeological remains can reduce the field work and rely on three dimensional simulations for much of the time. Humanists now have their own version of the laboratory as almost all stimulants can be experienced via the same screen. To a degree, the senses are caught between the linguistic turn and a digital existence.

The emphasis on the senses is designed to create alternatives to the linguistic turn; to upset well-established habits. It should not imply that linguistic analysis will fade away, because linguistic analyses are enjoying a renaissance with digital technologies, just not in the way postmodernists imagined it. For example, Derrida gained further renown by plucking the word "umbrella" from an unpublished Nietzsche text. The selection of a random excerpt fit the playfulness of postmodernism and allowed a single word to be surrounded by a massive corpus of interpretation. Digital language techniques are, however, anathema to the excerpt. The excerpt suggests a uniqueness with which the digital wants nothing to do. The digital world extracts items but always with the assumption that the piece of language that had been identified could be discovered somewhere else; it wants repetition, and it wants to look for more. It never does its work without this assumption, although it might frequently yield one result. If Nietzsche had only used the word umbrella once, the digital tool would still have looked for other occurrences. The tool cannot prevent the analyst from focusing on a single result, but the analyst will know that the tool is looking for more; it is a different situation to know that something continues to seek.

Digital technologies have opened doors to substantially more linguistic analysis. Fortunately, this does not undermine anything that has been said so far. On the one hand, the digital methodologies are sufficiently different from standard approaches of the linguistic turn and therefore, as cognitive linguistics makes clear, not all linguistic analysis operates on the same epistemological principles. On the other hand, the method has a pedigree. These digital techniques have ancestors in the 1950s, when scholars toyed with the links between computers and language. In many circles, interest has arisen in the works of earlier scholars who employed computational methods before the advent of the Internet. These methods are being revived now that technologies make singular references to a word such as umbrella look quaint. These methods are being paired with large databases, such as the ones at German universities in Saarbrücken and Munich, which are establishing paradigms based upon computer linguistics.[59] Linguistic analysis has become dramatically more complex and has made humanistic study that dabbles with word usage obsolete.

These databases can track subtle structural changes over time. In Shapin and Schafer, language is frozen on both sides of the language game. In the vast majority of postmodern instances, absolutely no effort has been made to comprehend slow temporal linguistic change. The appropriation of terms is always noted but does not reveal incremental change (which is an altogether divergent exercise from looking for *différance*). In part, this has to do with the general premises of postmodernism: so tightly associated with power and control, intentionality lies at the heart of its mission. That is, actors intentionally exert linguistic power, such as with totalitarian regimes. By contrast, evolutionary revelations of language may diminish human agency because no identifiable entity is responsible for the change. If language evolved haphazardly over time, how can a government be said to control a language? In the process, a tension between accidental and intentional aspects of language will surface.

The sheer digital volume of linguistic examples will also impact our understanding of translation.[60] In postmodernism, translation has been most closely associated with incommensurability to maintain the independence of knowledge systems and hence relativism based on language. The absence of linguistic expressions is also significant. If German does not have its own word for _____, then it can be said that Germans don't have the concept and live on their own epistemological island. Intuitively, this assertion loses its impact in a world of vast databases, since it is almost impossible to imagine a situation where a computer is unable to find an expression or syntax which cannot be made understood in another language. As long as one resists insisting upon an elusive exact translation, the computer algorithm will perform admirably. This works at the level of the past and present. In older environments, the question is slightly different because historical actors lacked access to digital translators; these contemporary translators can, however, show that translation possibilities were available, although an individual speaker may not have recognized the possibility. In today's world, where these translators play the role of active intermediary, it is easier to see how they overcome practical obstacles and extract the necessary components to satisfy the parameters of effective communication. Quine's *gavagai* example, in which translation is obscured because the reference to the rabbit part is ambiguous, would have had a completely different meaning if the man pointing at the rabbit had had an iPhone in his palm.[61]

Evidently, major changes are at hand. When embracing these digital opportunities, one has to bear in mind their relationship to the traditional position of the linguistic turn. The linguistic turn came to light in a unique social and academic environment and served the needs of thinkers who wanted to distance themselves from rationality. The movement was effective but not without its excesses. It had the quality of a drug that could lead to overdose and outliers such as Spiegel, who labored to escape its gravitational pull, confronted difficulty after difficulty. As a result, the linguistic turn has left behind thousands upon thousands of studies that followed the same basic pattern and drew the same basic conclusions, thereby cementing the hegemonic position of language. In retrospect, one can easily demonstrate where the enthusiasm went awry.

Consequently, equally reasonable options were sidelined. In particular was the notion of the senses as an independent object of study and not one that had to be rerouted through language simply because academics present their results in writing. Unfortunately, the classic dominance of the visual had a negative impact on the other senses. When postmodernists sought to subordinate visual autopsy to linguistic knowledge, the other senses were forced to go the same way and therefore lost their independence. Nevertheless, it should be clear that a non-linguistic interpretation of the senses is a perfectly viable option. This steps away from the linguistic turn, though the current focus is not on the senses per se.

In light of the observations made about the senses, a broader conclusion has to be drawn. The linguistic turn did excellent intellectual work for generations, but it did so with philosophical blinders because no other alternatives could seduce as easily. This cannot, however, continue endlessly. The digital methods, only briefly sketched in this chapter, will systematically change the position of language. As the next generation slowly moves on from discourse and *différance*, it will recognize the sweeping impact of a new intellectual hegemon. These digital databases will change research methods and the conclusions that emerge from them. They won't meekly continue the same traditional linguistic analyses, for they force the reinvigoration of theories of language, a process well underway.

The linguistic turn was more than a moment in the history of Western philosophy because it embodied a deeper desire to embrace the abstract world of theory. Theory became such a critical designator, and the linguistic turn represented the theoretical avant garde. A move away from raw empirical data and a focus on language was an opportunity to theorize about the world without getting caught up in the factual analysis that was starting to draw yawns. The gap between the real world and interpretive mechanisms grew exponentially as thinkers toyed with endless possibilities and, within a given intellectual framework, gave their imaginations free rein. The start of the linguistic turn gave enormous impetus to this theoretical urge. Would it then not follow that the end of the linguistic turn foreshadows the end of theory?

Notes

1. Johann Gottfried Herder, *Abhandlung über den Ursprung der Sprache* (Stuttgart: Reclam, 1969).
2. Gottlob Frege, *The Foundations of Arithmetic: A Logico-Mathematical Enquiry Into the Concept of Number* (New York: Philosophical Library, 1950).

3. Rorty, *Philosophy and the Mirror of Nature*, 8.
4. Richard Rorty, *The Linguistic Turn: Recent Essays in Philosophical Method* (Chicago: University of Chicago Press, 1967).
5. Martin Heidegger, "Der Weg zur Sprache," in *Unterwegs zur Sprache* (Frankfurt am Main: Vittorio Klostermann, 1985).
6. Jacques Derrida, *Margins of Philosophy*, trans. Alan Bass (Chicago: University of Chicago Press, 1982).
7. Gabrielle M. Spiegel, *The Past as Text: The Theory and Practice of Medieval Historiography*, Parallax (Baltimore: Johns Hopkins University Press, 1997), xix.
8. Gabrielle M. Spiegel, "History, Historicism, and the Social Logic of the Text," in *The Past as Text: The Theory and Practice of Medieval Historiography*, Parallax (Baltimore: Johns Hopkins University Press, 1997), 27.
9. Spiegel, *The Past as Text: The Theory and Practice of Medieval Historiography*, 177.
10. Dominick LaCapra, *History and Reading: Tocqueville, Foucault, French Studies* (Toronto and Buffalo: University of Toronto Press, 2000), 52.
11. Foucault, *The Order of Things*, 286–9.
12. Allan Megill, *Prophets of Extremity: Nietzsche, Heidegger, Foucault, Derrida* (Berkeley: University of California Press, 1985), 238.
13. Antoine Prost, *Republican Identities in War and Peace: Representations of France in the Nineteenth and Twentieth Centuries*, The Legacy of the Great War (Oxford and New York: Berg, 2002); Stephen Kotkin, *Magnetic Mountain: Stalinism as a Civilization* (Berkeley: University of California Press, 1995).
14. White, *Metahistory*.
15. Leonard Bernstein, *Leonard Bernstein at Harvard: "The Unanswered Question," Norton Lectures 1973*, videorecording (Kultur, 1992), 15–16.
16. Bernstein, *Leonard Bernstein at Harvard*, 29.
17. Bernstein, *Leonard Bernstein at Harvard*, 15–16.
18. Bodenhamer, "The Spatial Humanities."
19. Arthur C. Danto, *Analytical Philosophy of History* (Cambridge: Cambridge University Press, 1965).
20. Arthur C. Danto, *The Transfiguration of the Commonplace: A Philosophy of Art* (Cambridge, MA: Harvard University Press, 1981), 82.
21. Danto, *The Transfiguration of the Commonplace*, 176.
22. Steven Pinker, *The Stuff of Thought: Language as a Window Into Human Nature* (New York: Viking, 2007).
23. Kotkin, *Magnetic Mountain*. See also Stephen E. Hanson, *Time and Revolution: Marxism and the Design of Soviet Institutions* (Chapel Hill, NC: University of North Carolina Press, 1997).
24. Chakrabarty, *Provincializing Europe*.
25. Bernard Comrie, "Causative Verb Formation and Other Verb-Deriving Morphology," in *Grammatical Categories and the Lexicon*, ed. Timothy Shopen, vol. III, Language Typology and Syntactic Description (Cambridge: Cambridge University Press, 1985), 309–48.
26. Moretti, *Distant Reading*.
27. Martin Jay, "In the Realm of the Senses: An Introduction," *The American Historical Review* 116, no. 2 (2011): 309.
28. Henry Staten, *Wittgenstein and Derrida* (Lincoln and London: University of Nebraska Press, 1984).
29. Heidegger wrote: "*über die Sprache sprechen ist vermutlich noch schlimmer als über das Schweigen schreiben.*" Martin Heidegger, "Die Sprache,"

in *Unterwegs zur Sprache* (Frankfurt am Main: Vittorio Klostermann, 1985), 10.
30. R. Murray Schafer, *Voices of Tyranny, Temples of Silence* (Arcana Editions, 1993), 9.
31. Schafer, *Voices of Tyranny, Temples of Silence*, 57.
32. Schafer, *Voices of Tyranny, Temples of Silence*, 49.
33. Schafer, *Voices of Tyranny, Temples of Silence*, 47.
34. Schafer, *Voices of Tyranny, Temples of Silence*, 51.
35. Schafer, *Voices of Tyranny, Temples of Silence*, 15.
36. Friedrich Nietzsche, "Die Philosophie im tragischen Zeitalter der Griechen," in *Werke in drei Bänden* (München: Carl Hanser, 1966), 391.
37. Ludwig Wittgenstein, *Philosophical Investigations*, ed. G. E. M. Anscombe, 3rd ed. (Oxford and Malden, MA: Blackwell, 2001), 31.
38. Wittgenstein, *Philosophical Investigations*, 66.
39. Quoted in Ginzburg, "Clues: Roots of an Evidential Paradigm," 108.
40. Heidegger, "Die Sprache," 26–7.
41. Mark S. R. Jenner, "Follow Your Nose? Smell, Smelling, and Their Histories," *The American Historical Review* 116, no. 2 (April 2011): 335–51.
42. Jay, "In the Realm of the Senses," 309.
43. Jay, *Downcast Eyes*, 591.
44. John Berger, *Ways of Seeing* (London: British Broadcasting Corp.; New York: Penguin Books, 1972).
45. Berger, *Ways of Seeing*, 28.
46. Marcel Proust, *Du côté de chez Swann* (Paris: Gallimard, 1987), 46–7.
47. Marcel Proust, *Le Temps retrouvé* (Paris: Gallimard, 1992).
48. Proust, *Le Temps retrouvé*, 232.
49. Proust, *Le Temps retrouvé*, 232. The French is a "vue optique des années."
50. Wolfgang Schivelbusch, *Disenchanted Night: The Industrialization of Light in the Nineteenth Century* (Berkeley: University of California Press, 1995).
51. George Kennan, *Tent Life in Siberia* (Salt Lake City: Peregrine Smith Books, 1986), 329–30.
52. Heidegger, "Die Sprache," 9.
53. Burke, *Eyewitnessing*.
54. Even if there were grammatical changes, most researchers don't bother to find out.
55. Wittgenstein, *Philosophical Investigations*, 366. "Imponderable evidence includes subtleties of glance, of gesture, of tone."
56. Alain Corbin, *Village Bells: Sound and Meaning in the 19th-Century French Countryside*, European Perspectives (New York: Columbia University Press, 1998).
57. Tim Harte, "Stalinism's Sights and Smells in the Films of Aleksei German, Sr.," in *Russian History Through the Senses: From 1700 to the Present*, ed. Matthew P. Romaniello and Tricia Starks (London: Bloomsbury Academic, an imprint of Bloomsbury Publishing Plc, 2016).
58. Gerhard Paul and Ralph Schock, eds., *Sound der Zeit: Geräusche, Töne, Stimmen; 1889 bis heute* (Göttingen: Wallstein, 2014).
59. Wolfgang Krischke, "Sprachwissenschaft: Altbewährtes frischgemacht," *Frankfurter Allgemeine*, May 10, 2018, www.faz.net/aktuell/feuilleton/hochschule/digital-humanities-eine-bilanz-1-6-sprachwissenschaft-15579104.html. See, for example, Hans-Martin Gauger and Herbert Heckmann, *Wir sprechen anders: Warum Computer nicht sprechen können: Eine Publikation der Deutschen Akademie für Sprache und Dichtung* (Frankfurt am Main: Fischer, 1988).

60. The study of translation has its own history in analytic philosophy. As one example, see Donald Davidson, "Indeterminism and Antirealism," in *Subjective, Intersubjective, Objective* (Oxford and New York: Oxford University Press, 2001), 69–84.
61. Willard Van Orman Quine, *Word and Object* (Cambridge: Technology Press of the Massachusetts Institute of Technology, 1960).

4 The End of Theory in the Humanities

In its heyday, the confrontation between postmodernists and their opponents was often presented as a battle between those who were theoretical and those who were empirical or fact-oriented. The juxtaposition was overdrawn because it made light of interpretive distinctions, but it became a convenient means to distinguish between two camps. The emphasis on theory was certainly the promotion of a unique vision but also an expression of fatigue, a reaction against a longstanding positivist tradition. Facts had developed such a cult following since the start of the nineteenth century that advocating theory became its own form of opposition. Without even a need for explicit explanation, theory rejected the positivism of Auguste Comte and the empirical obsession of Leopold von Ranke. Theory became a synonym for antirealism.

Thus theory was not value neutral; to be labeled theoretical, the theory had to press in a specific direction. For example, Comte, the father of positivism, had a theory, but it was too empirical to be accepted as one in the 1960s. This worldview denied Comte a theory because positivism was too much invested in the facts of the matter, and if the facts were determinant, how could one speak of a theory? Alternatively, postmodernists developed theories to undermine these facts; these were the real theories that did real work in an antirealist fashion. Everything else was dismissed as a theoretical aberration or treated with disdain. This notion of theory was unique to the humanities, where the most vociferous positions were taken. In the sciences, theories continued with regularity, even monotony. Scientists in all fields postulated theories about black holes, genetic molecules, and electron flow. They could still work with a traditional definition of theory, though scientific practice continued to change as it always had. Theirs was a much less polemical approach to theory.

The digital world has, however, put its own stamp on scientific theory. More specifically, the idea that scientists even require a theory has been questioned. The end of theory has become a catchphrase to draw attention to the radically changing research environments brought about by Big Data. Chris Anderson shifted emphasis to the ability of algorithms to sift through massive data sets and present researchers with identifiable trends. Hypotheses become redundant when algorithms perform so much legwork and overwhelm the researcher; the statistical collections have an irresistible attraction.

If the hard sciences have to deal with this concept, should the humanities do so as well? Unlike the scientific end of theory, the end of theory in the humanities refers to a shift away from the theoretical enthusiasm dominant in the 1980s; it suggests historical and cultural change rather than the complete abandonment of theory. Superficially, if the humanities accepted an end to theory, this would immediately necessitate a rethinking of all postmodern positions: how could a movement so dependent upon theory survive the end of theory? The end of theory in the humanities would have dramatic consequences. Without accepting the most extreme scenarios, the digital age will reposition theory; it will be fundamentally transformed and cannot exist as it did during the 1960s and 1970s. Big Data will alter its status and therefore either change the definition of an older movement or give birth to an alternative movement.

In anticipating a state-of-the-art role for theory, a trajectory has to be determined that traces transitions from a pre-theoretical age in the nineteenth century to a theoretical age at the end of the twentieth century. By initiating the discussion in the early nineteenth century, the positivism of Comte can reemerge from its obscurity. His positivism became a foil for generations of theorists even if they could not be bothered to mention him by name. Although Isaiah Berlin noted that Comte had faded from view only because he had done his work too well, postmodernists were fully aware of his specter.[1] Positivism was a central foe of postmodernists and has therefore been dismissed for a generation; it even became a central term of opprobrium. Yet positivism's relation to theory has to be revisited. It came as a strong reaction to metaphysical abstraction; it therefore fought the same battle as postmodernism but in the exact opposite direction. As a consequence, almost since its inception, it faced opposition from thinkers who wanted more theory as in more abstraction. Despite its diminished influence, it is on the verge of a comeback. The collection of data and the identification of trends would be familiar to Comte's followers.

After Comte, the intellectual scene pushed for more abstract models, and these need a short introduction to situate the postmodernists of the 1960s. Wilhelm Dilthey and Friedrich Nietzsche, two historically inclined philosophers, pushed against positivism and set a groundwork for postmodern theories. While a detailed theoretical genealogy would become unwieldy, a look at those two authors reveals the germs of postmodern theory later on. From there, the discussion can move ahead a generation and explore Heidegger's style (not content) of theorizing. A true forerunner of Derrida, Heidegger's later works clearly indicate a jump away from the facts of the matter. His comments on technology, a familiar theme since they led to his admiration for the Nazi regime, receive a moment's attention because they explain why a postmodern theorist might feel threatened by Big Data.

Lastly, the apotheosis of theory in its Derridaean and Foucauldian form requires explication to give a sense of how these authors delved into abstraction at the expense of factual analysis; how they sought to obscure straightforward factual presentations in favor of theoretical dominance. They approached the world with words such as ambivalence, absence, imaginary, trace, and myth. Beyond the mere act of theorizing as a scientist might, the strategy was to enter an abstruse megacosm in which boundaries were blurred and uncertainty prevailed. The uncertainty permitted the advocacy of provocative claims and embodied a particular spirit of theory which postmodernism promoted. That brand of theory played a huge role in the 1980s and does so today. It reached such an exhilarating climax that positivistic approaches could be declared dead.

Unfortunately for these theorists, a handful of positivist values are creeping back into analysis and will upend what has become an established definition of theory. Instead of theory pushing ever deeper into abstraction and away from concrete reality, it will confront large data sets and have to deal with them much like scholars of the nineteenth century did. Under current circumstances, declaring a return to positivism would be too extreme because it would implicitly support a circular or elliptical vision of history in which we return to older methods. Similarly, a resurgence of positivism appears unlikely because the intellectual climate has changed dramatically. Yet a selective rebirth of relevant positivist ideas should not be counted out since strong ties bind positivism with Big Data.

After attending to the position of theory from the last thirty years, the discussion has to consider how data and a muted positivism might change things. How has the recent flood of data challenged theoretical usage? Digital phenomena will impact abstraction and return humanists to the basic premises of positivism. As the end of the linguistic turn will not end the study of language, the end of theory won't prevent conceptualizations. It will, however, necessitate reformulating the dominant and exclusive definition of theory that began with combative gusto but is now no more than a bromide. A more pluralist, a more positivist definition of theory, one that takes the data phenomenon into consideration, is in the offing.

In an age of digitization, Comte is an appropriate starting point because he taught at French technical schools. Born in France at the end of the eighteenth century, his youth was shaped by memories of the Enlightenment in the French milieu. He harbored a mistrust against the metaphysical ideas that had fueled the Enlightenment and suggested positivism would overcome metaphysics. He transformed this disdain into a three-state law that boldly divided the history of humanity into three phases—first, the theological, then the metaphysical, and then the positivist, which he believed to be around the corner. The theological is of less interest;

overcoming the metaphysical was designed to eliminate inherent abstraction. Comte wanted a system grounded in data to predict the behavior of society (which in his case was designed to predict his vision of a positivist society): the data would produce immutable laws. He mocked theological and metaphysical approaches precisely because they were characterized by a "preponderance of imagination over observation."[2] Thus, "though the positive philosophy offers the vastest and richest field to human imagination it restricts it to discovering and perfecting the co-ordination of observed facts."[3] As would any thinker with a grand scheme, he rejected limiting the possibilities of positivism. The positivist imperative subjected "social phenomena" to "invariable natural laws."[4]

The process eliminated speculation in abstract ideas that had no relation whatsoever to real phenomena. If an aspect of scientific pursuit were too abstract, Comte dismissed it as of no concern to the positivist. For example, some of Newton's propositions about attraction were considered insolvable.[5] In chemistry, Comte distinguished between an abstract pursuit of the science and one based on observation in which "observed facts" helped with the establishment of a rational system.[6] These observations were the basis of chemistry, from which generalizations could be made. Comte was not developing a method for the fact collector because determining the laws of nature required generalizations, which themselves risked becoming abstractions insofar as there was no one-to-one correspondence with a single example and the generalization that encompassed many examples.

The link between the observation and a general law was critical because the observation guaranteed the validity of the law. Here law is presented in the singular, which can give the mistaken impression that Comte wanted to reduce all experience to a single, universal covering law. That was not the case. He wrote that it was his deep, personal conviction that those "attempts at universal explanation by a single law" were "something so chimerical."[7] Yet the laws are based not on a speculative idealism but on the signals the earth sends to its inhabitants—they are grounded, as an electrical engineer might assert.

Although positivism later became associated with a factual objectivism, Comte's method shied away from specifics. He left the details to individual disciplines and encouraged thinkers in these disciplines to seek them out without interference from the positivists. The positivists could synthesize knowledge from the sciences to foreshadow societal developments, that is, the future form human society would take. In this guise, positivism was a social program, a political platform, and an exercise in theorizing.

Comte also framed his ideas according to standards of exactness. Exactness, no friend of the later Wittgenstein, played a key role for Comte because it had a progressive function and was something that could be aimed for in the future. For example, "sociological precision" is "founded upon the exact general knowledge."[8] Or, "the exact preparatory knowledge" might "have allowed a cultivated reason to foresee the progress proper to each period."[9] Not surprisingly, exactness was also a goal in observation: "the ancients observed with exactness a degree at the utmost. Tycho Brahe carried up the precision to a minute."[10] Inevitably, methods improved, and so did claims to exactitude.

The observation, the precision, the laws, and the exactitude were the long-lasting legacy of positivism. The content of these terms were the key targets of postmodernists, but they are silently reemerging in the world of Big Data. The theoretical (not metaphysical) abstraction of the postmodernists risks being replaced by lightly modified tenets of positivism. Comte's linear and progressive thinking would inherently reject a return to past models, but the familiarities with a data-oriented world are readily recognizable. Big Data prefers processing discrete pieces of factual information, encourages the belief that collecting more and more information is an essential part of persuasive argument, and relies on a process of synthesis that amalgamates all the information into an acceptable generalization.

Another instructive parallel can be made with Leopold von Ranke, often considered the modern founder of history because he established the study of history as a professional discipline. Regrettably, this midnineteenth-century historian is often derided today for having embraced positivist methods, though he had no formal or intellectual relationship with positivism whatsoever. Ranke was born at about the same time as Comte, so he was subject to common European influences. As a historian, he shared a general suspicion of metaphysical approaches because of their abstraction. In a German context, this implied hostility to strong currents of German idealism and a greater recourse to observational and documented facts.[11] Ranke urged historians to gather as much data as possible and let the facts speak for themselves.

In the twentieth century, Ranke suffered the same fate as positivism—philosophers of history dismissed the idea that a historian could take a value-neutral approach to their subject matter. Already in the 1930s, he was discarded as outmoded because of a naïve desire to pursue what his contemporaries called a noble dream. Charles Beard rejected the noble dream of objectivity as a leftover from the nineteenth century and showed that even Ranke had his biases. Ranke, as a Protestant, far from being aloof, espoused his own views in contemporary politics. Instead, Beard promoted philosophy and urged historians to embrace this field as a means to transcend the simple facts. He wrote, "the wider and deeper philosophic questions involved in the interpretation of history should be considered as having an importance equal to, if not greater than, the consideration of documentation."[12] Historians did not accept Beard's philosophical direction, but they did use his thoughts to place Ranke in the camp of positivists.

Although Ranke no longer inspires historians, he was instrumental in the nineteenth century for giving history scientific and empirical credibility and pushing historians to do archival research in a novel way. Unlike Comte, Ranke was not searching for historical laws, did not postulate grand historical phases, and was reluctant to admit a linear progress. If progress could be said to exist, then it was more like a winding river.[13] He therefore did not see a need to transform the cause and effect of specific events into a general law or rule.

Ranke explained his method by contrasting two German terms: *Geschichte* and *Historie*.[14] *Geschichte* stems from *Geschehen*, which implies actual happenings. This represents the scientific component of historical research because the historian must dig out facts; it is objective because it relays a simple search for the truth. *Historie* is more subjective because it reflects the actual subject matter, the selection of which depends upon the whims of individual historians. Nevertheless, once the subject matter has been chosen, the historian must act scientifically.

This juxtaposition of Ranke with Comte highlights subtle nuances that gain in significance when contemporary tendencies are already identifiable. Ranke revolutionized the ordering and collecting of information for historians, but he was hardly interested in data sets. He had a factual, not quantitative, approach and essentially wanted to hold the facts in his hands. These facts had rough edges and awkward shapes and sizes that depended upon the environment. The conceptualization of science was also by and large different in the Rankean system because it lay with the observational rather than analytic aspects of science; it meant confirming and documenting, but not introducing math or physics. In the Comtean system, science played a dominant role; hence the immense respect given to mathematics and the use of extensive analytic tools in the social sciences. Modern historians who present graphs, quantifying and evaluating data, are doing something more to the tune of Comte than Ranke.

Comte's larger social project never really established itself, and the few communities he inspired soon fizzled. The philosophical substance of his ideas struggled in a cultural world moving away from realism. In the arts, Impressionism and Cubism introduced degrees of subjectivity and inexactitude. In literature, Anton Chekhov explored the psychological uncertainties of modern individuals, and in psychoanalysis, Sigmund Freud questioned the rational and logical impulses which were supposed to be at the core of decision-making. All these late nineteenth-century movements upset the tidy scientific vision of society that Comte had presented to his audiences. Historians at major German universities persisted with their facts and sociologists searched for overarching models, but the winds of change were in the air. Another century would have to pass to overcome the Comtean mystique, but a process had been started.

The parameters of this transition can be explored through the thoughts of Wilhelm Dilthey and Friedrich Nietzsche. While the selection of two characters from an epic cast can cover only so much ground, it will demonstrate both opposition to positivism and the nature (not content) of theory which each thinker adopted. Dilthey never mounted the same philosophical challenge as Nietzsche and never became a central figure amongst postmodernists, but he carefully wove his way between conceptual generalizations and the facts of the matter. He therefore put theory within the context of abstraction, a significant juxtaposition. Nietzsche, who was less directly concerned with positivism, gave the strongest theoretical models to detach observation from experience and erected a relativist model for postmodernists in the middle of the twentieth century.

Dilthey treated Comtean followers with contempt—the "so-called positivists" who had "erected a makeshift structure."[15] He had equally harsh words for the Historical School, a specifically German phenomenon, which had made a "disastrous error" when it rejected "the world of abstractions."[16] Dilthey advocated theoretical abstraction while still insisting on paying attention to the living world and the cultural context of individuals. He developed the notion that abstraction could be "unintentional" and unwittingly shadow a historian: "Without intending to, indeed without knowing it, he is also constantly abstracting." The eye of the historian "loses its fresh receptivity for those facts which recur in all historical phenomena" and then gets abstracted into generalizations.[17] The antidote to this unintended abstraction was closer attention to the raw material of history. He was attempting to overcome the sweeping aspects of positivism while not allowing the naïve empirical aspects of historical study to eliminate abstraction.[18]

Dilthey freely employed the words abstraction and theory as necessary qualities: scholars had to embrace abstractions and develop theories. Dilthey's abstraction had nothing to do with the artistic abstraction emerging around this time; it did not imply Malevich's objectless Black Square or, later, Dali's clocks melting over a branch. The abstraction was not attached to myths or any effort to bend reality. Dilthey had more staid hopes for abstraction. In a simple way, abstraction meant no more than taking a distance from the facts, removing oneself from them if only for a moment. Thereafter, it implied thought and analysis and an effort to explicate "the uniform behavior of partial contents" of reality.[19] Abstraction could refer to the "substructure of what always remains the same in human nature" but goes unnoticed or is not spoken about; abstraction is latent whenever a broader generalization is made. It does not have to be a conscious effort, as one would expect from an artist of the period, but could take the form of passive assumptions as long as those passive assumptions respected the factual base and made an effort to understand real human experience.

Theory proceeds from this definition of abstraction but plays a more active role: "The totality of socio-historical reality must be examined theoretically to determine what can be explained in it."[20] One had to look away from the unique and the singular and look outwards to other disciplines to explain intersections amongst phenomena. The pursuit of theory is synonymous with the pursuit of "the interconnectedness of the whole."[21] This way of thinking suggests a more scientific attitude to the definition of theory and is light years apart from the common definition of theory in the 1970s and 1980s. Theory is a linking rather than a separating device. Theory is not associated with a specific academic discipline, such as literary criticism, but invites all partners to the table. Finally, theory is not combative and does not pit schools of thought against each other, though anyone might choose to disagree with Dilthey.

Dilthey can be considered a transitional figure between Comte and Nietzsche. He denied Comte's empirical obsessions and insisted upon the presence of abstractions for which Comte showed no interest as he pursued the discovery of natural laws. Dilthey was floating away from observed facts and looking to land somewhere between pure observation and complete abstraction. Georg Iggers readily admits that the structure of Dilthey's thought revealed irreconcilable subjective and objective tendencies, between the singular and the universal.[22] He nevertheless had a deep respect for the facts as he invited a host of other sciences to weigh in with their interconnected theories.

Nietzsche refrained from expressly discussing theory, but his disregard for the facts established a huge gap between fact and abstract contemplation, and thus the interconnectedness so central to Dilthey lost its meaning. Blending the methods of the philologist, the philosopher, and the aesthete, he transcended his own Alpine environment to give the world a thoroughgoing relativist theory. Although his relativism was first overshadowed by his existentialism, he always gave his readers puzzles to contemplate the truths of the world around them. He promoted irrational impulses, reversed the order of cause and effect, and questioned the sanctity of the self ("*der Täter ist zum Tun bloss hinzugedichtet—das Tun ist alles*").[23] After existentialism ran its course in the 1950s, Nietzsche became a principal inspiration for postmodern relativism. Although he had a deep interest in history and was quite content to present his readers with historical facts, his works had enough appropriate aphorisms to satisfy the relativist.

The aphoristic, poetic, and metaphorical nature of Nietzsche's writing, published or not, gave it a disordered feel. He played with language and promoted the idea that grammatical fictions, and not metaphysical entities such as the mind, were the source of action. In the *Genealogy of Morals*, he examined the historical origins of good and bad to argue that morality was a function not of God or a categorical imperative, but of the needs of the highest caste; their social requirements determined what was right or wrong. As a philologist, Nietzsche was most fascinated by word usage. The theoretical step was to take a word which had universal and absolute connotations, such as good, and contextualize it. (This became a fundamental methodological tool for postmodern work even if, strangely enough, many of the chosen words never had any universal connotations, thus emasculating the method itself.) In Nietzsche's terminology, 'gut' was etymologically linked with 'vornehm' and 'edel.' Similarly, 'guilt' was not a human condition but instead came from the practical, material matter of 'debt'—'Schuld' and 'Schulden' in German. Guilt and the associated punishment were part of a "contractual relationship" between a debtor and a creditor. The creditor retained the right to determine the moral code in the relationship. Thus Nietzsche detached morality from a fixed Christian meaning.

Nietzsche once wrote that one should not admire the height of a tree but the depths of its roots. He may have admired deep roots in trees but, when it came to morality, he pulled out those roots, and it was this practice of deracination which served postmodernists so well. In 1971, Foucault wrote *Nietzsche, Genealogy, History* in which he promoted the genealogy as a means to undermine truth claims and naïve claims about factual accuracy. Foucault emphasized that the Ursprung or origins in a genealogy do not return the historian to a pure birthing moment. Rather, the genealogy evinces the "vicissitudes," "accidents," and "chimeras." Similarly, in tracing the *Herkunft* or descent within a genealogy, the historian is not trying to identify a straight path into the past; this method was to be replaced by attempts to reveal deviations, mistakes, and "false appraisals."[24] All the accidents and vicissitudes created a gap between words and reality, a gap that later generations could fill with their own theoretical ambitions. Instead of a tight link between a word and its object, Nietzsche established an interpretive zone. The larger that zone, the more room theory had to play.

Nietzsche did not completely subscribe to the world of abstract theory because he did use empirical devices. In Nietzsche's view, *Schuld* was a value (*Wert*) and, as Heidegger pointed out, values are earthy and can be measured and weighed. Nietzsche's genealogy is based on physical and quantifiable relationships, a position seemingly at odds with postmodern usage of his thought. Heidegger even went so far as to suggest that Nietzsche's *Werte* were a "positivist substitute for the metaphysical."[25] Heidegger's own 'positivist' version of Nietzsche was in part motivated by a desire to place a distance between Nietzsche and himself, thus situating his own ideas on the far frontier. Heidegger was not the only one to point Nietzsche in this direction. Since interpreters will ultimately have to decide on their own digital Nietzsche, views at odds with standard postmodernism interpretations are worth a short stop.

Most of the alternative views come from philosophy and not history or literature departments. Arthur Danto, who had great respect for postmodernism, suggested that Nietzsche exhibited "attitudes toward the main problems of philosophy, which are almost wholly in the spirit of Logical Positivism." Danto argued that both Nietzsche and the later Logical

Positivists promoted the concept that propositions are meaningful if they "fall into one of two classes: propositions verifiable through sense experience and propositions certifiably true (or false) by virtue of their meaning alone."[26] Maudemarie Clark remarked that in the *Antichrist*, Nietzsche celebrated the Greek and Roman "sense for facts, the last and most valuable sense."[27] In the *Twilight of the Idols*, Nietzsche affirmed that "we possess science precisely to the extent that we have decided to *accept* the testimony of the senses."[28] Allan Megill has suggested an anticonceptual and antitheoretical strain in Nietzsche's thought precisely because his works are filled with abundant life-tested examples.[29] Nietzsche did not promote empiricism, but he had great confidence in the senses, just like he trusted human instincts whose characteristics transcended specific time periods and linguistic irregularities.

Neither Heidegger's earthy interpretation nor the empirical presentation of the analytic philosophers prevented postmodernists from drawing upon the anti-empirical strands of Nietzsche's thoughts while simultaneously pulling from Heidegger's own unsettling oeuvre. Heidegger's definition of theory eliminated the straightforward clarity of vision so crucial to a positivist concept of the world. Thus Heidegger's own theory, which was to seek out the lofty and mysterious, could be paired with all the previously noted thoughts and paved the way for antirealist postmodern theories.

In terms of theory itself, Heidegger analyzed the statement "Science is the theory of the real." Heidegger wanted a definition of theory that disabled the scientist's claim to universalism. Thus he began with a quick history of the term real, suggesting that only towards the seventeenth century did it become associated with factual objectification. In Greek, it had closer association with an immediate presencing, "a self-bringing forth into full presencing." German from the Middle Ages followed a similar pattern insofar as the real, *das Wirkliche*, was related to work and implied "to bring hither and forth."[30] In contrast, as science gained in prominence, boundaries were drawn between the object and observation of that object; the process of presencing no longer inhered in the single object. As the real came to represent a growing separation, theory itself changed in meaning and lost its connection with a presence becoming visible. Heidegger claimed that "The essence of theory as thought by the Greeks . . . remains buried when today we speak of the theory of relativity in physics, of the theory of evolution in biology, of the cyclical theory in history."[31] Modern theory defines a region, a narrowing, a spatio-temporal coherence, a securing, a specialization, and a delimiting, characteristics foreign to a Greek of Antiquity or a German of the Middle Ages.[32]

He differentiated a proper understanding of theory from a debased German version associated with *Betrachtung* or observation. He showed how the Greek version of theory differed radically from future versions which had a more formal structure. The Greek word *theorein* meant "to look attentively on the outward appearance wherein what presences becomes visible and, through such sight—see it—to linger with it."[33] This was a "lofty and mysterious meaning" at odds with the Latin equivalent of *Betrachtung*, contemplation, which "sunders and compartmentalizes." With the German *Betrachtung*, theory moves closer towards pursuing or entrapping something "in order to secure it."[34]

Heidegger believed that the Greek concept of wonder had slowly been replaced by curiosity, a celebratory word for most but a limiting term for him. Curiosity was that "which expresses the tendency towards a peculiar way of letting the world be encountered by us in perception."[35] The emphasis on seeing placed the experience as a function of ordering in the mind. Curiosity then "has nothing to do with observing entities and marveling at them."[36] In a distracted manner, it only briefly engages with an external world—the wonder of intersection, of the blurring between subject and object, is equally lost. The interaction between subject and object gets undermined as the subject becomes the disinterested observer, that is, the traditional positivist.

This was no mere etymological game. Heidegger emphasized that the Greeks looked upon theory as the "highest doing." The *bios theoretikos* was the way of life of "the one who looks upon the pure shining-forth of that which presences." It contrasted with the *bios praktikos* which focused more on activities and being productive; one could not be a practitioner of theory. Rather, one had to develop a theoretical craft such that it saw beyond the functional aspects of science and transcended the boundaries which separated the subject, in this case the theorist, from the object. The modern scientist would struggle with this, but the humanist could look with deep marvel into the object as the object presenced itself. This lived process of theorizing was antithetical to positivist theorizing, which depended upon isolating and essentially freezing objects in space. Heidegger was not just making a critique of modern science, for he also wanted to revive a forgotten lifestyle, a lifestyle determined by a commitment to a specific form of theory: "Theoria in itself, and not only through the utility attaching to it, is the consummate form of human existence."

Heidegger's criticisms of scientific theory came at a time when positivist precepts were still active, though increasingly vulnerable to vocal opposition. In a broader picture, Heidegger was not unique and tapped into the main currents of twentieth-century thought. In a narrower sense, the linguistic play, the unsettling of terminology, and the debunking of a technological regime became core elements in the postmodern canon. Whether they surfaced in Foucault's assault on the panopticon or in Derrida's presentation of the trace, they spurred a new generation of thought and ensured a continued energy flow. Postmodernists did not merely cut and paste from Heidegger but took him a step further. Gone was the fascination with the Greeks, the medieval Germans, and all their words as greater emphasis was placed on the contemporary world. Whereas Heidegger wrote admiringly about peasant shoes and wooden bridges, his successors clouded the physical world with intricate social theories. Since the contemporary world was filled with political movements, theory developed a combative edge. As Foucault stated, "theory does not express, translate, or serve to apply practice: it *is* practice."[37] As practice, theory was a weapon. Although Foucault's version of theory encompassed the *bios praktikos*, it also fully promoted the *bios theoretikos*, the ideal to which Heidegger aspired.

Theory defined as practice should not distract from the core components of a postmodern theory which was more synonymous with abstraction and antirealism than it was with practice (hence Foucault's insistence on emphasizing practice). As an intellectual vehicle rather than as a party platform, it influenced generations of interpreters who built upon specific abstract theories to argue against positivism. The abstract component to theory allowed it to drift easily among disciplines. Much of this theoretical work was done in the sphere of literature—works with fictional facts—so the most intense readers of these theories were found amongst literary critics. All of a sudden, familiar figures disappeared. Roland Barthes argued there was no such thing as an author. Derrida poked fun at John Searle, who had argued on behalf of unique individuals. Derrida advocated multiple authorship in SARL (a play on the American philosopher's name and the French version of a limited responsibility company).[38] Theory may have been practice, but it was always identified with a push into a more abstract milieu. When Robert W. Fogel and G.R. Elton wrote about a tendency to "subordinate facts to theory," it was precisely this definition of theory to which they referred.[39]

In the case of Derrida, the theory negating the existence of the *hors texte* came to imply that reality is contained within the structure of grammar and has no need for an external referent; thus the proliferation of talk about self-referentiality. Titles such as "The End of the Book and the Beginning of Writing" reduced the role of a factual object and instilled writing with a playfulness that could drift off wherever it chose.[40] Deconstruction, another classic theory, became deeply associated with play because it demanded a shifting, moving, and unsettling of words. The prime act of deconstruction, which was a twist on Heidegger, is to cross out all words. To cross out the word eliminates the power of the original word and denies it a stable meaning.

In *Of Grammatology*, Derrida wrote that "it is a necessary fact that empirical investigation quickly activates reflexions upon essence."[41] Not surprisingly, Derrida offered an alternative. Whereas Nietzsche had been disinterested in the nimbus surrounding origins because they were not relevant to his genealogical point, Derrida wanted not just origins but the manner in which these origins were fed by substances around them. An origin was not a mundane birthing moment which provided the world with an essential presence, but the start of an unpredictable journey; whenever one looked back from some point on that unpredictable journey, one could change the nature of the origin. The idea has come to be known as the presence of absence and is most closely associated with the French *trace*, a term that links to the *Holzwege* of Heidegger because the French word has precisely the connotation of *Weg*.[42] The trace is a lingering trail, but it also embodies contempt for the empirical. The trace reflects a theoretical attitude that emboldened an endless abstraction that could not be anchored in a convenient reality.

As Judith Butler points out in her introduction to the latest English edition of *Of Grammatology*, the translation of the original French alters the meaning of the original so that one can never settle into the birthing moment of that classic work.[43] What is striking about these comments is that they give the impression that time has not moved. Butler warns the reader that we are not working on a "sequential grid," but her own comments are fully within a Derridaean tradition and pay scant attention to any recent developments in society, which might have changed our attitude to translation. Writing for the fortieth anniversary edition, her comments would be as appropriate for the fifth anniversary edition had they been written then. In particular, there is no sense for how technologies have revolutionized translation (not functionally but as a process of understanding). We are faced with the rather commonplace claim that translations are problematic. In the same volume, Spivak mocks the "positivist reductions" of the Internet but does so with a vocabulary from the 1960s when the World Wide Web did not exist.[44]

The previous words reveal the dilemma that the rest of this chapter must elucidate: the postmodern version of theory is simply dismissive of the impact of data, an untenable position in current circumstances. Try to imagine, for example, the theory of the trace when faced with thousands upon thousands of recurrences of the same term. The presence of absence depends upon a singularity that evolves in specific situations. If one knew, however, that multiple instances existed, how could one pretend to understand the majority of cases? Knowing about the 'presence' of all those other invocations, would one have a responsibility to examine each one individually, or could one afford to make generalizations about all these cases that had been identified without being investigated? Would we have expected Heidegger to identify the nuances amongst all uses of the Greek word *theory*, when they were available in a list? These questions lay bare the conclusion that the availability of data changes the nature of theory.

At the surface, the emerging theoretical deviation can be seen as close in spirit to positivism. In Comte's worldview, the positivist did not have to know each individual detail to generate a law but had to respect the role details played when drafting a law. The drafting necessarily required theoretical abstraction because the law-maker did not have access to all the facts, much like the contemporary user of a database. As in the positivist world, the meaning of the data can be extrapolated and transformed into general laws (in the plural). Talk has shifted away from the term *law* because it connotes a form of positivism. Yet the process has parallels when applied to these vast databases. In fact, law might be even more appropriate than in Comte's time because the conclusions or laws will apply to a much vaster field than Comte ever dreamed possible. It is, of course, this inherent power that makes an appeal to databases such a temptation. Clearly, this positivism is not what Spivak had in mind with her pithy remark; hers was a harmless poke at the raw facts of the matter

With this theoretical direction in mind, the nature of theory in the digital world requires a firmer explanation. In the humanities, one can speak of the end of theory insofar as an abstract and antirealist theory is inadequate to the digital age. If every end is a new beginning, one still needs to know what will replace it. A world in which Big Data dominates will not prevent elegant conceptual extravagances amongst humanists, so some form of theory will emerge. It will contain elements of the positivism postmodernists derided, that is for sure; but this does not fully anticipate what lies around the corner. How will this innovative theory push away from antirealism and abstraction? What will it mean for a humanist to identify trends and transform those trends into generalizations? How can a humanist use a database inductively to confirm a conceptualization?

The first theoretical element concerns the inductive nature of the database. Because one starts with a huge amount of particulars, a deductive process which goes from the general to the particulars is out of place. In other words, the discrete facts of the matter are the starting point. As long as the theory depends to some degree on these facts, it cannot deny the veracity of the database; one is never forced to employ a database, but one cannot do so while rejecting the validity of its contents. Since the theorist cannot look at every individual component of the database, they have to trust the empirical basis for collecting that information (whether entered by hand or collected secretly from Facebook users). Algorithms stand between the researcher and the individual items in the database, so an intermediary in the process, absent in previous theoretical examples, has emerged. Even without any knowledge of the algorithm, the humanist is presented with conclusions that shape theory.

For example, databases can often communicate socially unacceptable results, such as when Google Maps pointed searchers of N_____ House to the White House during the Obama presidency.[45] Apparently, enough users tagged or associated the two to solidify the connection in the eyes of the machine, producing the result. The unfortunate event speaks to the interaction between data trends and social prejudices but also shows how a data-driven process can present an unexpected social theory to the humanist. The conclusion about racism can easily be drawn by looking no further than Google, and the humanist would find herself in the position of the scientist. The data has revealed a trend, and therefore there is no reason to develop an independent theory; the general hypothesis stands before one's eyes. The algorithm may have been socially unacceptable, but it nevertheless revealed a state of affairs that could not be undone. Even if Google eventually changed the algorithm, the original case revealed a trend, a truth of the social world. It also offers a prime example of the ability of a positivist approach to reveal improprieties at the margins of experience (the margins being the isolated locations of the users).

This example leaves out theories that involve observation or language, a contrast to both positivism and postmodernism. The process does not involve any visualization per se. The user who inputs the search word is looking at a screen, but it is the mental connection between the pejorative term and the residence of the American president that gives the example social significance. This is especially true since the users who generated the search and impacted the algorithm have no necessary contact with each other, though their discrete actions do have a serious impact. Similarly, the example is not one of language, though a word is central to the offensive nature of the action. Yes, language is being invoked, but in the ostensive manner, linking a word with an object, that was so inimical to postmodern thought. It was precisely because the pejorative became linked with a specific object that it evolved into an identifiable offensive trend. The strict coupling was a function of a digital environment that reinforced this link. It therefore must be attached to a different theory.

The repetitive use of the search word is notable because it accepts the value of the word in a different way; the original or ur-usage is less significant. The question of origins will always remind one of Nietzsche's claim about *Schein* becoming *sein*, but this process is not at issue because the origin of the word does not play a role in helping us understand the societal values being reflected and generated by the Google search. A historian, for example, could look back at an often-cited reference to show that the term did not always mean the same thing, but this would not bear weight on the actions being preserved in the database. Similarly, Derrida's key moment was to prevent the meaning of a term from settling so that everything remained in flux. In the Google example, the origins of the word are not at issue, though usage of the word has changed over time. The critical component is the link between a pejorative, whatever that pejorative happens to be, and a physical site, and then the subsequent fixing of this link in the database (this move fixes a social moment in the database, but not the meaning of the term for all time). This then becomes a fixed reality, which can be quantified if never fully understood.

The Google example continues to allow nuances in the meaning and uses of the term. For example, the term can have regional variations, and some users have already appropriated the term, transforming the pejorative into an accolade. While all this may be true, this lies outside the parameters of the database. This is to say, the database has its limitations precisely because it is not concerned with those nuances and instead creates a vast quantity of identical usages. This is a cautionary note about relying too strongly on a database but also another way of emphasizing the positivist elements of working with databases. Since one is faced with so many examples, one is pushed towards broader generalizations, much like the scientist whose device makes millions of measurements. One could look at each case individually, but the task is overwhelming and, as will be discussed in a later chapter, the results from the database are too tempting. More and more frequently, scholars point to the trends these databases produce.

A trend incarnates repetition, a key component of any theory that builds off the database. As Butler's comments on the translation of Derrida's work suggest, repetition is completely foreign in that world because one never experiences the same thing twice. In contrast, the Google Maps example would be uninteresting if one did not have repetition. This repetition is not referring to the internal logical loops of the algorithm but confirms that individual actors are contributing the same action to the database; in this case, searching for the same thing. The repetition has the lightest of parallels with the repetition of a scientist's laboratory experiment, though no one is controlling experimental conditions. Individuals can inhabit unique experiential worlds, but their point of interaction with the database is similar and thus repetitive.

A theory has to take these developments into consideration. The automatic collection of data and the various outputs it provides most closely approximate the positivist ideal. Much like the positivist, the humanist will increasingly interact with a parsed individual whose actions have been neatly tailored to the parameters of the database. The fluidity of multiple human actions will not be revealed because the experiential output reflects a single and easily identifiable action of an otherwise dynamic individual. Furthermore, when one examines the results, one is essentially examining the generalizations embodied in the database and not those who performed the action. The database fails to register the fingerprint of the user who typed the letters or pay attention to the surroundings in which the information was produced. The close ties to positivism cannot be overlooked, though the world of the nineteenth-century positivist depended upon more direct access to the facts. The database is an intermediary between an individual action and the social impact of that action. Access in the digital age is mediated by a database, which exists in real time (no researcher assembled the data for the White House example; it was simply there). Theory will therefore have to adapt, since the data world is slowly putting together a composite picture of all those individual actions.

A database exists somewhere between the real world and the outcome of a digital world. The humanist will struggle to develop a theory that recognizes data's massive impact on human activity without sacrificing the nonuniformity so characteristic of life. Because the two ends of a classic spectrum, the humanist and the scientist, are becoming increasingly intertwined, theories made to oppose one end or the other will lose their purchase and drift. They won't perform the necessary labor, or they will become so detached from reality they will speak to a reality long since having flowed under the bridge. Thus, to keep obsolescence at bay, our conception of what a theory is clamors for rejuvenation. Humanists still work without a comprehensive digital theory or digital philosophy.

Evidently, changing does not mean ending, so we can refrain from making sweeping claims about the death of theory. Nevertheless, the end of theory can be defined as the end of a narrow and combative version that has been the standard bearer for so long. Two changes have to be made. First, the rigid association between postmodernism and theory has to be dissolved to open the way for novel theories, with inspiration coming from a digital world once foreign to humanists. In this spirit, the predominant view that theory reflects a destabilizing antirealist agenda also has to be abandoned. The digital world is not one of absolute certainty, but it cannot be reconciled with the singularities and oddities that reinforced the backbone of antirealist theories. Working with concepts such as repetition requires a revised attitude.

Fortunately, humanist theories can intersect with rather than depend upon the database—the theory will not be dependent on the database, nor will the theory be independent of the database. The humanist may come close to embracing the basic principles of the positivist, but they won't have any problems identifying its limitations or superimposing other principles. The database limns the real world and extracts from it, though it is not a holistic representation of that world. Just because it selects samples from that real world is not a sufficient reason to dismiss it—its impact is formidable. With an understanding of its limitations, humanists can promote a form of neopositivism without worrying that the real sense data will be swept away. When cognizant of these limitations, one will always be ready to seek sense data somewhere else as well and then develop a theory that merges both worlds.

Underlying this attitude to theory is a force that has barely been mentioned, the algorithm. More must be known about the algorithm because it has become such a key player in bringing the results back into the real world. As Google admitted with the White House example, the results were not pre-programmed but a matter of an unexpected outcome of the math. The detailed math is less important than the realization that a tool is so powerful, it can unexpectedly generate information of critical social significance. The nature of algorithmic decision-making therefore requires examination so that it can be compared with methods of decision-making familiar to humanists. Once again, it will become clear that the logical step-by-step attitude is inherently foreign to the postmodern methods of theory described earlier. Humanists have raised algorithmic alarms but have done so with a focus on the output of the algorithm. Moreover, even those who decry the power of algorithms don't hesitate to employ them. The algorithm has proved too useful a tool to ignore, but its internal relationship to theory is still unsure as its raw output gathers most of the attention. Thus, something more must be said about the algorithm.

Notes

1. Berlin, *Historical Inevitability*, 3. There is, in fact, a postmodern equivalent. Many researchers have never read Foucault but, in one way or another, continue to promote his ideas. In Peter Novick's book, Comte is not in the index but positivism comes up all over the place. See Novick, *That Noble Dream*.
2. Auguste Comte, *The Positive Philosophy of Auguste Comte*, trans. Harriet Martineau, vol. II (London: G. Bell and Sons, 1896), 211.
3. Comte, *The Positive Philosophy of Auguste Comte*, II:212.
4. Comte, *The Positive Philosophy of Auguste Comte*, II:216.
5. His attitude is not surprising given how long it took to demonstrate the validity of Newton's theorems. See Thomas S. Kuhn, "The Function of Measurement in Modern Physical Science," *Isis* 52, no. 2 (June 1961): 161–93.
6. Mike Gane, *Auguste Comte*, Key Sociologists (London and New York: Routledge, 2006), 61.
7. Auguste Comte, *The Positive Philosophy of Auguste Comte*, trans. Harriet Martineau, vol. I (London: G. Bell and Sons, 1896), 17. On this as a general trend, see other comments in Mike Gane, *Auguste Comte*, Key Sociologists (London and New York: Routledge, 2006).
8. Comte, *The Positive Philosophy of Auguste Comte*, II:219.
9. Comte, *The Positive Philosophy of Auguste Comte*, II:230.
10. Comte, *The Positive Philosophy of Auguste Comte*, I:166.
11. Leopold von Ranke, "On the Character of Historical Science (a Manuscript of the 1830's)," in *The Theory and Practice of History*, ed. Georg G. Iggers (London and New York: Routledge, 2011), 15.
12. Charles A. Beard, "That Noble Dream," *The American Historical Review* 41, no. 1 (October 1935): 86.
13. Leopold von Ranke, "On Progress in History (From the First Lecture to King Maximilian II of Bavaria 'On the Epochs of Modern History,' 1854)," in *The Theory and Practice of History*, ed. Georg G. Iggers (London and New York: Routledge, 2011), 22.
14. Leopold von Ranke, "Pitfalls of a Philosophy of History (Introduction to a Lecture on Universal History; a Manuscript of the 1840's)," in *The Theory and Practice of History*, ed. Georg G. Iggers (London and New York: Routledge, 2011), 19.
15. Wilhelm Dilthey, *Introduction to the Human Sciences*, vol. 1 (Princeton, NJ: Princeton University Press, 1989), 57, 75.
16. Dilthey, *Introduction to the Human Sciences*, 99.
17. Dilthey, *Introduction to the Human Sciences*, 140.
18. Georg G. Iggers, *The German Conception of History: The National Tradition of Historical Thought From Herder to the Present* (Middletown, CT: Wesleyan University Press, 1983), 134–5.
19. Dilthey, *Introduction to the Human Sciences*, 78.
20. Dilthey, *Introduction to the Human Sciences*, 141.
21. Dilthey, *Introduction to the Human Sciences*, 142.

88 *The End of Theory in the Humanities*

22. Iggers, *The German Conception of History*, 138.
23. Friedrich Nietzsche, "Zur Genealogie der Moral," in *Werke in Drei Bänden*, vol. II (Muenchen: Hanser Verlag, n.d.), 790. In English, "the doer is merely a fiction added to the deed—the deed is everything." This is Walter Kaufmann's translation.
24. Michel Foucault, "Nietzsche, Genealogy, History," in *The Foucault Reader*, ed. Paul Rabinow, 1st ed. (New York: Pantheon Books, 1984), 80.
25. Martin Heidegger, "Nietzsches Wort 'Gott ist tot,'" in *Holzwege* (Frankfurt am Main: V. Klostermann, 1950), 209–10.
26. Arthur C. Danto, *Nietzsche as Philosopher* (New York: Columbia University Press, 2005), 83.
27. Quoted in Maudemarie Clark, *Nietzsche on Truth and Philosophy*, Modern European Philosophy (Cambridge and New York: Cambridge University Press, 1990), 104. Peter Berkowitz offered his readers the exact same excerpt to make a similar point. See Peter Berkowitz, *Nietzsche: The Ethics of an Immoralist*, 1st Harvard University Press pbk. ed. (Cambridge, MA: Harvard University Press, 1996), 10.
28. Quoted in Clark, *Nietzsche on Truth and Philosophy*, 105.
29. Megill, *Prophets of Extremity*, 54–5.
30. Martin Heidegger, "Science and Reflection," in *The Question Concerning Technology and Other Essays*, trans. William Lovitt (New York: Harper Perennial, 2013), 158–60.
31. Heidegger, "Science and Reflection," 165.
32. Heidegger, "Science and Reflection," 169–70.
33. Heidegger, "Science and Reflection," 163.
34. Heidegger, "Science and Reflection," 166–7.
35. Martin Heidegger, *Being and Time*, trans. John Macquarrie and Edward Robinson (London: SCM Press, 1962), 214. For this discussion in visual terms, see Jay, *Downcast Eyes*, 270–1.
36. Heidegger, *Being and Time*, 216.
37. Quoted in Megill, *Prophets of Extremity*, 195.
38. Jacques Derrida, *Limited Inc* (Evanston, IL: Northwestern University Press, 1988).
39. Robert William Fogel and Geoffrey Rudolph Elton, *Which Road to the Past? Two Views of History* (New Haven: Yale University Press, 1983), 126.
40. This is a chapter title in *Of Grammatology*.
41. Jacques Derrida, *Of Grammatology*, trans. Gayatri Chakravorty Spivak (Baltimore: Johns Hopkins University Press, 2016), 81.
42. The French 'trace' is not the same as the English 'trace.' It can also be noted that Heidegger's *Weg* is a completely different invocation from Wittgenstein when he writes about a *Wegweiser*.
43. Judith Butler, "Introduction," in *Of Grammatology*, edited by Jacques Derrida, trans. Gayatri Chakravorty Spivak (Baltimore: Johns Hopkins University Press, 2016), X. The trace in *Of Grammatology* is primarily presented as a linguistic phenomenon though Derrida does link it to gesture in a slightly modified form. See Derrida, *Of Grammatology*, 255.
44. Spivak, "Afterword."
45. Brian Fung, "If You Search Google Maps for the N-Word, It Gives You the White House," *Washington Post*, May 19, 2015, www.washingtonpost.com/news/the-switch/wp/2015/05/19/if-you-search-google-maps-for-the-n-word-it-gives-you-the-white-house/.

5 The Influence of Algorithms on Humanistic Thought

In *Once Upon an Algorithm*, Martin Erwig explains with a humanistic sensitivity how algorithms work. Erwig's strategy is to contrast the logic of the algorithm with a fairy tale, a literary device which would seem to have no connection to logic whatsoever. He retells the story of Hansel and Gretel, popularized by Jacob and Wilhelm Grimm at the start of the nineteenth century. The parents of these two children lead them into the forest and abandon them because the household did not have enough food for everyone. The children are fortunate enough to overhear the parents' plot, and Hansel has the foresight to collect pebbles that can be dropped in the forest so they can find their way home after their parents bid them adieu forever. In the fairy tale, the children face a number of adventures before a white bird leads them to the famous witch whose plan was to eat them. As everyone today knows, the children manage to stuff the witch in the oven and find their way back home.

Erwig suggests a better way than pebbles for the children to navigate the dark woods of medieval Germany. An algorithm, "a precise description of computation," can be developed to ensure that the kids make it out of the forest.[1] The algorithm consists of steps (not the steps taken by the children's small feet) that break down the decision-making process as the children make their way back. The journey is segmented into discrete elements, and with each step a simple yes/no question is asked to determine the direction of the next step. The moment Erwig shifts away from the fairy tale, the decision-making process is analytic and follows a strict computational logic to make the route back home as efficient as possible. The transition to the precision and binary logic embodies the algorithm's desire to save energy and find the most efficient routes possible. The same approach can help the UPS driver find addresses in a modern urban forest.[2]

Erwig's introductory paradigm is defined to soften the logic of the algorithm, but it can easily be contrasted with another story in a German forest. In *Holzwege*, Heidegger wrote about mysterious forest paths. The paths, though overgrown, were like the traces left by a derelict railway over the plains; maybe a ridge, a bump, or a pattern of shrubbery that gave a sense of direction to the trained eye. Only loggers (*Holzmacher*) and forest wardens (*Waldhüter*) really knew where those paths were, but they were reliable guides: "Holzmacher und Waldhüter kennen die Wege. Sie wissen, was es heisst, auf einem Holzweg zu sein" [Loggers and forest wardens know the paths. They know what it means to be on a forest path].[3] *Auf einem Holzweg* would normally suggest getting lost, but not for the loggers and the forest wardens who have an innate sense for the forest; they have an instinct for their environment.

The poetic meaning of Heidegger's example could not survive the logic of the algorithm because his paths are identifiable only with a unique set of humanist skills. It is a matter not of selecting which path to take, but of identifying subtle features and unremarkable aspects of the landscape that reveal the path to the warden. Reducing the Holzwege (or Holzweg in the singular) to a series of algorithmic steps would be a destructive exercise and undermine the nuances in Heidegger's own ambiguous word usage. In recasting the story of Hansel and Gretel, Erwig is providing a heuristic device, but not without risk: the beautiful Wege will be reduced to the mechanics of machine code, annihilating the poetry of the forest for Martin, Hansel, and Gretel.

Erwig used a story as an entryway to explain math but, more frequently, scholars move in the other direction, reducing the algorithm to language. Ed Finn has proposed the concept of "algorithmic reading," which does no more than turn the clock back to Speaking Bolshevik from twenty-five years ago.[4] Leaning on another author, Finn also asserts that software is a "metaphor for metaphor," but provides no explanation for why this should be accepted as a metaphor.[5] The "Regime of Computation" is a light tweak of regimes of technology.[6] All this does is return the algorithm to the same old principles, once again as if nothing has changed in the interim. When algorithms are cast with much older terminology, it obfuscates how they work and how their inner mechanisms impact methodologies.

The trend is, in part, motivated by two old foes meeting again. The promotion of the universal qualities of algorithmic power has entrenched both sides. If one side insists on situating it within language, the other side promotes it as a technological cure-all. Pedro Domingos, a proponent of the Master Algorithm, envisions a Master Algorithm that has "power across all fields." His description of the Master Algorithm hooks into themes that would be familiar to Auguste Comte, because the Master Algorithm leaves detailed work to the specialist and focuses on developing a broader synthesis: "Within field X, it has less power than field X's prevailing theory, but across all fields—when we consider the whole world—it has vastly more power than any other theory."[7] This algorithmic world echoes that of the positivist.

Neither position is that instructive, so the humanist has to find a meaningful way to adapt to the increasing presence of algorithms. To be sure, the algorithm is long past its age of innocence. Safiya Umoja Noble has written extensively about the racist qualities of algorithms, noting that "algorithmic oppression is not just a glitch in the system but, rather, is fundamental to the operating system of the web."[8] Tarleton Gillespie suggests that "the seemingly solid algorithm is in fact a fragile accomplishment."[9] Further, "though algorithms may appear to be automatic and untarnished by the interventions of their providers, this is a carefully crafted fiction."[10] In a humorously depressing overview of chaotic Google-driven searches, James Grimmelmann writes, that "Everything that Google's automated ranking system does, it does because Google programmers told it to. A computer is just a glorified abacus; it does what you tell it to."[11] These authors are a small sampling of those who refuse to accept the algorithm as a neutral arbiter in human affairs.

In the *Black Box Society*, Frank Pasquale has questioned the secret nature of algorithms and exposed why programmers have such a vested interest in preventing others from looking inside their algorithmic code. The Black Box is a "system whose workings are mysterious; we can observe its inputs and outputs, but we cannot tell how one becomes the other." The gap between the inputs and outputs is critical because "knowledge is power."[12] Pasquale employs the expression in a Baconian sense; the knowledge is secret, but there is no secret about what the knowledge can do. His examples refer to the financial industry, where large firms transform all the data into scores and interest rates that have an immediate impact on our lives. She who holds the facts holds the power. If the financial industry were to release the contents of the Black Box, which in Pasquale's example exists non-problematically, they would relinquish power and hence be considered weak. The key to happiness, then, lies within the black box.

The black box metaphor captures an uneasiness about the dark corners of algorithms that answer to invisible puppet masters. It also suggests, as testified by the examples in the previous paragraph, that the data input and social output of the algorithm garner most of the attention. Moreover, the focus lies on the algorithms of others rather than on the increasingly common phenomenon of humanists taking advantage of algorithms to solve their own problems. Although the algorithm is rightly being criticized, much more needs to be said about what's inside that black box. Pasquale's ambiguous reference to knowledge and power clearly highlights issues from the last chapters. That look inside won't solve the dramatic social problems to which Noble refers, but it will show how humanists are skirting the edge of new methodologies. Humanists still use older terminology to describe current events, and thus a shadow of uncertainty surrounds those assertions.

One therefore does not have to question the conclusions outlined here in order to take another approach. Instead of seeking out additional instabilities in the output of algorithms, a humanistic look inside the black box can analyze the algorithm methodologically, that is, understand how algorithmic decision-making can actually anchor a definition of knowledge and power in virgin soil. Since numerous projects in the Digital Humanities require the use of algorithms, one is not just developing a critique of Google or of large financial corporations. Instead, internal questions about the behavior of humanists gain center stage; algorithms modify everybody's behavior. Humanists are developing stronger and stronger ties with algorithms, so it pays to look at the algorithms in a self-reflexive manner. Of course, those points of greatest interest relate to methodological irregularities—when you look into the black box, does postmodernism look back?

Humanists have been preconditioned to deny binaries, but this is the internal format of the algorithm, a format that humanists are happy to engage with in their everyday lives. The introduction of algorithms into the work of humanists requires acceptance of a method which turns fluid situations into discrete entities that meet only whenever a logical decision—IF, OR, AND—has to be made. (What should AND be a metaphor for? What is the grammar of OR?) A little more acceptance of the logic of the algorithm is required to better define the boundary that separates Erwig's forest paths from Heidegger's Holzwege, and thus to better understand where they overlap on the edges.

Algorithms are remarkable because the individual binary decisions can manufacture pluralistic outcomes that should satisfy the goals of anyone advocating diversity. Yet the sheer volume of data gives algorithms the feel of an industrial meat grinder. Sometimes they appear perilous not because they make lots of decisions, but because they make many decisions unnecessary. Nevertheless, they need to be examined in a way that respects the mathematical integrity at their heart, and not in a way that sidelines their inner structure to the external desires of righteous social commentary.

The intricacies of algorithms are poorly understood for good reason—they quickly become so complex that even computer scientists who began their careers before the algorithmic explosion have difficulties with them. Although a handful of humanists have demanded that their peers should learn how to code, too much coding can distract from central humanist issues. One should not actively discourage coding for those who choose that trajectory because tools already abound to facilitate the process for non-experts. Nevertheless, as the tools themselves suggest, too many intricacies will put the humanist on the Holzweg of the casual visitor to the forest. The compromise is frustrating, but if a discussion gets pushed too deeply into technicalities, the overarching consequences of the algorithm will be meaningless. Brevity risks being linked with triviality, but even if the simplicity strips the algorithm of its mathematical wonder, it inches a basic understanding forward.

Fortunately, Erwig has explanations that show where algorithmic differences cannot be ignored. The algorithm's dislike of ambiguity, its methodological step-by-step process, and its dependence on feedback loops are all qualities that don't currently have a home outside the world of the scientist. Once the decision-making process has been clarified in an accessible but impactful manner, the algorithm can be put in context with its predecessors to gain a sense for its novelty. Algorithms, as will be explored later, can be compared to cliometrical analysis of the 1960s and 1970s. Long before the digital age, historians collected massive databases and processed them with statistical formulae; the method relies on databases but is procedurally different from algorithms. Similarly, classification has been a subject of much analysis for its false claim to objectively order an existing world so comparing algorithmic techniques can reveal peculiarities of note. When algorithms are positioned in this context, they won't be falsely equated with grammar or other devices with which they have no inherent connection. If connections should exist, they have to be elucidated rather than assumed.

When an algorithm executes computations, it does so by reducing problems to their most trivial elements so that the decision taken is unambiguous—algorithms dislike ambiguity because they are ultimately designed to make a final decision.[13] An algorithm runs into problems when it meets ambiguous linguistic constructions such as homonyms. The algorithm must define a way to distinguish between trunk as part of a tree and part of a car; the definition cannot leave room for doubt. These ambiguities are a regular part of everyday language, but they upset the functioning of algorithms. As Erwig notes, "ambiguity is a *bug* in a language's syntax definition."[14] Therefore, the language of music or of the algorithm requires rules to prevent these situations from cropping up: "Any notation that violates the rules cannot be properly executed as an algorithm . . . [it] must represent effectively executable steps that can be interpreted unambiguously."[15] The precision and the lack of ambiguity pull the algorithm in a scientific direction. Firmly separating the meaning of homonyms into discrete units represents a remarkably anti-postmodern approach to language.

The distaste of ambiguity is closely linked to the binary parameters of the process; one could hardly expect a system based on yes/no decisions to appreciate vagueness. Despite this mathematical air, one should not forget that the algorithm makes multiple decisions. The vast majority of algorithms process lots of data and make thousands upon thousands of decisions along the way. Each single decision may bear an oversimplified air of clarity, but the millions of decisions can return effectively ambiguous results, though each single question answered en route was not ambiguous at all. This perspective offers a moment of relief from science, but it is not a reason to ignore the effectiveness of binary decision-making.

Internal ambiguity is especially awkward for the algorithm because it wants to search, sort, and isolate whatever data it combs through. The most advanced techniques thus break down problems into their most simple elements. For example, if an algorithm is programmed to determine the order of inheritance in a family tree, it needs to isolate and label each member of the family and then sort them according to rules.[16] The algorithm proceeds through the lists step by step and orders them accordingly. Since programmers seek to make the algorithms as efficient as possible, thereby reducing steps and run times, they figure out complex techniques to approach specific problems. To explain alphabetization, Erwig discusses a binary search tree defined by the fact that each node of the tree has only two sub-values; with these trees an algorithm can determine whether a certain letter (stored as a value) appears in a word. The algorithm thinks of letters as values depending upon their alphabetic location and makes a binary decision (smaller or larger in comparison with the alphabetic position of another letter) only to determine which branch it should look down. If c, for example, is at the top of the tree, and the algorithm is searching for b, it would look to the lower branch because b has less alphabetic value than c. It then looks at the letter at the node below the c and does the same test—is b larger or smaller than a? B would be larger, and therefore the algorithm would look to the higher branch. When it determined there were no more branches to go down, it would either have already found e or determined that it does not appear in the sequence.[17]

This is only one of numerous algorithmic variants, but it embodies the binary nature of decision-making almost always present in one form or another. The irony embodied by such resurgent binaries cannot be overlooked. Binary oppositions have been anathema to scholars for decades, so how can one base decisions on binaries? Why would one not reject the process altogether (as opposed to accepting the result and then subjecting it to a social critique)? Humanists have immediately dismissed naïve claims about the neutrality of algorithms and have rightly suggested that programmers have biases of which they might not be aware but have been more concerned with the programmers than the actual decision-making process. The irony is only mitigated by the fact that the volume of single decisions permits pluralistic results.

The individual binary decisions do not continually reference each other as a postmodern model of a trace would desire. The closest the algorithm comes to this behavior is the feedback loop or *recursion*. Although a decision made is a decision made, the output of any decision can be reintroduced into the input of an upcoming decision. This aspect of the algorithm might be familiar to many in the form of a flow chart. As the loops become more complicated, they feed back information, and these conditions get reconsidered with each subsequent execution of the algorithm. The feedback is essential in larger algorithms as a control structure that transforms or connects "primitive operations into larger algorithms for describing meaningful computations."[18] The feedbacks are fascinating because they bring the past back into the present (as memory can influence our present decisions) and modulate—bring more precision—to the end decisions. They play with time because they continually return to the past to ensure a desired future result. While this alters a present state to overcome a past inadequacy or inconsistency, the algorithm needs the recursion only until a final decision has been made.

Self-referentiality is a critical postmodern concept and, in the spirit of Derrida's trace, has been invoked to undermine a metaphysical presence. In an algorithm, an output can be looped back into its own input so that the actual output is a function of changing itself. It refers back to itself and is a case of self-referentiality. The parallel with the algorithm, however, only goes so far. First, the algorithm is designed to provide a specific result and stops when it reaches an end condition; it can fluctuate internally but the output is clear and concrete. The trace that returns is a digital trace subject to a digital decision-making process; it can exert influence within a self-referential code but itself is a simple command or index. Finally, Derrida's recursive trace does not act as a loop (though the Hegelian dialectic has been described as a helix, this is still not a loop). Derrida's version reflects a back and forth, a push and pull of elements, so no simple input or output can be identified. In the algorithm, recursion is regular and predictable even if it is self-reflexive. Although the feedback suggests that decisions are never really final because they are always subject to subtle changes, the algorithm wants to come to a conclusion.

The technical parameters for the preceding thoughts come from Erwig's basic introduction to algorithms. Surprisingly, his work is littered with references to language and makes every effort to cast algorithms as a language, a strategy long familiar to humanists. The book has references to the "*signifier* and the *signified*," to "grammar rules," "a visual language" and so on.[19] On the one hand, humanists should be thrilled to see the impact of the linguistic turn in scientific writing. This would appear to corroborate Ed Finn's claims about metaphorical qualities, mentioned at the outset of this chapter. On the other hand, a closer look shows that despite all the references to grammar and the sign and the signified, the text has little in common with standard notions of the linguistic turn. Instead of revealing family resemblances, it reinforces the unique qualities of the algorithm.

All Erwig's references to grammars with specific elements refer to the grammars of natural languages; the work does not make an attempt to parse and dissect grammatical elements of the programmer. Therefore, natural languages perform the role of metaphors or, more clearly, act as a heuristic aid. The references to the sign and the signified do not describe how the programming language works, much like knowledge of a few English words won't tell the user anything about the structure of the

English language. Moreover, Erwig presents the sign and the signified as an act of labeling, precisely the move that Wittgenstein derided in the first few pages of the *Philosophical Investigations*. As far as the programming language is concerned, the signified is a placeholder in an equation. A list of suspects' names in a Sherlock Holmes case refers unambiguously to the individuals who bear those names. In those cases, such as in homonyms, where one "signifier can represent different signifieds," the example is presented to show how algorithms sort through ambiguities to produce clarity.[20] This usage does not meet the expectations of the linguistic turn.

The more significant example concerns time, because there is absolutely no connection with an algorithm's understanding of time and the manner in which natural languages store or present time. Whereas a natural language expresses time with features such as aspect, a programming language marks time in a raw numerical manner. The programming language is not indifferent to the passage of time, since it must take efficiency into consideration. The algorithm can be designed to reduce the number of steps to solve a problem or to reduce the run time of the algorithm. This is an outcome rather than a feature of the programming language. If one absolutely insists on stating that the programming language has a grammar, then one would have to add that the grammar has no tenses or any capacity to express time. Time can be expressed only with numerical references and indexed values that are not part of a grammatical system; this is the same for English when it comes to making exact statements about when something happened.

These considerations impact the humanist because humanistic methods increasingly rely on these algorithmic functions. While steering clear of individual programmers' peccadilloes, this look into the black box of the algorithm reveals unresolved tensions. Much like Martin Jay ran the senses through discourse, commentators on algorithmic languages want, out of habit, to treat them no differently from natural languages. There is a continued reluctance to differentiate between the properties of a programming language and Russian or Spanish because an older theoretical template is being superimposed upon the programming language. If, however, language determines thought and the humanist relies on the language of the algorithm, the algorithm will alter the structural thinking of the humanist. Looking inside the black box thus reveals layers of deeper interest than expected.

Translation is another prism through which to explain the gap between the algorithm as language and the natural languages of everyday experience. Erwig makes no attempt to translate a natural language into a programming language; the examples are always metaphorical, and metaphor is not a translational device. This leads one to correctly suspect that algorithms cannot be translated in the same way that natural languages are. For example, one cannot introduce an algorithmic phrase into Google Translate and expect a return in Haitian Creole, Corsican, or Southern Sotho. The reverse does not work either. You cannot enter a phrase in Sinhala or Sindhi and get a programmer's phrase in return.

Another way to emphasize the same point is to consider Quine's notion of the indeterminacy of translation: "manuals for translating one language into another can be set up in divergent ways, all compatible with the totality of speech dispositions, yet incompatible with one another."[21] Quine was urging readers to look beyond one single, unique, and correct translation of a word. As the quote suggests, the indeterminacy of translation did not impact the functioning of the language or its translation, though the translations were not unique. A programming language, however, could not survive the indeterminacy of translation.

Algorithms are often described in common English before their functions are realized in a programming language. English thoughts can then be translated into a programming language, seemingly refuting many of the considerations noted earlier. This 'translation' might appear unproblematic, but the programming language has to tighten all the screws to make it work. If one then took the translated programming language and asked a third party to translate it back into English, we would have two English versions with no exact correspondence between them (this was Quine's point). The inexact translations would fulfill their descriptive duties in English, but the algorithm would lose its way with all the variants. The best way to contemplate the interaction between an algorithm and natural language is to think of it as a unidirectional translation.

Most often, this version of the indeterminacy of translation is unproblematic because everyone understands the difference between a natural language and the programmer's language. The more common role an algorithm plays in translation is as a blind intermediary between natural languages. It never sees the light of day, but it facilitates communication between two external languages. Google Translate exemplifies the gap between the algorithm and the natural language because no visible link connects the algorithm with the translated languages; the algorithm knows absolutely nothing about the languages per se.

Google Translate has been criticized because of its inexactness. Professional translators have toyed with it to show how quickly it transforms and muddles an expression (for example, by continually translating the same message back and forth between two languages, the message eventually gets distorted; this game is the digital equivalent of the game of telephone). If cognitive linguists and Artificial Intelligence researchers lament its imperfections, it is precisely these imperfections that fit the postmodern mold.[22] Google Translate, though beautifully awkward, fits the concept of the Wittgensteinian *Wegweiser* or signpost: The signpost is in order—if, under normal circumstances, it fulfils its purpose.[23] One should not try to create an artificial form of skepticism when Google Translate can perform effectively in many situations. Google Translate often offers imperfect translations, but, as a matter of experience, it is highly effective at pointing the communicant in the right direction. As long as the translation gives a general sense under normal circumstances (and yes, it sometimes can be wrong), then criticisms fall by the wayside. As Google develops new algorithms, the translations improve and the signposts function more effectively.

As the algorithms keep changing and reach ever increasing levels of logical complexity, Google Translate identifies patterns in already translated texts (such as those produced by the United Nations) so that it can reapply this translation whenever it reencounters the same pattern. It works effectively because it canvasses billions of potential patterns. This can lead to anomalies—languages with a smaller written presence will be harder to translate or will produce shakier translations. It can also happen that Google Translate only has a single pattern upon which to base a translation. A reader can have an English translation of a German text and wish to verify the accuracy of the English translation. If Google Translate has only a single pattern, which has been taken from that same English translation, it cannot verify anything because it will regurgitate the same phrase one wanted to verify. It can assist someone struggling with the German edition but cannot check that the English is correct because it has not compared it to anything. In this case, one has to hope the original human translator did her job properly.

The machine translator does not learn German or English grammar before embarking on its task; a postmodernist should welcome the freedom it exercises outside of state language commissions. It is indifferent to the home language and bases the translation on common language usage. Since the first data sets came from the United Nations, it originally excelled at diplomatic and bureaucratic translations and was less effective with street jargon. Recent algorithms are better at mapping the semantics of language, but whatever innovation occurs, the method of translating has little in common with translations performed in the 1960s. The machine does not learn a language per se but processes it without having the slightest clue about the meaning of what has been translated or communicated.

A slight parallel with logical positivists such as Rudolf Carnap emerges in this case.[24] A lead figure amongst the logical positivists, Carnap wanted a more scientific language with empirical undertones. He encouraged scholars to unearth the logical metalanguage that underlay our common language (a position that the later Wittgenstein and almost everyone else would abandon). The structure of the metalanguage was supposed to be independent of the practical language because it was embedded in logic much like the algorithm is independent of the language it translates. Yet the programming of an algorithm has no interest in mapping common language to anything or creating a metalanguage. The programming language is designed to execute efficient instructions that get realized in any form in the real world; it does not attempt to create a universal grammar, though it employs logical universals.

In this respect, the algorithm and the languages it translates lead isolated lives. The success of the algorithm depends upon the collection of massive amounts of data paired with logic rather than the learning of verb tables or listening to tape recordings. Google Translate and its equivalents have nevertheless become essential tools, though a human cannot learn the Google algorithm in order to speak German. The algorithmic language cannot be translated into German, but it can, and does, impact our understanding of German based on a set of logical rules foreign to the experience of speaking German.

Google Translate is seen as a convenient device that assists translation when necessary but, for many of the reasons mentioned earlier, is not integrally attached to the home languages; the two parallel tracks will never meet. Over time, however, the Google machine translations will impact linguistic usage and penetrate into the grammars they never really understood. In other words, Google Translate will encounter patterns that it was influential in creating—it will have left a trace on linguistic usage that is barely detectable. This echoes the postmodern process of appropriation whereby a community accepts a pejorative moniker, such as queer, and empowers itself by appropriating it. The translation algorithms are more abstract and inanimate, but they slowly appropriate aspects of the language they translate.

These thoughts corroborate the intuition of a Gillespie or Noble, both of whom have noted the instability of the algorithm, but the thoughts presented here do so at a much different level. They certainly reinforce the notion that the algorithm has an artificial and unreliable quality to it. Furthermore, they indicate that the algorithm is neutral and invisible only as long as we choose not to look deeper into it. Yet the conundrum outlined earlier speaks to internal dynamics rather than to a readily identifiable and empirical output. When Noble writes of all the problems that "are part of the architecture and language of technology," one can fully agree with the sentiment but have no idea which language is being referred to or what precisely is meant by language; the ascription is a function of habit and not anything particular to language.[25] Thus, the focus on the internal dynamic reflects an imperative because otherwise, the humanist risks identifying the problem while misunderstanding the cause of that problem; she will then only be able to offer a placebo rather than a comprehensive treatment and ignore the extent to which the analyst has been infected by the malady as well. The algorithm, however, forces new modes of thinking that both underlie the problem and creep into the way humanists now make decisions. The latter is as important as the former, especially considering the central role of language in all of the works noted thus far.

If the algorithm neither learns grammar in a traditional manner nor functions like a dictionary which pairs words, it is more akin to an English-to-Spanish version of Bartlett's Book of Quotations because it looks for patterns. So much postmodern literature has focused on identifying and analyzing words because they are readily identifiable in a sentence (ironically, just as our eyes identify single discrete objects in a cluttered room). One can then write about the discourse of that word. In contrast, the algorithm seeks out patterns—and a word can be considered a pattern as well—in the semantics of a sentence. Because it seeks patterns, it is much more sophisticated than any analysis based on words. Take for example the clichéd claim that a specific language has no word for X; it therefore cannot conceptualize that thought or emotion, and thus the speakers of that language have an incommensurable worldview compared to speakers of languages who do have the word X. The algorithm would not see the lack of a word as an obstacle, though it might run into other barriers.

Translation with algorithms, then, embodies a few paradoxes. The present inability to offer exact translations fits the general needs of the postmodern manifesto. Yet the current desire to make Google Translate more perfect and more efficient fits the aspirations of a scientific community. The current outcomes are based on a binary decision-making mechanism that is completely opposed to postmodernism and the languages to which it normally refers. Lacking an internal grammar, it understands how to link natural grammars without necessarily understanding those grammars: an algorithm does not have an "imaginative" grammar, though it might link two imaginative grammars.[26] Words such as language and grammar must be treated with extreme caution so as to respect the layer that separates the algorithm from the language it translates. Its features are of a different sort, and one should not feign a similarity for the sake of conceptual convenience.

The algorithm also establishes a moment to explore casual references to metaphors. As grammar cannot be thrown around loosely, some constraints have to be placed on metaphors—not everything is a metaphor. A programming language could be a metaphor for something just as a stage can have a metaphorical function relative to the world; the metaphorical relationship must be identified explicitly because some metaphors don't work. The story of Hansel and Gretel can be used metaphorically to explain the algorithm, but the algorithm language cannot be used as a metaphor to explain Hansel and Gretel. Similarly, the programming language does not have metaphors within it: could the programming language state that all the world is a logical IF? *Software* might be a metaphor for something in the English language because the term has such broad application; but the guts or components of the software, the programming language and its individual steps, don't have the same metaphorical capabilities as the term software in written English. The only way to identify metaphors in a programming language would be to identify how they act as metaphors within that language. Yet they cannot conjure the requisite imagery to function metaphorically. What imagery would emerge from a programming language that would be imagery within the linguistic world of programming? What type of functionality could a metaphor in a programming language have if the programming language, as Erwig asserts, hated ambiguity? These are not easy questions to answer, and that is why they are most frequently dismissed.

This brief excursus on metaphor shows how quickly confusion arises if the distinction between the inner functioning and the outer face is not made clear. The same issue can surface with the term trope, a favorite word of postmodernists in no small part because it stems from the Greek *tropos*, or turn. One author writes that with the help of the algorithm, "the trope that persists hidden through the centuries can now be traced effortlessly."[27] The algorithm has nothing to do with tropes, but it can identify tropes in medieval writing because it is identifying patterns. In fact, in looking for tropes in the previous excerpt, the algorithm is performing searches that cognitive linguists have been doing for decades—scanning languages for fragments to establish recognizable patterns and therefore draw conclusions about grammars over time and space (though the historical and social context is of less interest to these individuals). The algorithm is performing a positivist duty by identifying tropes.

The Greek term for pathway (ατραπός—atrapos) is etymologically close, if not identical, to trope. In a sense then, the algorithm is being asked to identify the Holzwege so important to Heidegger, especially since the Greek term can be associated with a shortcut. Yet the Holzwege of the logger and the forest warden have absolutely nothing to do with the algorithm and its search for these tropes. They are operating on their own levels and the algorithm's identification of a trope can be said to undermine the poetic moment of the Holzweg itself. The algorithm, in finding the trope, identifies the precise location in the forest, so the traveler no longer has a treed path to navigate; the skills of the forest warden are irrelevant. A stranger to the forest has been dropped into a *Lichtung* or clearing. This individual no longer experiences the whole forest.

This further explains why the algorithm itself is not a trope; if the algorithm were a trope, then it would be representative of a specific style. Imagine a situation in which a historian or literary critic gained renown not for the style of her writing but for the style of the algorithms she produced. The experiment is not completely far-fetched because many digital humanists have urged colleagues to code and software programmers have their own unique style. A style in this case only means differences in practical approaches rather than a full-scale difference in linguistic being.

The algorithm has also been praised because it can "perform the same analysis over and over again."[28] The "over and over again" refers not to the internal feedback loops of the algorithm, but to the ability to take the same algorithm and press the start button in a variety of situations. This repetition sounds convenient but contains qualities that run afoul of postmodern theses; it is not quite clear how postmodernism deals with something happening over and over again. More existential than postmodern, Nietzsche introduced the concept of eternal return which encompasses an emotional and moral form of repetition, but this formulation is still distant from an algorithm repeating itself.

Intuitively, one would expect postmodernism to reject repetition for almost all the reasons stated in previous discussions. Derrida's notion of the trace prevents one from returning to a starting position and rerunning an experiment because the starting position already contains a trace of everything that came after it; a dialectic relationship has been established. The algorithm knows of no such difficulty; it can repeat on an empty stomach, so to speak. Repetition suggests a sealed laboratory in which a practitioner can control an environment to ensure the stability of results. An algorithm is past the laboratory stage, but its taste for repetition can easily be understood in that context. Repetition does not have to be conceptualized as a circle, like the circle line on the Moscow subway, but can be thought of as a city walk that loops back to its start at the end of the day. The regularity of the same route, like the Kantian walk through Königsberg, defies the diversity of experience postmodernism emphasized. Relativism does not go round and round.

The repetitive nature of the algorithm indicates that the algorithm likes to look for regularities; in a sense, the algorithm can be trained to discover regularities but would struggle to make sense of irregularities. It could look for an irregularity within a regularity, but the irregularity has to have a pattern or regularity of its own. The algorithm is then being asked to look for an anti-pattern within a pattern, which it could produce as well. It is much more effective at identifying the presence of specific tropes in medieval literature than the absence of tropes (unless it were asked to look for the absence of a specific trope). It can find a trope only because it has an internal continuity across separate cases. The algorithm therefore prefers continuities over discontinuities (it is as yet unclear to me how an algorithm might be used to identify an infinite series of discontinuities). As such, it pushes 'special cases,' marginal examples, to the periphery.

The repetitive nature of the algorithm also has a tinge of the formulaic, though an algorithm is not a formula per se. In thinking of the algorithm as a formula, it can be constructively compared to cliometrics. Cliometrics was a forerunner of contemporary data analysis and became popular amongst economic historians.[29] In the early days of computers, cliometricians constructed data sets from historical samples, such as the height of soldiers in the Habsburg army, and then processed the data to draw social conclusions, such as correlating height to increased food supply and a rising standard of living.[30] The data and the statistical mathematics employed to analyze it told a larger story about slavery or the impact of the Industrial Revolution on migrants to cities. Since the method reeked of quantitative analysis and paid scant attention to social or cultural history, it did not enjoy prestige amongst most humanists.

While both methods process data, their dissimilarities further highlight the unique position of the algorithm. Both methods are formulaic in the sense that something is calculated or computed and data is processed. The cliometric formula, however, does not involve step-by-step decision-making en route to providing a result. It has an analog flavor insofar as it does not reduce values to binaries to engage in a binary decision-making process. For example, it integrates values over fluid time with traditional differentials and sums. In contrast, the algorithm depends on basic logic functions that are designed to decide (not decipher) upon subsequent paths to take. The algorithm is more active with the data, a process that is reflected in the numerous feedback loops. In a comparative perspective, a reliance on algorithms shows a greater commitment to positivism than does cliometrics because of the dependency on binary decision-making.

Interestingly, cliometricians often published the formulae they used for their calculations; the formulae were mysterious to many but instructive for anyone who grasped mathematical analysis. A similar requirement could be asked of contemporary scholars who employ algorithms, satisfying at least one of Pasquale's wishes. Although major corporations guard their computational secrets in deep vaults, academics could place their logical steps in the public domain. The reader could then make her own decisions about the internal operation of the algorithm. If the algorithms were presented in this manner, the humanist analysis would reveal a deeper commitment to science because the interconnection with such a methodology would be self-evident.

Another comparison, this time going back further in time, can be made with classification, because classification can also be considered an older form of working with lots of data. In addition, classification has an uneasy status because it has been pilloried by postmodernists as a remnant of the Enlightenment. The name Carl Linnaeus, the eighteenth-century Swedish scientist, is synonymous with classification, and what was for him a glorious and grandiose exercise became a paradigm case of imposing a socially constructed order on the unsuspecting natural world. Postmodernists derided classification because of its ill-begotten attempts to mirror nature with names and because of its attempt to devise universal systems of order. What had been presented as an objective ordering of knowledge was criticized because it contained internal social, gender, and racial prejudices that influenced how users accessed and used knowledge. In the same vein, the Library of Congress classification system for books has been presented as an arbitrary system that promotes the needs of its creators. While classification produced long, long lists for admiring scientists in the nineteenth century, it did no such thing for humanists at the end of the twentieth century.

Algorithms have a similar feel and could easily be categorized as classifiers, but classification labels rather than processes data. One can think of the streets in a city. Classification is more interested in establishing a naming system for streets and avenues to make for more efficient street maps; it establishes a more convenient way to deal with lots of empirical data. The algorithm is indifferent to the naming system but takes the names given to it in order to compute the most efficient routes through the system; an algorithm might name items internally, but this is a means to a sophisticated end. The classifier of the eighteenth or nineteenth century was obsessed with an ordered and systematic manner for naming fauna, whereas the algorithmist simply uses the names as labels as a component of a more powerful service for those who wanted to track the movement of animals in the jungle.[31]

The world of photography offers a poignant example drawn from the nineteenth century. Scientists and photographers of the nineteenth century did extensive visual studies of personalities to classify beauty, emotion, and personality. In 1862, Guillaume-Benjamin Duchenne published *Mécanisme*, a positivist effort to chart human facial expressions.[32] He created synoptic tables which demonstrated these facial expressions and took full facial photographs such as the one designated "The Muscle of Fright, of Terror."[33] The viewer sees a man whose face is being nudged into the right expression with the assistance of scalpels. This method has clearly been discredited, but like so many nineteenth-century projects, it still fascinates historians and art curators; Duchenne's approach opens doors to the values and emotions of another era. Algorithms can identify these nineteenth-century figural differences and identify facial trends, but they are not designed to confirm socially constructed categories of classification. The algorithm would be more focused on visual recognition, or on expanding the sample set and exposing further examples of similar facial features in these older documents without heeding the antiquated classification system. Algorithms are not actual classifiers despite sorting information. Of course, the algorithm can still produce morally and socially unacceptable outputs, but it does so by trending rather than classifying information.

A system of classification creates a system that influences or steers users once they enter that system without processing the data. A library classification system sorts and sticks labels on books, but the system sits there passively until a user stumbles upon it; it then actively steers but does not force a user to land at a specific section or alter the contents of the books. It subtly influences the access process. Similarly, the classification of plants assists scholars in identifying their place in the natural world and, of course, can artificially or accidentally create a distorted vision of that world.

The algorithm, on the other hand, is much more flexible since it continually processes the information and creates dynamic results. A Netflix algorithm has the ability to steer users away from the expensive blockbusters, but this is not a fixed category; it depends upon an ever-changing list of blockbusters. In essence, the algorithm passes each bit of information or action by the user through a series of checkpoints and then spits out a result depending upon how the information fared at each checkpoint. The processing is much more active and classification harmlessly passive in comparison. Furthermore, the inner workings of the algorithm don't permit for the same ambiguity as a classifying system. The algorithm is always correct relative to the input it receives; if it is told to find a word or expression, it will (which will inevitably lead the scholar to trust it too much). This does not mean the result is correct or neutral or stable relative to the external world; only that the checkpoints follow a predetermined logic.

The distinctions indicate that both methods depend upon a rather empirical attitude to facts, but the algorithm takes it a step further, since it essentially respects each individual input then processes it to give a desired outcome or to order the inputs so that trends can be identified. It more closely approximates the positivist method because the trends it identifies and establishes are similar to the laws that positivists wanted to establish. Law is too strong a word, but here it can be mentioned in the same breath as trend, if one takes into consideration the limitations of the algorithm. The individual who objects to classification should harbor the same reluctance to accept the algorithm. This will be much more problematic, however, since the algorithm is a much more energetic and intrusive tool and is slowly becoming the bedrock of humanistic decision-making.

Since the algorithm can have such an influence, how much of an understanding must the humanist have of the algorithm? How much logic will the humanist need to adequately use these algorithms? (How much postmodern theory, if any, did a humanist need to cite postmodern theory?) Recently, a gerrymandering case in Wisconsin arrived at the Supreme Court of the United States because some view gerrymandering as a threat to democracy.[34] The gerrymandering has become incredibly effective because algorithms maximize electoral results in favor of one party. The gerrymandering case is quantitative from start to finish and therefore compels humanists to extend a horizon beyond the confining parameters of language. Will the future political scientist and historian have to comprehend the basic elements of the gerrymandering algorithm to grasp the broad significance of this political case?

The discussion has focused on basic internal parameters of the algorithm but has not addressed the pedagogical or methodological requirement that makes humanists dip deeper into a logical world to learn more about algorithms. The humanist could trust the algorithm, pay scant attention to its inner workings, and be happy with whatever results it gives. Without succumbing to the logic of the algorithm, the analysis will still benefit because the algorithm will have pointed research in a new direction, much like Newtonian physics of the seventeenth century impacted humanistic philosophy of the eighteenth century. In contrast, as others have urged, the humanist could learn how to code; this would be the equivalent of learning the DNA of the algorithm. The humanist could take lessons in quantitative methodology, a step that would dramatically shift the nature of the enterprise because quantification would leave its mark.[35]

The overlap between the humanist and the scientist is not new. Amongst historians of science, a wide range of attitudes prevail from those with a deep understanding of scientific phenomena to those who focus on the scientists first and the science second. The level of scientific commitment varies immensely and often corresponds to the scholar's determination to espouse the objective qualities of science. The less interest shown in the science, the greater chance the narrative has of being placed in a postmodern direction. Postmodernism was exceptionally effective at creating a boundary between itself and the hard sciences (the persistent attempts to eliminate the distinction between the hard and soft sciences ironically did just that) but this boundary, which will respect the methods of the hard sciences, will become more porous.

This chapter kicked off with a work that blended humanistic stories with the mechanics of the algorithm. The tale of Hansel and Gretel was fortuitous because it took place in the beloved medieval forests of Heidegger; their walk could be contrasted with the walk of the forest warden. In the algorithmist's dream, Hansel and Gretel would make their way home following a set of discrete steps, each step embodying a single directional decision. Heidegger's forest warden would wither away under such conditions, overcome by a logical malaise. One does not have to pick sides—either help the lost children or follow the forester on his daily routine—but one must recognize how different they are. They cannot be pulled together artificially with a few convenient catch phrases. This is not about separating the scientist from the romantic, but about feeling comfortable enough to recognize a boundary where one exists.

Consequently, the positivist elements of algorithms weaken the postmodern component of humanist writing and cannot be brushed away by pretending that the internal decision-making process of the algorithm is irrelevant to the larger social issues it may be instrumental in revealing. If the humanist works with the outcome of the algorithm, he is accepting the internal workings of that algorithm and this acceptance requires shifts and changes in other methodologies. As scholars working in the digital world clearly agree, the algorithm cannot be treated as a black box that one looks upon from the position of the external observer; one must feel involved in the algorithm itself. To argue that one can remain completely isolated from the workings of an algorithm is an intellectual colonialism that can be compared with British citizens who believed they could have an empire without having their own values transformed by all the other cultures in that empire. The internal logic of the algorithm will ineluctably transform the attitude of the external user.

The initiative over the last pages aspired to promote the novelty of the algorithm by distancing it from the pull of older ideas. It is mistaken, for example, to cast the algorithm as a language; the elimination of this refrain essentially removes the algorithm from the twentieth century and situates it in the twenty-first century. The metaphor as malapropism was a big part of the argument but by no means the only part. In the straightforward case of Google Translate, one immediately sees the complexity of the riddle when asked to translate the programming language of Google Translate into a natural language; the process contains too many hairpin turns to be fully effective. The algorithm is also different from its closest ancestors. It is reminiscent of a fascination with cliometrics but depends on a slightly different worldview and even transforms the elegant analog curves of the cliometrician into the sharp turns of binary codes. Before dismissing the algorithm as another misbegotten classifier, one has to remember that it is not a classifier per se. Although the algorithm loves to sort information, as the first examples from Erwig indicate, it is not a classifier at heart.

The acceptance of this logical, if uncomfortable, process does not eliminate the algorithm's ability to focus on societal issues; the humanist can withstand the centripetal pull of a scientific world with its naïve sense that technology is a magical solution to social problems. In *Where the Animals Go*, James Cheshire and Oliver Uberti have a final chapter called "Where the Humans Go" in which they marvel at the ability of the algorithm to trigger an alarm about a grandmother who has lost her way.[36] The optimism is admirable, but the work fails to mention how governments, such as the one in the People's Republic of China, employ algorithms to monitor the movement of their citizens and assemble a moral score depending upon locales frequented and services used.[37] When the algorithm has been called upon to perform aesthetic and emotional judgments, the SOS has been immediately sounded. Algorithms have been employed as connoisseurs to identify subtleties in paintings provoking the obvious objection that algorithms cannot replicate human experience tout court.[38] The objections define an area where the algorithm has no right to be—say, in the emotional world of a human. The abuse of the power of the algorithm can easily be recognized without inserting it into a postmodern critique a close reader could not accept because it relies too strongly on the method it chooses to denounce. In short, the philosophical essence of postmodernism is at odds with the logic of the algorithm, though both can produce the same social conclusion.

Ultimately, the algorithm processes data and is not the data itself. The discussion therefore has to probe deeper into the digital world and look at that data and how the characterization of data makes its mark in the humanities. These massive sets of information are more than just impressive for their size. The concept of intersecting with such a foreign source of information is a novelty that can easily upset comfortable worldviews.

We are not as familiar with the data as the forest warden was with the woods, but this is not a reason to ignore Big Data. If learning about an algorithm is more than learning to code, understanding Big Data is much more involved than just listing strings and strings of information.

Notes

1. Martin Erwig, *Once Upon an Algorithm: How Stories Explain Computing* (Cambridge, MA: The MIT Press, 2017), 17. In the context of the current discussion, this book is fascinating because the author has made an extreme effort to employ postmodern terminology yet advocates a method completely at odds with postmodernism. As presented, the two approaches are impossible to reconcile.
2. Ed Finn, *What Algorithms Want: Imagination in the Age of Computing* (Cambridge, MA: MIT Press, 2017), 19. A variant of this theme appears in Arlindo L. Oliveira, *The Digital Mind: How Science Is Redefining Humanity* (Cambridge, MA: The MIT Press, 2017). Oliveira asks, what is the set of roads with [the] shortest total length that will keep all the cities connected?
3. See the opening page of Martin Heidegger, *Holzwege* (Frankfurt am Main: V. Klostermann, 1950). The title has been translated as "Off the Beaten Track" but this is rather misleading. The German original has wood/forest in the title; the material substance is critical to Heidegger's meaning and materiality resurfaces throughout the volume. The translation also suggests what the Holzwege were not rather than what they were. True, they were not the main roads; but they were paths, and they were beaten by the soft soles of individuals who really knew their forest environment. See Martin Heidegger, *Off the Beaten Track*, ed. Julian Young and Kenneth Haynes (Cambridge and New York: Cambridge University Press, 2002).
4. Finn, *What Algorithms Want*, 5.
5. This reference appears in Finn but relies on the work of Wendy Chun. See Wendy Hui Kyong Chun, *Programmed Visions: Software and Memory* (Cambridge, MA: MIT Press, 2011).
6. See the title heading to chapter one in Katherine Hayles, *My Mother Was a Computer: Digital Subjects and Literary Texts* (Chicago: University of Chicago Press, 2005).
7. Pedro Domingos, *The Master Algorithm: How the Quest for the Ultimate Learning Machine Will Remake Our World* (New York, NY: Basic Books, 2015), 47.
8. Noble, *Algorithms of Oppression*, 10.
9. Tarleton Gillespie, "The Relevance of Algorithms," in *Media Technologies: Essays on Communication, Materiality, and Society*, ed. Tarleton Gillespie, Pablo J. Boczkowski, and Kirsten A. Foot (Cambridge, MA: The MIT Press, 2014), 169.
10. Gillespie, "The Relevance of Algorithms," 179.
11. James Grimmelmann, "The Google Dilemma," *New York Law School Law Review* 53 (September 2008): 944.
12. Pasquale, *The Black Box Society*, 3.
13. Erwig, *Once Upon an Algorithm*, 162.
14. Erwig, *Once Upon an Algorithm*, 162.
15. Erwig, *Once Upon an Algorithm*, 145.
16. Erwig, *Once Upon an Algorithm*, 75.
17. Erwig, *Once Upon an Algorithm*, 92.

18. Erwig, *Once Upon an Algorithm*, 182.
19. Erwig, *Once Upon an Algorithm*, 51, 145, 181, emphasis in original.
20. Erwig, *Once Upon an Algorithm*, 54.
21. Quine, *Word and Object*, 27.
22. For a more philosophical perspective, see John R. Searle, "Minds, Brains, and Programs," *Behavioral and Brain Sciences* 3, no. 3 (1980): 417–57.
23. Ludwig Wittgenstein, *Philosophical Investigations*, ed. G. E. M. Anscombe, 3rd ed. (Oxford and Malden, MA: Blackwell, 2001), 87. Der Wegweiser ist in Ordnung—wenn er, unter normalen Verhältnissen, seinen Zweck erfüllt.
24. Rudolf Carnap, *The Logical Structure of the World*, trans. Rolf A. George (Berkeley, CA: University of California Press, 1967).
25. Noble, *Algorithms of Oppression*, 9.
26. Finn, *What Algorithms Want*, 27.
27. Elias Muhanna, "Islamic and Middle East Studies and the Digital Turn," in *The Digital Humanities and Islamic & Middle East Studies* (Berlin and Boston: De Gruyter, 2016), 9.
28. Muhanna, "Islamic and Middle East Studies and the Digital Turn," 230.
29. Alfred H. Conrad and John Robert Meyer, *The Economics of Slavery: And Other Studies in Econometric History* (Chicago: Aldine Pub. Co, 1964).
30. John Komlos, *The Habsburg Monarchy as a Customs Union: Economic Development in Austria-Hungary in the Nineteenth Century* (Princeton, NJ: Princeton University Press, 1983).
31. See James Cheshire and Oliver Uberti, *Where the Animals Go: Tracking Wildlife With Technology in 50 Maps and Graphics* (New York: W. W. Norton & Company, 2017).
32. Robert A. Sobieszek, *Ghost in the Shell: Photography and the Human Soul, 1850–2000: Essays on Camera Portraiture* (Los Angeles: Los Angeles County Museum of Art; Cambridge, MA: MIT Press, 1999), 40–1.
33. Sobieszek, *Ghost in the Shell*.
34. Jordan Ellenberg, "Opinion: How Computers Turned Gerrymandering Into a Science," *The New York Times*, October 6, 2017, sec. Opinion, www.nytimes.com/2017/10/06/opinion/sunday/computers-gerrymandering-wisconsin.html.
35. These discussions abound amongst Digital Humanists and are well represented in the *Debates in the Digital Humanities* volumes. See Matthew K. Gold, ed., *Debates in the Digital Humanities* (Minneapolis: University of Minnesota Press, 2012).
36. Cheshire and Uberti, *Where the Animals Go*, 160.
37. Mara Hvistendahl, "In China, a Three-Digit Score Could Dictate Your Place in Society," *WIRED*, accessed July 2, 2018, www.wired.com/story/age-of-social-credit/.
38. Muhanna, "Islamic and Middle East Studies and the Digital Turn," 171.

6 Digital Space

The algorithm is a magical mathematical device, but it must be fed, for otherwise it has no raison d'être; without an everlasting string of inputs, it cannot influence the world with its outputs. These inputs and outputs have commonly and collectively come to be known as Big Data. Big Data is a rather vague expression because it merely quantifies a phenomenon, but it captures a certain spirit. Olympic in size, Big Data inspires thoughts of grandeur about something larger than life. In the days of old, the *New York Times* quipped that if it did not appear in the *New York Times* index, then maybe it did not happen.[1] As Roy Rosenzweig, the doyen of digital historians, noted, the same can be said of the world of Big Data—if it cannot be found in a database, maybe it never happened. He also recognized the temptation to be lured into the belief that digital technologies could potentially offer humanists an "essentially complete historical record."[2]

Although these massive databases reflect a contemporary moment because of their association with algorithms, large data sets have a long ancestry. In the first half of the nineteenth century, Charles Darwin had access to zoological databases to assist in determining the global distribution of species.[3] In the late nineteenth century, Francis Galton employed databases in his work on hereditary genius to separate men of intelligence from mere idiots.[4] Half a century later, more ambitious projects sought to make active databases available to teams of researchers. Rebecca Lemov has referred to a database of dreams to describe how American social scientists pooled data on people's dreams by placing them on microcards. The accessible database could then be manipulated by all future users (rather than having single dreams on scattered storage devices).[5]

The placement of dreams on a microcard evokes the paradox of space in a world of Big Data. Intuitively, a dream occupies no space at all. It simply emerges in our bodies when we are asleep. The process of cataloging the dreams on microcards gives them a spatial dimension foreign to their origins. Since the dreams could be preserved with smaller technologies, they could be distributed with greater frequency to interested researchers. This act of storing something that originally occupied no space onto a card that takes space was designed to save space. In this rather twisted example, space is synonymous with size and the ability of databases to contain massive amounts of information in the smallest of spaces. The focus on these savings is done in a quantitative fashion, having us marvel at condensed pieces of information. This should not, however, be our only understanding of space in the digital world, especially since it will mistakenly cement a functional conceptualization of a database. Big Data permits all sorts of spatial changes that remain hidden behind one-dimensional analyses.

The common concept of distant reading is a spatial metaphor, but it is not about space per se. Space must be examined from a perspective that revolves around the tension between the spaceless storage of objects that we assume occupy space and our understanding of them in space. These issues are slowly revealed when one briefly explores what it means to study objects when you barely have to move to access those objects. This preliminary facilitates a move into the spaces of Big Data and concrete examples of databases that necessarily shift our conception of space. The Digital Panopticon project, a database of prisoners, offers a fundamental spatial contrast to Foucault's panopticon, and the digitization of museum objects explains how an object can be fragmented and then viewed in a way which no one ever intended. The Internet Archive's Wayback Machine answers questions about objects that never existed in real space because they came into being in an Internet environment. This examination evolves into a question about digitally born objects and what it really means to give birth in a digital milieu—what happens if a baby has no dimensions?

Space also impacts an understanding of facticity. In this spatial process, the nature of facticity and knowledge changes. What is the status of a fact whose dimensions keep changing? How should we characterize knowledge when it occupies so much space and yet hardly any at all? Does the volume of information influence our conceptual understanding of how that information fits in the larger world? Postmodernism urged a material component upon its adherents as an alternative to a disembodied metaphysics, so the concept of Big Data, a fragmented and disembodied form of knowledge, is troublesome. Big Data tends towards the elimination of the third dimension and, much like Georges Braque's cubism, only toys with a third dimension without fully replicating it. This quality is difficult to characterize, but this chapter attempts to find a way to understand the alternate materiality of facts sitting in a digital environment by looking at the process of mapping.

It is easiest to begin on the outside, that is, with the impact of the phenomenon on the material practices of the researcher. Professors often explain the intellectual impact of walking the battlefields of World War I to undergraduates; the bloodied landscape is long overgrown with pretty flowers, but the experience offers a deeper meaning of the war. It makes the broader point that the serious scholar has to make every effort to integrate herself into the physicality of those they studied. A scholar of provincial Russia could not write a book without going to the Russian provinces, and an expert on Honoré de Balzac has to visit the site of his marriage in Berdychev, Ukraine.

The world of data has put these habits at risk as scholars find they can access information in more familiar places. Lara Putnam has already raised an alarm because historians have started to find their way without visits to the archives; archives are not battlefields, but they bring scholars closer to their subject of study. In her opinion, we risk "creating an increasingly partial aggregate portrait of the wide world's past."[6] The process is metaphysical insofar as it eliminates materiality and allows a scholar to sit in a single location and contemplate those parts of experience significant to her research. It is a modified version of Descartes's *cogito ergo sum*. To be sure, experience persists outside the mind, but the spatial parameters of experience have been severely reduced if not eliminated. Philosophers have often been criticized for reducing experience to a drop of metaphysical rationality, but thinkers in other disciplines are inching in that direction. Now the most empirically minded historians are faced with a dilemma whenever they decide to cull sources from the comfort of their own home. A spatial dimension of their research has been lost to a digital convenience. Visits to the archives, where old documents await, have been replaced with visits to websites, which do not require any movement at all. The world is at our fingertips, but it is not held in our hands.

A future generation of scholars, trained with analytics, might look back at the mid-twentieth-century man of letters and see the modern equivalent of the alchemist—a few books here, some scattered notes there, and a pen lying haphazardly on the desk. Intellectual hypotheses can be overturned from generation to generation, but the intimate environment of the scholar should not be so readily dismissed. The pen and the torn pages of a book are not nostalgic tokens but a reminder that holding a pen was holding an implement and a physical activity requiring space. When one ceases to envision the scholar in three dimensions, one won't have anything left to grasp Big Data with.

Scholars of spatiality are less concerned with the sedentary historian because they realize how Geographic Information Systems (GIS) can recreate a diversity of landscapes. Versatile software, however, creates a whole new set of problems because it can give naïve viewers the impression that they are reliving space in its original. A historian could don an Oculus Rift headset and come to truly believe she is watching an Apollo mission take off from the NASA control center. David J. Bodenhamer has expressed concern that the role of technology as mediator will quickly be forgotten because the visual experience provided by the technology is so compelling.

Bodenhamer, however, frames his alternative with equally rigid postmodern language. In an attempt to prevent a sweeping technological victory, he reminds his readers that GIS is "epistemologically branded." To see through this branding, users have to recognize the ability of "critical discourses" to explain the mediating role of technologies. Moreover, the humanities have a responsibility "to draw the technology further out of its positivistic homeland."[7] These are all standard phrases that have been in circulation for decades. The only novelty is that they are now being applied to spatial software. This is an awkward position relative to space because instead of rethinking positivism for the digital age, it continues to treat positivism with disrespect. The attitude is disorienting because the author is an advocate of technology. It is much like having a best friend who one handles with continued suspicion.

Space, then, has to be looked at in another way. The major concern in these external cases is the manner in which digital technologies impact the habits of researchers. In Bodenhamer's case, the focus naturally fell on mapping broadly conceived because maps deal with the representation of space. Mapping will be discussed in more detail towards the end of the chapter, but all the initial examples deal with databases and how they shift our perception of space. Objects are spacelessly stored in a database and then take on space when they become accessible to a user. This transformation is at the heart of the next few pages.

The Digital Panopticon project is an ideal starting point (though a little small to fit the precise definition of Big Data) because it contains a contradiction in its title. Most contemporary thinkers would route their understanding of the panopticon through Foucault. The panopticon, a nineteenth-century surveillance device in prisons, became a means for Foucault to make more general statements about the control of knowledge. The term became so tightly associated with Foucault, scholars referenced the panopticon without ever connecting it to an actual prison (this can be considered an extremely successful metaphor). In contrast, the panopticon in the Digital Panopticon project refers to the actual prisons, because the website "allows you to search millions of records from around fifty data sets, relating to the lives of 90,000 convicts from the Old Bailey."[8] The *Digital* adjective in the project's title neutralizes the postmodern understanding of the panopticon; the two words together have a more functional definition than the standalone noun *panopticon*. For better or for worse, the spatial component of the Foucauldian panopticon is removed. The metaphorical power of Foucault's theoretical device depends upon an intervening space; one has to be able to conceptualize vision transversing space. Whenever a scholar invokes the panopticon theoretically, the reference implies space. The same is true in other Foucauldian contexts; the analysis of *Las Meninas* traverses a variety of spatial zones. The Digital Panopticon circumvents spatial referents, though its creators would recognize the existence of a physical prison. The prison is treated as an object in space rather than as a component in a series of spatial relations.

The user of the Panopticon project can search information on the fate of prisoners or employ the database to investigate the nature of criminal justice. The prison database represents data drawn from its original context, digitized and then made available through algorithmic techniques; intermediary steps act upon the facts before they arrive at the user. One study has combined data from the Digital Panopticon and other databases to distinguish between typical and atypical prisoners. The databases reveal that one prisoner had been "convicted for uttering [offering for sale] base coin in 1880."[9] In the real world in the 1880s, a woman sold counterfeit money. Since she was apprehended, her actions were recorded in a ledger of the British criminal justice system. This act encapsulated only a tiny fraction of all the activities of that woman because the justice system was really interested only in actions that transcended the law. The registration of the crime sits on the ledger, essentially forever. In her own lifetime, it defined her position in society and standing relative to the law. More than a century later, the entry finds its way into a database where it is stored, no longer as the fate of an individual but as a series of discrete chunks of information. The chunks can be reassembled to reconstitute the original criminal, but more frequently, the chunks are used as pieces in building projects that have little concern with the woman in any holistic sense; the woman becomes disembodied and loses the space she once occupied.

The process is intensified because of the search means available. The Panopticon project encourages searches according to partial metrics. Personalities can be searched based upon height, hair color, or distinguishing marks. The digital database is just presenting the original prison sources in a more accessible format, but the ease of delivery discourages a look beyond the statistics. The database can also graph results, so the prisoners quickly become averages rather than individuals, and all sense of their original being is lost. To be sure, the database offers useful information, but it fragments and dissects nineteenth-century prisoners. All that information has been compartmentalized, so the individuals do not exist in the database until they are specifically called upon. Then they reemerge, but in the format desired by the user. Thus the database has repositioned the initial sources in space.

The Panopticon project facilitates the entryway into a discussion on space because the prison began as a spatial architectural project. Although the next few examples are not as self-evidently spatial as the panopticon, they demonstrate how a multidimensional object undergoes a spatial transformation when it enters a database. The object—a museum piece—is converted into another shape and occupies another space that has no physical or metaphorical connection with the original. The transformation of space in these instances gives another way to understand the link between digital space and the facticity of objects.

A museum can make its collection available online. It then has to design a database with specific categories, categories that were not tied to the original objects. Once the software has been designed, a museum employee can enter the details into the database according to the predetermined categories. The curator will have an easy time inputting the date of creation, the artist's name, the size of the object, the location where it was made, and other rather uncontroversial essentials. More subjective decisions will inevitably arise when the provenance of an artwork has to be entered or an aesthetic description of the object is required. The database will absorb these selections and transform them into digital segments or fragments that will evolve to be as important as the original 'whole' object. The database will digitize these objects into a spatial form foreign to their original existence. Although the museum would ensure a user had access to an image of the object (and an effective 3-D representation), the professional process digitally fragments the original object into a series of discrete parts, much like a database of prisoners eliminates huge swaths of their original personalities and places the emphasis somewhere else (i.e. by defining a human by a discerning mark such as a scar). These fragments don't occupy space even when a user might look at the actual dimensions of the object supplied by the museum. The provided measurements are only an approximation for most users because they don't have mastery of the measuring system.

Since the majority of those who experience the object will do so through the database, the fragmentation becomes experientially more determinant than the original object itself. The user will interact with a sampled version of the object, and those sampled fragments become the bedrock as entities unto themselves; what was once a three-dimensional object has been de-spatialized and stored in fragments in the database. In particular, each subsequent user will experience a different version of the object; the database will recreate the object specific to the environment in which it is called upon. Each search of the object in a database presents the object anew because the search engine will return unique characteristics; no two users will ever receive the same object twice.

The natural temptation is to draw a straight line between these shifting forms and postmodern relativism because postmodernism is so closely associated with pluralism. The pluralism in the previous cases has no connection with postmodern explanatory devices. For example, the fragmentation inside the database, where space is stored, has no relationship with discourse or language. The problem is more closely related to the concept of a physical device that stores information that can be released at a moment's notice. When the information is released and manifests itself on a device, discourse and language play absolutely no role; language does not intervene between the storage device and the representation on the screen. Similarly, the shifting spatial dimension is not epistemological, or if it is epistemological, then not in a way conceived by postmodernists. For example, postmodern relativism drew on the limitations of eyewitnessing; the unique perspective of each eyewitness to a series of events implies there is no such thing as one singular, correct description of events. With the objects, however, no one would ever say one is looking at the same object. Viewers see a variety of different objects, each of which they take to be the real one.

Sometimes the transformation of an object has no meaningful significance. Humanists who work with intellectual texts can avoid this tangle altogether because they are more concerned by the accuracy of the text than they are by the manner in which it is displayed; the format is a peripheral matter. The materiality of the text, the paper upon which it might have been printed on, is lost, but not all readers are concerned with this. They do not have to worry about the spatial transformation and can be satisfied with the ability to read a copy otherwise unavailable. In this case, the disappearance of a text into the storage of a database has no relationship to postmodernism; nor does its reemergence in a modified spatial form on a screen.

The Wayback Machine, a component of the Internet Archive in San Francisco, also recreates space when it retrieves websites from storage. The Wayback Machine crawls the Internet with sophisticated software to preserve as much digital knowledge as possible.[10] It reproduces entire websites rather than just crawling the web for data, thus operating much more like a storage facility in a museum which holds physical objects than the museum online database that describes the objects in its collection. In this respect, the Wayback Machine presents its viewers with a static one-to-one copy or visual map of the original, absent the dynamic qualities of the object. The Wayback Machine allows visitors to recreate a website history of popular sites, for it can produce a glimpse of a CNN webpage from 1999 or a *New York Times* page from 2001. It has millions upon millions of snapshots accessible to anyone with an Internet connection. Since the Wayback Machine takes snapshots, it has the same restrictions as that of a photograph when recording an instant in the real world (hence a traditional anti-ocularist might denounce the Wayback Machine as just another doomed example of photographic realism).

The Wayback Machine is a powerful crawler, but it cannot capture complete and dynamic replicas of older websites, so the user has to understand that they have only a fragment. When a user looks at a BBC website from 1997, she cannot interact dynamically with all layers of that website. Nor does one have access to the exact webpage a user saw because these webpages change dynamically depending upon the digital coordinates of each individual user. The Wayback Machine cannot track the dynamic moment of the website or identify when and where the website was accessed, but it can map the original digital content and situate it with coordinates fully comprehensible within the digital landscape.

Despite these limitations, the Wayback Machine is spatially significant because it is completely digital; it begins and ends with digitally stored information. Essentially, all the work of the Wayback Machine is done below the surface and exists on servers. When the information is collected, it is done silently and subtly; it reveals itself only when called upon. The websites it collects spend the overwhelming portion of their time in fragmented digital form, and only rarely does a human intersect with that information as an original website. This process of reconstitution has no parallel in the pre-digital world.

When a user forces the Wayback Machine into action, it recreates a two-dimensional website in a visual format; it has no relation to the objects in the website it displays. It searches only for digitally born content, so even if an object existed in the real world, the Wayback Machine will return the object only in its digital form (theoretically, it can reproduce a website that never saw the light of day). It neither validates the content of the website nor confirms whether the BBC website of 1997 reflected anything that happened in the real world; it just returns a copy of the original two-dimensional website. If the question of holistic knowledge should arise, it does so only in conjunction with the website itself and not with objects in the website that might have had a multidimensional existence somewhere else.

The Wayback Machine is part of an archive, so the way in which it reproduces documents should be of most interest to historians. The Wayback Machine raises questions about the facts of the matter because it stores so much information in a spaceless and disaggregated form foreign to the common historical understanding of facts. If you are accessing facts, what type of facts are you accessing? Since you are accessing something that does not seem to exist, on what basis should the historian question the facts of the matter? How should the historian understand the Wayback Machine as an intermediary? Is it a neutral translator, or does it put its own spin into the recreated website?

Intuitively, most humanists will accept the recreated websites as exact digital replicas; they won't cast philosophical doubt on the efforts of the Wayback Machine. They will also show little interest in the computational tools used to produce the two-dimensional visual. One should be aware that the archived websites have an awkward relationship to the real world because the websites are uneven reflections of that world. The humanist will lean towards accommodating these novelties and downplay the spacelessness of the Wayback Machine. This is a practical step, but it also limits the ability of the humanist to cast those facts culled from the Wayback Machine in a familiar theoretical framework. It is extremely problematic to draw an object from the Wayback Machine, accept its existence as a three-dimensional object, and then cast the factual status of the object in relativist terms; the information undergoes so many transformations. The historian cannot extricate a single fact from an ancient website and highlight its relativism without recognizing the process through which that fact was provided to him.

The Wayback Machine also implicates materiality in two significant ways. Because the stored information is spaceless, it has no material component. Material historians have cast a suspicious eye on this because so much research has linked meaning with the material with which objects were crafted: the feel of velum of the Magna Carta impacts our interpretation of the Magna Carta. The Wayback Machine never intersects with materials because it has no space for those materials. At best, it acts as an intermediary for objects which had a material existence somewhere else. Intermediary forms are slowly becoming surrogates for the real thing; they are making the transition from intermediary to reality itself. Since the Wayback Machine bypasses materiality, it also transforms the aging process; an object that occupies no space cannot be said to age. A website might have a retro look to contemporary eyes, but that is a stylistic rather than physical aging. The digital signal that produces the website can be endlessly reenergized to produce the same result. Museums take pride in their efforts to preserve objects to resist the withering impact of time, but the Wayback Machine has no such concern. The distinction is again seen between the server, which is physical and can decay, and the information on the server, which need never decay.[11]

The association of the Wayback Machine with spacelessness should not lead to the false conclusion that it occupies no space at all. The fascination with digital databases often obscures the physical infrastructures that secure these projects; the Internet Archive has to find space for its servers in San Francisco. In Chandler, Arizona, the noise of servers from the CyrusOne data center drives residents nuts.[12] One might well imagine archaeologists centuries down the road digging through layers of earth only to come upon a buried and forgotten server farm. Recovering the data from the antiquated servers would have its parallel with archaeologists who tried to piece together ancient artifacts or translate Egyptian graffiti without the Rosetta stone, though the archaeologists would be working with spaceless objects.

The Wayback Machine deals exclusively with digitally born materials. The term 'digitally born' is often casually employed to distinguish between traditional sources of information and information generated within the digital world. Yet digitally born is better understood when coupled with birthing and a birthing moment. A birth is a mammalian event, and thus digitally born represents a compromise between the automated premises of Big Data and the humanistic needs of its users. A birth is also a caesura in time, as it cuts between the past and the present by bringing something new into the world; the world has gained another object. Digital births are tricky to describe because the object is not readily identifiable (nor are the parents—the press of a button, the transmission of a word, or the output of an algorithm). At the moment of its birth, it has no dimensionality whatsoever and only enters space once someone or something stumbles across it. It has a latent potential that can be triggered at any time.

The closest analog and historical parallel comes from Erik Hobsbawm and his ideas of invented traditions. When Hobsbawm wrote of invented traditions, he was thinking of a similar process—at a specific moment in time, a tradition is brought into the world, and this marks a real and objective birth of the tradition. Similarly, digital facts have a birthing moment, so in the spirit of Hobsbawm they have an objective existence that cannot be questioned. The birth of each digital fact cannot be easily identified, but its 'invention' is structurally no different. It just does not necessarily occupy any space at that moment.

The Wayback Machine as a digitally born tool is easier to understand because the user can readily visualize how it replicates a past website; it still has a deeply empirical quality to it. In a naïve sense, one can just think of it as a one-to-one mirror of an image from the past. Other cases of Big Data are more complicated because the mirroring function is absent. Often Big Data reproduces materials in a form completely different from its original existence. The information in a database may have lost contact with its original dimensions, or it may have been extrapolated from activities that never occurred in space. For instance, a database can collect information on voting, driving patterns, and shopping habits. All these real-world activities enter the world of Big Data, where they are decomposed into fragments. The votes are fragmented into yeses, nos, or the names of individual politicians. The experiential component of voting, the whole ritual surrounding the activity, gets lost. A car-driving database that carefully gathers information on every single movement of its drivers is not operating in space. The cars and the passengers move in space, but the data collected in the database and frequently referenced is not spatial. When data is stored, the data and the space it will be asked to portray don't correspond with each other in any way. Similarly, shopping gets reduced to the shopping list because Big Data eliminates the need to explore the experience outside the items in the list. In fact, Big Data has a strong functional affinity to the shopping list because of its instinctual desire to itemize. The itemization is a fragmentation that does not respect the original spatial identity of whatever was itemized.

In contrast to the Wayback Machine, which actively reconstitutes something, the previous instances of Big Data reproduce only a fragment of the original activity. If Big Data did not have such a gravitational pull on users and exert such an influence on experience, this could be ignored as trivial. Yet its outputs have become irresistible, and the spaceless decisions it makes are returned back into experience. This generates complex philosophical problems because the underlying digital structure based upon rigid mathematical systems plays such an instrumental role. For example, anything that enters the database will be reduced to fragments, but these fragments have an enduring relationship with the original item that entered the database.

In this regard, the digital layer beneath is instrumental. We tend to make judgments from the output and then assume a straight line back to the source. In between, however, an act of translation occurs as the fact or item travels from one layer to the next. This process of translation is not one of language. The humanist can ignore the rules of translation, but she must be aware that the translation converts from a world of positivism into a more imperfect world of experience. The translation binds both sides to something concrete. Although the spaceless storage would seem to allow for endless pluralism, a tie always exists between the Big Data hidden in the underworld and any single expression of it. Translation impacts but does not wreak havoc with it.

These multiple instances of decomposition and recomposition ensure that data waits spacelessly until called upon. When commenting about the study of history, E.H. Carr wrote that facts do not speak unless called upon by the historian; the historian must activate them.[13] Carr made this remark in the early 1960s when he recognized his contemporaries were pushing back against positivism and flirting with relativism. As a compromise, Carr did not question the objective status of the fact, but he allowed the subjective priorities of the historian to play an instrumental role in determining how that objective fact will be received. Although few historians may choose to admit this today, their views probably align with Carr—through a thicket of discursive slogans, one can normally detect strong traits from Carr.

Carr offered the example of Caesar crossing the Rubicon and asked why, of all the people who crossed the Roman river, his crossing should be the most well known. Beyond the historian making the choice, there is no reason. Carr had in mind historians who read Latin texts and visited the river, and not historians who worked with large databases. In the digital world, his example changes dramatically because the immense flow across the river makes it increasingly difficult to individuate anything. The volume of information, here equivalent to more people crossing the river, prevents the historian from making any neat individual choice. The more information that flows across the river, the more difficult it becomes for the historian to play a role in making these facts speak. An irony emerges in the process because the database fragments its own internal version of individualization, but hinders the historian from doing the same.

Carr's example is imperfect because the historian selects Caesar not just for what he did crossing the river but for what he did in Roman history. He was a pivotal figure in a much larger story. In the world of data, it will still be possible to individuate the narratives of these heroes and villains who had a major impact on society. Their stories will not disappear in a sea of data and will be recovered with relative ease. Nevertheless, the volume of data will make the process more difficult for all but the most recognizable, especially since Big Data represents such a seductive force. Every knowledge-seeking community finds it increasingly irresistible. Though we might never lose sight of Caesar, everyone else crossing the river becomes a blur.

Clearly, nothing prevents a continued reliance on traditional sources, which occupy a familiar concept of space. Humanists can rely on narratives in which people walk in and out of rooms and leaf through atlases that vividly depict shifting borders on rugged earthy landscapes. It is, in fact, easier than ever for the humanist to spend a week along the shores of the Rubicon and contemplate the significance of the Roman river before the Industrial Revolution led to the construction of railway bridges from shore to shore. The physicality of the river will always be there to explore, though the temptation of Big Data makes it seem farther and farther away.

As such, humanists need a concept to keep Big Data at bay, to recognize that Big Data should not be allowed to exist on its own. It must be paired with Little Data, the traditional analog scraps that have always been at the heart of humanist endeavor. Little Data does not have to be defined with quantitative metrics. It is enough to suggest that it occupies a different type of space from that of Big Data. It has a materiality that can be conceptualized in any number of dimensions. It has length, width, and depth that are malleable qualities and can be manipulated as such. Little Data, much like the bricks from the Bastille Prison in revolutionary Paris, can be continually moved to new environments where it takes on additional meaning. It has a flesh-and-blood quality absent in Big Data. Furthermore, Little Data is neither less nor more objective than any other knowledge. It satisfies all of Carr's components for facticity.

Little Data should not be confused with local knowledge, a standard explanatory device in the postmodern lexicon. Local knowledge gained currency because it suggested a geographic dimension designed to undermine universal knowledge; each culture had isolated knowledge. Little Data, however, has no geographic dimension whatsoever. It occupies space in a way that Big Data does not, but it is not Little Data because of where it happens so much as how it happens. It reflects knowledge produced at the ground level anywhere and anytime. It lacks the cultural specificity of local knowledge though it is no less rooted in a unique milieu. As far as Little Data is concerned, the smells, sounds, and social dynamics of a small Swiss bakery are no different from the activities of a small restaurateur in Heihe in northern China. They both produce knowledge at the level of Little Data, and their position relative to Big Data is the same (similarly, Big Data produced in each of those countries is Big Data by virtue of qualities other than its location). Little and Big

Data can emerge in the exact same location, so neither one is tied to local knowledge.

Distant reading occupies a rather intriguing position in this regard. Since it scans thousands of texts for word patterns, the established reputation of authors is irrelevant, and the algorithmic machinations can revive or rediscover authors who have been marginalized for centuries. Ironically, it has the ability to place the literary center of gravity onto the periphery. It identifies thousands upon thousands of pieces of Little Data while it simultaneously parses those literary oeuvres into digestible pieces to feed Big Data. Distant reading shows both sides of the coin: a revival of the ignored and the speed with which the marginalized can be absorbed and forgotten in the crowded milieu of Big Data.

Relying on traditional sources has the air of the obvious, but Big Data has already begun to impact our attitude towards the haphazard information generated without the aid of the algorithm. The vast world of Big Data threatens to reduce Little Data to anecdotal status—evidence that cannot be firmly anchored in a large database will not be taken seriously. In Russian, an *anekdot* is a joke appropriate for a dinner party, and in English, though not a source of laughter, anecdotes have a lightness to them. Little Data risks being treated as a light-hearted sidekick, much like oral histories were in the past. Scholars once dismissed the oral stories of laborers because they too were considered anecdotal; researchers preferred to spend their time with government decrees and political debates. Oral historians had to painstakingly overcome this intellectual prejudice, and one will continually have to fight to preserve the position of Little Data.

A practical step towards a solution for the humanist is to think of herself as a craftswoman rather than as an intellectual bound to mere ideas or as a programmer bound to recent technologies. Heidegger characterized peasants and lumberjacks as craftspeople because he spent his energies redefining *techne* to pull technology away from the laboratory. Techne was presented as a craft and a skill applied to material things, thus accommodating Heidegger's later obsession with *Dinge*.[14] When Heidegger painstakingly took apart words only to bring them back together again, he envisioned himself tilling the soil, turning it over again and again. It became a way to philosophize the inherent contribution of small things. The peasant and the forest warden were in much better positions to collect Little Data because of how they roamed the physical earth. The concept of the craftsperson may appear modest, but it belongs together when thinking about this back and forth between different worlds.

The spatial intersection of Big Data and Little Data, albeit in a modified form, has long since intrigued geographers who work with Geographic Information Systems (GIS). In a piece on the production of knowledge, Eric Sheppard distinguishes between institutional and local data to highlight the analytic impact of ignoring hand-picked data. Black and white farmers in post-Apartheid South Africa had different visions of the landscape when asked to sketch a map of their respective terrains.[15] Institutional databases were (or are) unable to capture these nuances. In contrast with Little Data, however, the farmers are presented as an emblematic example of local knowledge. According to this interpretation, the meaning of their spatial conceptualization depends upon the precise location of these farmers in the world. Little Data does not depend upon geographic coordinates to assert its significance; it has a distinct dimension but not a secured location.

The emphasis on the local production of knowledge arises because of the intellectual framework of Sheppard's thoughts. Specifically, he employs a postmodern 'frame of reference' with signposts familiar to geographers. He writes, "GIS software represents space as a Cartesian co-ordinate system, following Newton in representing space as an independent grid within which social processes are located rather than Einstein or Leibnitz's arguments that space is relational."[16] Here, however, Newton's ideas are presented in real, practical, and empirical terms, whereas Einstein's are offered metaphorically; that is, the two scientists are invoked in different modes. Einstein's spatial theory has absolutely nothing to do with wealth, gender, or race, but a focus on the word 'relational' or the word 'relative' can inspire the geographer to think of economic, gendered, or racial space. Einstein's ideas helped geographers conclude that an "American Indian conception of space [is] inconsistent with those used in GIS," though Einstein's theory would argue otherwise. An American Indian and a sixteenth-century farmer who both occupied the same slice of spacetime would experience space in the exact same way; if their spouses shared a common slice of spacetime but different from their mates, the two women would have the same spatial experience, though it would differ from that of their husbands. When one looks beyond a metaphorical Einstein, it does not matter who you are, you will still experience space according to certain relational laws of the universe. (The exact same can be said for time, to be discussed in the next chapter.) One cannot rely too strongly on these standard tropes to explain a tricky contemporary phenomenon. These comments do not deny that an early modern French farmer had a peculiar attitude to space, just that the attitude had nothing to do with Einsteinian concepts. We can study the farmer's knowledge of Little Data without linking that Little Data with Einsteinian relativism (or local knowledge).

The map example foreshadows a conflict between the two forms of data. Spatially, Big Data and Little Data definitely collide because the borderline between the two is ill-defined. No ready parable exists to explain how space shifts between the two, but better and worse ways do present themselves. Big Data can display itself in numerous ways, many of which are not spatial. For example, the artwork of Jer Thorp discussed in Chapter 8 on data visuals has no spatial component. No spatial relationship exists between the imagery stored in the database and the manner in which the artist invites the viewer to perceive it.

Maps fulfill an explanatory need because maps embody space, and the study of maps has attracted humanists as much as geographers. In his work on the landscape of history, John Gaddis employed a map of England as a heuristic device to communicate his attitude to relativism.[17] Other historians have presented maps as the paradigm case of social construction.[18] And though not related to relativism, the ability to lie with maps has also been a source of fascination.[19] Whereas Sheppard the geographer presented the institutional and local as two separate spheres, the humanist has to follow the trail from Big Data to Little Data and back again; they interact with each other and cannot be separated. In the digital age, mapping is often an interactive process and the cartographer records the human trail as it is being made, thus the parameters have changed yet again. The transition between the two data forms must be presented according to the requirements of the humanist.

The case of the Native American can drastically highlight the spatial problems of the digital age. Sheppard's example, though designed to overcome universalizing tendencies, is in fact steeped in the stereotypical image of a Native American roaming the virgin plains of America. Today, most American Indians live in urban centers, including places such as Los Angeles in the United States and Winnipeg in Canada (in Russia, large native populations live in cities such as Yakutsk).[20] With respect to maps, they navigate cities following the same traffic patterns. More important to the current argument, they have iPhones like everyone else and have no problem making their way through urban streets (and highways, many of which follow routes they set centuries ago). They have the same spatial habits, though they might not take the same roads and could visit different destinations. They input their own trail back into the system when a system gathers data on the movement of their automobiles; their movement contributes no differently to the system. The digital mapping system reinforces their spatial conception within the urban environment. It is quite possible that their spatial conception differs in other regards, but here there is a correspondence that both weakens Sheppard's claim and suggests the problems that emerge when separating the local from the institutional. The routes carved with real movement (Little Data) feed a larger database (Big Data) only to further influence the real movement again. Separate spheres don't really exist.

The interactive component ensures the growth of a vast database, but it does not determine how the map will be represented. The representation of the map is significant because that is traditionally where scholars have identified the imposition of institutional attributes on local knowledge, thus eliminating the "relational mapping" of local communities. In the digital age, where a representation does not have to be fixed, the data can be presented in an infinite number of ways so that it is tailored to whatever the needs are. The flexibility is not infinite because whichever manifestation is selected, it is tied to the data below. Let each representation of the data be a social construction; the data below is not.

When John Gaddis invoked a map of England to make a point about the limits of relativism, he did so by referring to measurement. Depending on the scale used to measure the coast, larger or smaller, one would always emerge with a unique length because the length would depend upon the measurement fragments employed. Since Gaddis's example is frequently cited, its position relative to a digitally reconstructed spatial representation warrants elucidation. Gaddis is envisioning the actual coast being recorded by someone who physically traces it. The trace is recorded and then measured, but, as he points out, the coastline is accurately traced regardless of the measurement. In sum, the various measurement scales do not hinder our understanding of the landscape despite the multiple measurement possibilities.

In the digital milieu, the measurement is not an issue because of the sheer variety of display options. Gaddis showed three details of a map of England, each section zooming in a little closer to the coast. In an interactive screen, the viewer could just as easily stick with one piece of detail and change its size on the screen, thus shifting the measurement instantaneously. With all these digital maneuverings, the substrate below would remain the same. Gaddis's maps have a fixed relationship to the coast much like the digital map examples have a fixed relationship to the data.

In contrast, Gary Lock, an archaeologist steeped in GIS, notes that "maps are not objective representations but rather the product of a specific culturally positioned point of view and set of power relations [that] is now well established."[21] With all the spatial possibilities outlined in this chapter, it is difficult to distinguish the type of power to which he is referring: is it raw power, or is it capillary power? Google Maps, for example, exerts massive amounts of raw power on drivers when they allow it to find their way home (sometimes through sound, and not through the driver identifying anything visually). This is not an epistemological power because the power is exerted from a representational level we consider objective. It follows the identifiable and easily marked roads. Therefore, it represents a transparent force, the majority of whose motions trace identifiable landscapes. These bold Google decisions push you through a landscape, but the driver can still choose how to perceive the space they move through. The map can certainly provide prejudiced and unacceptable choices, such as avoiding specific neighborhoods because of their ethnic composition.

So much of the power is raw, the capillary power seems almost insignificant. This assertion seems to be confirmed by the observation that GIS scholars rarely provide messy local maps to identify those subtle power relations. In the volume in which Lock's comments appear, the claim that local spatial concepts get marginalized appears frequently; but all the maps have a scientific air, as if the GIS scholars could not convince themselves that the local map was worth reproducing (most of the GIS maps are so obviously schematic no one would ever mistake them for a realistic portrayal of anything, though they make interpretive sense). The closest map to Lock's essay provides a "Spatialized user interface for exploring a news wire archive."[22] Moreover, most humanists are learning a techne closely associated with an ability to read these abstract scientific maps. This simply suggests that the raw power of the data representation is much more significant than the capillary power associated with the notion of a set of power relations. The insistence on making these claims stems from an intense focus on the local/global paradigm rather than a deeper exploration of space as it transitions from Big to Little Data; the means of representation follow the latter, not the former.

The map examples facilitate explanation because they are directly spatial and involve the spatial humanities; it therefore makes it easier to envision the process. They show a handful of interpretive weaknesses as well as the light drift of the humanities into the world of science. The digital mapping, however, is not entirely consistent with the panopticon, the Wayback Machine, or the other examples because those digital databases were not committed to the representation of space. They were not about cartography insofar as they did not attempt to assist in the navigation of earthly space. More fundamentally, they make the user reshape the perception of an object (since the user is not moving through space, as the maps imply). The presentation in the earlier examples impacts a spatial understanding of the object when it flashes before the mind and when one shares the object spatially with someone else. In addition, the person with whom the object is being shared may have experienced the same object in a completely different spatial manner (most likely visually, but also as an aggregate of fragments). These 'spatial relations' surface from the digital substrate and take on many possible forms.

The whole story is one of pluralism, but not of postmodern pluralism. At the risk of repetition, it serves to reiterate the postmodern tropes to which this pluralism is not attached: the metaphorical Einstein, narrative or language, and cultural differences. Individuating the specific components of postmodernism moves the discussion away from the sweeping generalizations that so often appear the moment, say, Einsteinian relativism is invoked. If the scholar still insists on invoking relativism, more digging is required. Without any ready alternatives, one can still promote a radical spatial individualism anchored no less in the digital world.

Digital space is undeniably elusive and might not be space at all, but it has identifiable characteristics. The two panopticons revealed the transitions underway in that sea of data—the first metaphorical, the other real; the first deeply spatial, the other spaceless; the first postmodern, the other suitable for the digital age. The Digital Panopticon project divulged this transformation in its unadulterated simplicity. The more common practice is to interact with space in the manner of the Digital Panopticon; as long as space is experienced through this form of intermediary, our understanding of space has to adjust (the metaphorical but not the spatial qualities of Foucault's panopticon can still find applications). Similarly, the museum object drifts from tradition because the focus shifted from the manner in which it floats in our minds when we are not with it to an understanding that the floating image is determined through our interaction with a museum database; since we might never have contact with the real object, the database determines the interaction. The Wayback Machine does not involve traversing space in any significant way but it also claims its own position. Never having occupied real space, every drop of space drawn from its servers is digital space, the parameters of which are determined by the ability of the digital world to shift and move at will. One could try to imagine mapping the locations where users accessed the Wayback Machine, or even trying to map the space occupied by the webpages produced by the Wayback Machine. This last exercise has the potential to become convoluted almost instantaneously. If one pursued this option, one would need a contemporary solution adequate to the task.

The transition to Little Data made the basic observation, already made by others, that the world of three dimensions cannot be ignored. But Little Data is not just a re-labeling of traditional source materials because it urges a rethinking of the position of traditional materials. Instead of thinking of Little Data as local information, it sought to spatially understand how Little Data interacted with Big Data. The interaction emphasizes entanglement rather than isolation, the preferred position of the GIS scholars. When the interaction is seen through mapping, the unwillingness to deal with the shifting spatial environment crystallizes because the GIS examples hang between the old and the new.

In the GIS examples, the expectation persists that the digital GIS should be treated as a tool to represent 'reality.' The computer mapping is then handled as a modern version of older cartographic techniques and subjected to the same questions. Thus the underlying question becomes: does the digital tool represent the lived world in an adequate manner? In answering this question, one is essentially evaluating a measuring tool (as in: does the thermometer objectively record temperature?). With such questions, postmodernism can easily be called to the rescue. The entire scheme, both question and answer, fits with an older paradigm.

Hopefully, a newer if incomplete archetype emerges from the concerns mentioned here. Mapping should not be the paradigm for exploring space, for, while helpful, it insists on comparisons from an older world. The forward-looking approach focuses more on the digital transformation of space which effectively has nothing to do with cartography. It rests on the assumption that the existence of stored information creates conditions at odds with standard explanatory mechanisms. As such, it urges more daring searches and riskier ways to capture all the dimensions in which we live—Big Data, Little Data, and everything in between. This is the last thought here, but the first at the start of a bumpy road. Finding one's way is not easy when there is no space to find one's way in, especially when it never really settles into a fixed form. Yet the path is slowly taking shape.

Notes

1. Rosenzweig, *Clio Wired*, 217.
2. Rosenzweig, *Clio Wired*, 5.
3. See, for example, Clifford B. Frith, *Charles Darwin's Life With Birds: His Complete Ornithology* (New York, NY: Oxford University Press, 2016), 60–2.
4. Francis Galton, *Hereditary Genius: An Inquiry Into Its Laws and Consequences* (London: Macmillan and Co, 1869).
5. Rebecca M. Lemov, *Database of Dreams: The Lost Quest to Catalog Humanity* (New Haven and London: Yale University Press, 2015).
6. Putnam, "The Transnational and the Text-Searchable: Digitized Sources and the Shadows They Cast," 378.
7. Bodenhamer, "The Spatial Humanities," 31.
8. www.digitalpanopticon.org
9. Lucy Williams and Barry Godfrey, "Bringing the Prisoner Into View: English and Welsh Census Data and the Victorian Prison Population," *Australian Historical Studies* 47, no. 3 (September 2016): 398–413.
10. For archival criticisms of the Internet Archive, see Rebecca Guenther and Leslie Myrick, "Archiving Web Sites for Preservation and Access: MODS, METS, and MINERVA," in *Archives and the Digital Library*, ed. William E. Landis and Robin L. Chandler (Binghamton, NY: Haworth Information Press, 2006), 141–66.
11. Since technologies can change, the information can be lost. The decay is a function of neglect and not of the passage of time. The information can simply disappear rather than decay.
12. Story by Bianca Bosker, "Why Everything Is Getting Louder," *The Atlantic*, November 2019, www.theatlantic.com/magazine/archive/2019/11/the-end-of-silence/598366/.
13. Carr, *What Is History*.
14. Nietzsche had a similar attitude with respect to thought: "dass es zum Denken einer Technik, eines Lehrplans, eines Willens zur Meisterschaft bedarf,—dass Denken gelernt sein will, wie Tanzen gelernt sein will, als eine Art Tanzen." Friedrich Nietzsche, "Götzendämmerung," in *Werke in drei Bänden*, vol. II (München: Hanser Verlag, 1966), Was den Deutschen abgeht, 7.
15. Eric Sheppard, "Knowledge Production Through Critical GIS: Genealogy and Prospects," *Cartographica* 40, no. 4 (2005): 7–8. See also David J. Bodenhamer, John Corrigan, and Trevor M. Harris, eds., *The Spatial Humanities: GIS and the Future of Humanities Scholarship*, Spatial Humanities (Bloomington: Indiana University Press, 2010). This volumes shares a spirit with Sheppard. Interestingly, for all the talk about local space, the imagery and maps in the volume are scientific, and a nineteenth-century positivist would have no problem understanding them.
16. Sheppard, "Knowledge Production Through Critical GIS," 8.

17. John Lewis Gaddis, *The Landscape of History: How Historians Map the Past* (New York: Oxford University Press, 2002).
18. See Johanna Drucker's comments in the introduction.
19. Mark S. Monmonier, *How to Lie With Maps* (Chicago: University of Chicago Press, 1991).
20. See, for example, Nicolas G. Rosenthal, *Reimagining Indian Country: Native American Migration & Identity in Twentieth-Century Los Angeles* (Chapel Hill: University of North Carolina Press, 2012).
21. Gary Lock, "Representations of Space and Place in the Humanities," in *The Spatial Humanities: GIS and the Future of Humanities Scholarship*, ed. David J. Bodenhamer, John Corrigan, and Trevor M. Harris, Spatial Humanities (Bloomington: Indiana University Press, 2010), 91.
22. May Yuan, "Mapping Text," in *The Spatial Humanities: GIS and the Future of Humanities Scholarship*, ed. David J. Bodenhamer, John Corrigan, and Trevor M. Harris, Spatial Humanities (Bloomington: Indiana University Press, 2010), 112.

7   Digital Time

In *The Clock*, the visual artist Christian Marclay searched for tiny fragments of motion pictures that somehow indicate the time, whether on a wrist watch or alarm clock or church tower or whatever. His visual collage on the screen jumps from film fragment to film fragment, but time remains perfectly continuous and marches forward second by second even as the visual scenes wander around from bedroom to office or into a car; the space can change radically though time flows like the proverbial river. Time is a ghost that floats from scene to scene and embodies itself somewhere physically on the screen. To add to the complexity, when a museum exhibits the art piece, the scenes are synchronized with the local time of day—if a church bell rings in one of the movie segments, rest assured that a church bell is ringing somewhere out on the street. This was not the intent of the original film director, who did not care when his audience watched the film or if the time in a scene could be synchronized with another time grid. Marclay has therefore established a unique time universe in the museum theater, but one which can be seamlessly integrated into the outside world. Moreover, making the time in the segment correspond to real time conflates the factual with the fictional. When the last sequence ends, the twenty-four-hour cycle begins afresh and rolls through the same segments again.

The work is a beautiful example of slicing up time into little segments and then rebuilding it to serve other needs in a different environment. Viewers might be distracted by the occasional celebrity, but those whose eyes are pegged to the representations of time are drawn to a carefully woven tapestry. The piece can stand as a metaphor for the digital fragmentation of time, to be discussed in this chapter. What were once fluid elements in an original temporal environment are molded and transformed to fit in their new homes; Marclay's segments, for example, overstate the importance of time in the original feature films. Although not his intention, his creation can warm his viewers to the idea that if time changes its meaning when dissected in analog fragments, no less can be expected of it in a digital universe. The digitization of time is more ordered than an art piece that depends on earlier methods of time measurement represented in Hollywood films, but it also takes snippets from more holistic situations and places them with new partners in a database.

Whether couched in a verb, represented by a number, or depicted by a well-crafted object in Marclay's art, time has always fascinated the muse. Starting towards the end of the nineteenth century, time as a feature of a world independent of human beings became less attractive and more anthropocentric models took its place. As a physicist, Albert Einstein was not so concerned with properties inherent to humans, but he energized the notion that time just might have relative qualities. This premise strongly encouraged philosophers such as Henri Bergson to write about duration as a human phenomenon to be contemplated rather than as a natural phenomenon to be measured. In the spirit of the last century's animosity towards objectivity, further attempts were made to treat time as a cultural trait found in specific communities. The goal was to wrest it from interpretations that saw it as an external agent impacting human experience. Norbert Elias, in *Time: An Essay*, argues that until Galileo gave time the specific task of measuring an experiment, its definition existed relative to the social and political needs of communities (and not individuals). Hence rulers could whimsically change calendars, and African tribes trusted their priests to take care of timing because they satisfied distinct survival needs. Borrowing from Einstein, Elias urged an understanding of time as a "form of relationship."[1]

Elias was not blind to the increased mechanization of time in the period of the Industrial Revolution and knew how society had carved up experience into ever smaller slices of time. Yet his thoughts from the early 1980s did not address the digital age; Elias passed away before the Internet became a widely known phenomenon. The advent of Big Data does not undermine Elias's proposals, but it does suggest the need for a more contemporary assessment; it would not be enough to assert that time in the digital age simply continued the trend Elias described—it would fall short to claim no more than that the community of digital aficionados have a special social need fulfilled by their conception of time.

The digital world, as seen, has a spaceless quality because it is at once everywhere and nowhere. Alongside its spacelessness is its timelessness. Not in the sense of eternity, since all sorts of comments about technological decay have shown how digital technologies are subject to the passage of time, but time-less in the sense that time's intersection with users remains an ignored factor. The digital age, however, has had a fundamental impact on time in complex ways. Nowadays anyone with a cell phone not only shares the same conceptual understanding of the passage of time but is tied to a central system of time distribution as well. In other words, as expected, the Chinese owner of a bookstore in Yining and a soccer player in Buenos Aires both work on the principle of the twenty-four-hour day (a convergence Elias would have predicted). More importantly, however, when they both look at the time on their devices, that time will have been set by the same central authority—when they meet at a cultural exchange, the man from Yining won't be two minutes late because of systemic differences in the measurement of time. This synchronization and segmentation has become absolutely critical to the financial industry, which must "time stamp" orders down to the billionth of a second when they come from around the world.[2] Although time as an external phenomenon may have lost all its supporters, digital time has a creeping universality that fits the parameters of the Kantian categorical imperative, albeit not in a moral way.

Previously, the layered quality of the digital world has been the subject of much discussion. In the algorithm, the parallel lives of the programmer and the speaker of a natural language never really met. The binary form of the data internal to the data was incommensurable with its actual usage and appearance on the surface. With time, however, no layers bifurcate experience, for all levels of the digital experience measure or react to time in the same way. From clock functions in digital circuits to the clock seen on a desktop, time moves according to the same principle. The universality of digital time would seem to make it self-explanatory, an innovation of convenience rather than one of complexity. Yet the experience of digital time can be compared to the reaction of Ukrainian villagers after the Chernobyl nuclear accident, when they listened to scientists talk about the half-life of radioactive isotopes. They were presented with a concept of time for which they were wholly unprepared. Digital time, when looked at more closely, is equally perplexing.

The thoughts of Henri Bergson are an apt starting place because he sought to find a compromise between the sciences and the humanities. He did this in part by emphasizing the concept of duration, an idea that runs afoul of phenomena such as the digital partitioning of time. Bergson, in the tradition of the early twentieth century, wrote about the passage of time in consciousness, a consciousness that Elias would reject because of its egocentrism. Nevertheless, Bergson humanized time because he discarded the notion of a universal time that could be measured with tidy intervals and instead insisted on duration in consciousness. Duration was an indivisible quality that could not be measured in increments: "when we try to cut it, it is as if we suddenly passed a blade through a flame—we divide only the space it occupied."[3] Time still had an external dimension, but consciousness played by its own rules in creating these indivisible durations. Bergson offered the following example: "I draw my finger across a sheet of paper without looking at it" and thus "the motion I perform is, perceived from within, a continuity of consciousness, something of my own flow, in a word, duration."[4] Simultaneity was an outcome of duration. As Bergson wrote: "We therefore call two external flows that occupy the same duration 'simultaneous' because they both depend upon the duration of a like third, our own."[5] This lively illustration suggests that the key to grasping consciousness is to rotate our eyeballs so they look inside our head, an image that few would accept today. Yet he wanted to differentiate the personal experience of time with that of the physicist who kept staring at a clock.

Albert Einstein, the physicist, was a specific target of Bergson's because of his over-scientific view of time. The discord between Bergson and Einstein is more relevant than ever because it evokes a paradox of the digital era. Einstein, who used clocks as the basic timekeeping pieces in examples to promote his theories, has been popular amongst postmodernists for the obvious reason that he had a theory of relativity; unfortunately, the emphasis has always been placed on the relativity and not on the theory. This has led to some confusion because as a theorist, Einstein sought to develop a grand scheme to describe the universe, whether or not humans should inhabit that universe. As A.R. Lacey writes, "Einstein's world is as real and absolute as Newton's, but it is a set of relations, not of things."[6] Digital time is much closer to the Einsteinian than the Bergsonian concept because it establishes real and absolute relations between all the elements in the digital environment; the moment a fact or action enters the digital universe, it gains an address and position relative to all the other digital information in that universe.

The distinction between Bergson and the digital universe is heightened by a closer look at measurement. As Bergson wrote, "the time that endures is not measurable."[7] In duration, the distance between two points in time cannot be measured, and no fixed distances exist between these points, if there are any points at all. Duration is necessarily successive—the future follows the present and the present follows the past—but no standard exists to permit measurement. In contrast, digital time is eminently measurable as a relationship between phenomena. In the general spirit of both Einstein and Elias, digital time can embody different spheres of interest rather than a fixed representation that appears visually on a clock. Despite this, digital time has a universality foreign to Elias but all too familiar to Einstein.

In his continued effort to oppose the segmentation of time, Bergson famously took aim at what he called the cinematographer's version of consciousness, that is, the idea that images flash before the mind in a sequence of segments, just like the film reel composed of frames passes before a lens. Duration could not reconcile itself with such a vision. The target has disappeared because frames no longer exist in the digital film world; the digital reel is much more continuous, as duration would want, than its segmented predecessor. The paradox emerges that digital technologies have undone a heuristic device only to confirm a position on digital time embodied in that heuristic device, the film reel, a device Bergson sought to deny. Under these circumstances, Bergson would have been forced to find another counterpoint for his thesis. This serves not just the banal fact that philosophers choose their cases from their contemporary surroundings, but that time in the digital era has new reference points.

The shift in cinematography may have drawn Bergson closer to contemporary developments, but, in the main, his concept of duration runs up against the basis of digital experience where time segments are fundamental—even in simple cases where Google tells a user how long a search took. When juxtaposing duration with the nature of time encapsulated in Big Data, one quickly sees a return to the temporal values that preceded Bergson. Digital time is parsed by an external force and then imposes itself on human experience. The force is powerful enough to challenge the sense of duration that exists within consciousness. The casual individual's experience of time will veer from the structure of time anchored in Big Data, but will be hard pressed to resist its influence. The manner in which Big Data isolates, parses, and then returns values of time is of particular interest given all the twentieth-century efforts to return a natural fluidity to time.

While the individual consciousness may still experience duration in the manner Bergson hypothesized, the moment an object enters into the world of Big Data, it becomes subject to the rules of time within that world. Primarily, Big Data strips or demotes the original temporal framework and situates it within a grid. The grid is unnatural insofar as it is situated in the technological environment of Big Data, but it is an inescapable aspect of experience at the input and at the output. The user may not recognize the immediate influence of Big Data on her understanding of time or the impact of a symbiotic process, which is difficult to remain independent from.

Unfortunately, these paradoxes or subtleties rarely enter into digital discussions. Katrina Navickas has made use of QGIS, a tool to present geospatial information, to map protest and procession routes in England in the first half of the nineteenth century.[8] Navickas has assembled a number of processions, given the day when they happened, and then superimposed them on the geographical outlay of the city. Interpretively, this gives the researcher an opportunity to understand the spaces these processions visited and then judge the political or social significance of the route. The calendric time is presented unproblematically without any attention to the layers of time (the days) that span decades on a single map. Although the map has a small temporal component, the day when the procession happened, the research aid is primarily spatial; spatial parameters dominate temporal ones. The spatial relations in the map remain fixed and thus time is fixed in those spatial relations despite the events happening at markedly different moments. When you experience the map visually, you have no way of judging the separation of time except for looking at the legend which explains when the event took place.

In a traditional environment, this would go by unnoticed, but now that data has been entered to produce the map, the software generates an additional temporal component. On the one hand, digital technologies should allow a more dynamic representation of time, visually revealing the temporal layers, as the procession moves slowly through the city. Below the surface, the geospatial software has given each route specific time coordinates by creating a time tag for each individual component of the data, integrating it into the network of digital time. It adds further time tags whenever the data is accessed by a user; all these tags belong to the same digital time network. The impact of this continual and dynamic process is even more forceful with digitally born materials.

Another scholar working on the history of Damascus made a hand-assembled database of terms from late nineteenth-century local newspapers to explore shifts in language patterns; the results of the database were superimposed on a map so the viewer could see the geographic distribution of these terms in the city's neighborhoods. As to be expected, the bulk of the analysis was spatial and paid no attention to temporal distributions or what happened to the original times that were embedded in the cultural environment of the newspaper itself.[9] As a result, when glancing at the map, one immediately recognizes the spatial distribution of the words plucked from the newspapers, but otherwise the city is frozen in time; the 'when' of the word usage gets lost in a spatial grid.[10] The more curious viewer might well ask if the words were used before sunset or in the afternoon or want to know when they were published in the newspaper. Alternatively, the map could show the time of day when a reader would be expected to come across the words in the newspaper. All these various times could be presented on a map with layers representing a specific perspective on time. Adding these layers, an intricate process, would show the words existed as much in time as in space.

Contemporary methods illuminate the diverse temporal possibilities, but they still don't show how the process of digitization repositions time. In the Damascus case, a word is first extracted from a sentence that has verbs and other elements that imbue the word with a grammatical duration; if this last element is removed, it skews the original framework of time. The extraction is the most common part of almost all databases and thus is not unique to the single example here. When the words are presented on the map, they are presented within the context of a numerical indexing system, such as years and days, rather than the grammatical time environment the words originally inhabited. Thereafter, each piece of data is given more discrete time tags: the precise and unambiguous time it entered the database and the subsequent times it was accessed. It is therefore subject to an ongoing process of indexing. This occurs in a way the original author of the word or item could never have imagined.

Within the database, the elements of time are unified in a single environment but fragmented into discrete units that do no respect the original temporal identity. They have no spatial relation to each other, but they settle in a grid shaped by equidistant temporal relations metered by a universal digital clock. The digital grid secures a position in time for the data: what were originally unrelated curiosities succumb to the relations established by the grid. Its original fluid time, conducive to duration, becomes fragmented. Whether the grid is determined by a unique property of the external world or by the unique qualities of human consciousness is moot in this case. The grand phenomenon of tagging all these elements in one digital system standardizes the time-relationship of all of them. This concept of time is, in fact, quite close to Einstein's.

The subsequent time tags of the original word, fact, or piece of data may all too easily be dismissed with a shrug because they are just add-ons to the more significant birthing moment. Surely, the real time is when the item came into the world, and everything afterwards is just a manipulation distracting us from the original. This position is unsustainable because it runs against the view of so many commentators who, over the last hundred years, have demonstrated that the first event itself is only a fraction of the sum of experience. As Proust so mischievously suggested, memory is not anchored in an instant of the past but unexpectedly triggered and manipulated by intervening and contemporary circumstances. The concept of a moment forgotten in time has been debunked over and over again. Moments take on new lives, and nowadays the new lives reappear in a digital grid. Concepts designed to emphasize flow and flux leave no other choice than to accept that the entry of data into the databank must reflect significant temporal changes and cannot be brushed off; the digital fragmentation must have an impact as the data put down roots into its unanticipated environment. They, the elements entering the database, become woven into the fabric of a new story and, as expected, cannot be extricated from that cloth. They have, however, been woven together with the perfect loom so all the threads occupy neat spaces on a grid, and these threads continue to exist as threads without ever completely dissolving into the cloth. The more willingly we accept the idea that facts are not born in a single moment but evolve, the greater the impact of digital time tags.

The map examples offer a starting point, but they touch upon only one aspect of digital time. Literary examples are better suited to demonstrate how the time component of an item in a database differs fundamentally from its position in time before it entered the database. The literary selections that follow call attention to a process in which the original temporal surroundings of literary production can easily be overshadowed or forgotten when entering the digital world. If one drew expressions from Roman literature, what would happen to the original hexameter and pentameter when placed in a database? What if one searched for all references to a flâneur in French literature? Could one understand how quickly each of these flâneurs maneuvered through a crowd? (And, would the same individual who performed that search be interested in using GPS technology to map the specific movement of the flâneur by reducing the movement into equidistant steps?) Walter Benjamin, no stranger to the flâneur, once wrote about his extensive walks in Moscow.[11] Could that text be parceled into a database without ruining his temporal intentions? The man who wrote about technical reproduction may have wanted his steps reproduced not as herky-jerky movements on icy Muscovite streets but as indexed bits in a database; this would still represent a change from the original text. These individual examples remind the reader that time and rhythm can be invisibly present in the simplest of expressions, thus stressing the corollary that Big Data necessarily impacts the conceptualization of time as it partitions texts to satisfy its own structural needs.

Virgil's *Aeneid*, a classic stopping point in the Latin curriculum, permits insights into these temporal mutations. Borrowing heavily from the *Odyssey*, it recounts the adventure of a young man who makes his way from Troy to the northern shore of Africa through the Strait of Messina just off the coast of Sicily and northwards to form a settlement which was destined to blossom as the great city of Rome. On the way, he faces challenges presented to him by the Gods. As he traverses the Mediterranean, Juno raises a storm only to have Neptune, unhappy with Juno, tame it, making it possible for Aeneas to travel to the shores of northern Africa. Alongside these godly interventions, violent clashes and romantic moments shape his experiences. Over the course of twelve books, Virgil gave his audiences an opportunity to glory in the foundational story of Rome.

The poem was written in dactylic hexameter, so the prosaic description in the last paragraph robs it of much of its beauty. In dactylic hexameter, each line has six feet, so the parallel to a flâneur is hardly far-fetched. The meter did not have to correspond to the words in the line, and poets purposelessly shifted their rhythmic emphases from those expected in normal speech. The meter could then be used to rhythmically describe the actions of the verb. For example, Lee M. Fratantuono and R. Alden Smith remark that at the beginning of the *Aeneid*, an expression such as *"undique et undique"* has a neutral pattern that embodies the grand expanse of the sea and sky to which they refer.[12] This makes the point that the meter can easily be translated into something of empirical significance; it is not 'just' a rhythmic addition. Any example of meter embodies an aspect of time, so the extraction of *"undique et undique"* into a data list would necessarily modify its time structure and thus its meaning.

An even more appropriate instance of shifted time emerges in the middle of the fifth book, where Virgil writes, *"temporibus geminis canebat sparsa senectus,"* which can be translated as *envious age began to sprinkle my head with gray hair*.[13] The gray hair, *senectus* in this line, comes at the end of the hexameter and thus implies the onset of old age, a process that "crept up on" Entellus, the figure to whom the line refers. Thus *senectus* can sit seemingly immobile in that line, yet it bears with it a dynamic sense of time that is triggered by but not equivalent to the meter in the line.[14] Entellus was not aging according to the tempus of hexameter.

Naturally, the slow onset of time encapsulated in *senectus* is unique to its position in this line. In other Latin writings, *senectus* will be a placeholder for another time scale, especially since *senectus* won't always refer to hair but can more simply refer to old age. Words or sounds with a variety of meanings are a regular linguistic phenomenon, but that is not the concern here. The idea of *senectus* as a placeholder for a specific representation of time is critical. When it becomes clear that the term can absorb a variety of temporal positions, it follows that this variety is at risk when it enters a database as a single term. The database can accept all these words without paying attention to this rhythmic dimension; within the well-ordered database is a chaotic brew of varying times whose true identity is suppressed.

One might argue that the excerpt taken from the Aeneid is a linguistic oddity because hexameter is designed to saturate the line with rhythm, unlike the prose with which we are most familiar. Rather than seeing it as the exception, however, it should be treated as the rule, for the Romans were not the only ones to situate variants of time in the strangest of places. In the Middle Ages, an era of anxiety, writers often referred to natural catastrophes. Catastrophes in the modern world are familiar phenomena with ample explanations, but when the term catastrophe is invoked today, it does not have the same rhythm as its medieval ancestor (here is a non-digital example of eliminating time from an expression). Catastrophe originally had a dramatic meaning linked to the rhythm of a play. Not coincidentally, the Russian word for catastrophe, *stikhinoe bedstvie*, has the exact same phonetic roots in the Russian word for poem. It also embodies a poetic rhythm even if it should appear in the dullest of prose. Every word, utterance, or expression, then, has an element of time associated with it, no matter how subtle the association. The time element may be minimal, a trace, and in certain instances can be ignored (to avoid spiraling into a hopeless skepticism); but a significant transformation takes place upon entering the database where digital time superimposes itself on the textual time.

The same problem can be addressed by putting the feet of the hexameter into the shoes of the flâneur. In the 1920s, Walter Benjamin wrote about flâneurs, the nineteenth-century Frenchmen who walked through the crowds of Paris, following the random traces and clues the city had to offer. The flâneurs spent an inordinate amount of time performing autopsies of the urban setting, particularly in the commercial arcades that held such a fascination for Benjamin. In Benjamin's telling of the story, flâneurs also possessed a time component. The flâneurs walked, strolled, and changed their pace. In the 1840s, it became fashionable to take a walk with a turtle: "The flâneurs liked to have the turtles set the pace for them."[15] Even if they carried pocket watches or heard the occasional chime above the urban din, the feet beat a time of their own. Because each individual flâneur embodied a specific pace, it is not just a word that identifies an urban personality from the nineteenth century; each single reference to the flâneur has its own pace, and this pace risks being eliminated because it does not correspond to an easily repeatable calendric or digital time.

It is hard to imagine how one could digitally capture turtle time once the flâneur entered into a database. The database would necessarily segment the actions of the flâneur, rendering the turtle pace obscure. For example, how would one graph the movement of the flâneur through the city using digital technologies, as Navickas did procession routes, without forever altering the temporal component of the flâneur? This does not necessarily mean that the turtle pace will be absolutely and completely eliminated (a more ambitious individual always has recourse to the original; a software program could allow a user to set the pace) but it will be pushed into the background. One cannot predict how the temporal component will change, only that it will change.

In a well-known article on the work of art in an age of technical reproduction, Benjamin presents another perspective to complement these thoughts on time. In looking at the nature of authenticity, he was particularly obsessed with the 'original' and its "Hier und Jetzt" (here and now) because these established a mendacious authenticity. This situation changed dramatically with technical reproduction because these modern processes served to "untie" (*lösen*) the reproduced from tradition; in other words, the copy is liberated from the original.[16] Benjamin built his definition with the word *lösen*, which can mean untie but is also close to the word 'dissolve,' just like the dissolved chemicals that react with paper to form those photographs of which he was so fond. Then *lösen* is not so much an unforgiving severance but a transformation. The outcome of this process was a world in which the patina of elitism could be dissolved and in which art would be more responsive, more reflective of the mass movements of his day.

But what if we modified the idea ever so slightly and wrote about an 'original time'? Not in the sense of Adam and Eve to satisfy theologians or in the sense of the Big Bang to satisfy scientists, but to mean that objects have an original time within them that can be unwittingly modified later on. It requires little imagination to see that in all the cases mentioned to this point, each item was invested with an original time, a concept mentioned in the context of Proustian memory. This does not mean that the word or experience was born at an identifiable calendric time to be logged on a birth certificate, but that its creation was accompanied with an identifiable intent with respect to its temporality (i.e. rhythm, flow). In the hexameter example, *senectus* is given the time of the hexameter intended by Virgil. When invoked elsewhere, such as in a dictionary (which is also full of time moments), its original time will again be unique. This original time will be dissolved and centralized in the digital milieu; we will lose track of the fact that the same word had different temporal connotations in Virgil and in the dictionary. Somehow all these unique original times have to be reconciled with the mass time sequencing of the database they enter into.

The temporal transformation is significant because it corresponds in essence to the structure of Benjamin's social thoughts. He set his sights upon an original and individual piece of art and its meaning once it moved into the world of the masses, into a world of massive quantities. This transaction has its equivalent as independent pieces of information, such as a line from Virgil, get deposited into a swell of mass data and find themselves, just like the flâneur, in a crowd. When these terms enter into the world of digital reproduction, the original times become part of a mass transaction. The emergence of this large mass is accompanied by a process of temporal centralization.

The digitization of time will promote fragmentation, but it will not completely eliminate what Heidegger called historians' time, the basic understanding that years in the title of books are a convenient shorthand rather than a reference to a universal clock. Heidegger exaggerated the amount of attention historians pay to time—dates, yes, time, no—but the idea of historians' time suggests that more casual references won't be eliminated. Historians who recognize the social role of a clock (such as religious control though chimes) will continue to be interested in the moment when the bell rings rather than in the flow of time. Alain Corbin extended Elias's analysis with his neat mélange of time encapsulated in French church bells of the nineteenth century.[17] The study is fully aware of the manner in which a priestly caste determined the rhythm of village life and has endless references to standard calendric, whether Revolutionary or Gregorian, dates. Corbin is asking historians not to rethink time in their own works, but to analyze how levels of authority impacted the rhythm of the historical actors they study.

Although Corbin's work came before the digital age, a contemporary historian could revisit the extensive archival material and create a database of all the times related to the ringing of the bells; all of Corbin's time markers can be digitally tagged. The database could be searched not for words but for instances of time, and thus one would have established a database that could be approached as a temporal equivalent to distant reading. This database of temporal indices would honeycomb Bergsonian duration and establish another temporal parallel with distant reading insofar as it extracted time from complex social situations. Since Bergson was concerned about duration and not instants, it was a natural step for him to claim that "duration is thick," or *épaisse* as in his French original.[18] Thickness is normally an idea we associate with Clifford Geertz and his concept of thick description, yet it had a forerunner in Bergson.[19] Just as distant reading has a thinness resistant to thick description, the temporal subdivision in the database has a thinness that runs counter to duration.

All the previous examples involve a transfer from the pre-digital to the digital and don't take digitally born sources into consideration. If sources emerge digitally, does it still make sense to write of a transformation? What happens to the concept of an original time if the digital environment is the original timekeeper, for actions in digital time are tagged the moment they occur? The digital equivalent of the flâneur might be the casual cyclist in Beijing who rents a bicycle with the iPhone and then goes cruising through the city. The cyclist could enjoy the same experience meandering slowly through thick crowds, but the route would be timed and inserted in a digital time grid from the moment of the rental. To those looking in from the outside, the pace would be set with a universal clock and would keep track of stops along the way; a visit to a hotel lobby or the liquor store or to the library would be meticulously logged in a database according to both spatial and temporal coordinates. In such situations, the digital time takes over and overwhelms other forms of timekeeping. A grandfather clock chiming three times in a hotel lobby no longer tells time. It just makes noise because it stands outside the relational network of digital time.

The paradox with original time in the digital world is its inversion. Instead of the external entering into the internal, the internal invades the external. The timing of events already begins within the digital world, and this structure predetermines how time will be experienced on the outside. This reverse process was absent in Corbin's study of church bells—bells could be stored in the memory of villagers, but the villagers' experiences could not be stored in the memory of bells. The timekeeper in the digital world is able to record the temporal experience of those participating in the digital time world. Individual actions are metered by the time circulating in one's device; this is an almost inescapable corollary of the ubiquity of these devices. These actions—social, cultural, or otherwise—have no other option than to be registered in digital time. This represents a sea change from the history of time elucidated by Elias. The idea of the original is persistent but produced at the level of mass consumption and marked according to parameters internal to digital time.

Digital time easily baits us into accepting its parameters—so it must be harmonizing with something inside us—yet it cannot be coterminous with inner mechanisms of the brain (most likely because it does not yet have a correspondence with evolutionary aspects of consciousness determined by external experiences). In the past, the structure of a computer became a convenient metaphor of the human mind just like film had been before it. Digital time should not, however, be reduced to a philosophical metaphor because it actively impacts lived experience; there is no gap between digital time and our experience of it. The internal workings of the brain may remain a mystery, but digital time reveals a propensity to incrementalize lived experience.

With digitally born sources, it is critical to think of Big Data in terms of time and not simply subjugate time to space; whenever Big Data is collected, time samples are being collected as well, and the database can be searched solely on an item's position relative to its place in time. One commonly thinks of the GPS for car travel to navigate our position in space. Similarly, a Garmin device monitors the forward progress of a cyclist, but this is not all it does. It also records the cyclist with millions and millions of time tags, effectively synchronized with all the other cyclists linked to the same system (and everyone else linked to the system who is not necessarily a cyclist). One might look upon this as a chronometric surveillance system reified in the expression "We know when you are." One cannot be dismissive of time's role simply because it cannot be seen directly.

These time tags also influence human action. This does not mean that the eager cyclist looks at the Garmin device as a model of increased precision because it can present tenths of seconds. Heidegger, as mentioned much earlier, would interpret this as the onslaught of a technological obsession that insisted on more and more decimal points of accuracy. Moreover, the GPS time tags do not have to correspond directly to the visual display (they can be even more accurate, but the synchronization with a general system is the more significant component). Even when the cyclist looks away to enjoy the countryside, the system keeps recording these time tags. By virtue of the fact that all these digital experiences are accompanied by the device's incessant desire to register time, they also play back into personal experience. They absorb users into the grid, and thus users reinforce the system with their own actions. Oddly enough, this could be considered a temporal form of a Hegelian dialectic.

Similarly, the time on an e-mail is not a mere curiosity for users eagerly awaiting a response from an admirer. The time determines when plane tickets are purchased and when one shows up at the airport. This time sets the alarms that wake us in the morning and situates the user every time he interacts with a wireless network in a museum. One can still enjoy life in the woods or detach oneself from this network; live off the time grid, so to speak. But the pillars of experience are anchored in this grid, and true temporal moments of freedom have to be sought elsewhere. In effect, the system creates an example of Einsteinian simultaneity. The simultaneity is only attached to a specific relational network, but only one relational network exists, hence its impact. The system is so vast and imbricates so many users, it has an expansive presence. The more data entered, the more influential the grid becomes and eliminates other possibilities.

This impact belongs to the long tradition of timekeeping; church bells played a similar function. In contrast to older methods, however, the system requires feedback from users with constant inputs from outside to reinforce the system. In the Russian countryside of the eighteenth century, peasants did not ring their own chimes to reinforce the message from a belfry. Furthermore, the bells were a much more public event. They were audible in their surroundings, and bell raisings were also significant social occasions; the villagers knew where the source of time was located and could conceptualize how the bells made noise. Digital time lacks this public dimension because it is in a sense hidden, not visually, but in its continued efforts to tag, tag, tag.

The question of exactitude also has to be mentioned in this discussion because it appears as if digital time is seeking ever more exact measurements. This has a grain of truth when Wall Street demands smaller time intervals, but the ordering of time is more important than its exactitude. It is not that we perform actions at an exactly synchronous moment, but that the actions that are performed fit within the ordered parameters of digital time. Individuals are being sucked into a system of greater uniformity. As they enter this system, their subsequent actions will be more in accord with digital time.

The uniformity can be seen with the digital fate of expressions such as '24/7.' Trivially, it just refers to a store that is open twenty-four hours a day for seven days a week, and then the cycle begins all over again. Yet digital time does away with both the 24 and the 7. It never stops in the background, it is always ambient, and can be latched onto whenever by anyone; in the world of Wi-Fi, it lingers in the air, invisible, as all these signals have the same digital time frame. The *New York Times* no longer has a distinct morning edition; it just rolls through the day with articles tagged by a digital clock; *Izvestiia* in Moscow and the *Frankurter Allgemeine Zeitung* in Frankfurt follow the same principle on the exact same backdrop. Digital time might mark a change from Monday to Tuesday with a flick of a byte, but this is a mere formality based on convention and the internal mechanism of the timekeeper.

Where does this uniformity fit within the world of the postmodernist or with social histories of time? To be sure, digital time is a social phenomenon par excellence because it is a recent arrival in human experience. It does, however, embrace a uniformity at odds with the social time of Norbert Elias; the ordering and recording of time was not part of his explanatory apparatus. The ubiquity of digital time and its basis in logic alienate it from the precepts of the postmodernist. Digital time is not real time, as the time existing outside of humanity, but it is an idealistic form of time insofar as it has universal appeal amongst human beings (and can push other time frames to the margins). One might even imagine a situation in which all these temporal items are lined up in a dense, chronological packet that extends into infinity. The ability to order this time in neat arrays and to subject its passage to logical analysis cannot be reconciled with postmodern claims. A panopticon of time is not a completely ridiculous idea, since the source of time, unlike the sun or watch, is invisible to users. The advocate of digital time might worry about temporal power and find a postmodern friend on this issue, but her underlying motives would differ philosophically. Digital time can be considered relative in the manner which Einstein but not postmodernists defined the term.

If digital time does not quite fit the parameters of postmodernism, where does it fit in relation to positivism? The empirical nature so dominant amongst positivists is absent in digital time because the time is invisible to users and housed within a network of computers; it does not need to manifest itself empirically to play a role in empirical activities. It therefore becomes much harder to categorize, as it manifests itself only when attached to external actions. Drawing general laws based solely on digital time is nigh impossible from a humanist perspective and best left to the contemporary colleagues of Einstein. The best parallel with positivism is the ordering of time that is done logically, in the most elementary understanding of the word logic. It is not complex mathematical logic but a practically efficient logic that lets it be characterized by arrays and positioned on axes. Otherwise, digital time operates in its own sphere, far from the desires of positivists.

All this talk of order and logic does not imply, however, that the real rhythms of time will be eliminated. Thomas Boswell, the baseball writer, wrote that time begins on Opening Day.[20] As already intimated, birthdays will be celebrated based on a planetary cycle, and lunar markers will continue to interest astrologists. Similarly, calendar changes won't disappear. At the end of the seventeenth century, Peter the Great reformed the Russian calendar and right after the Bolshevik revolution, the communists did so again. Radical thinkers have tried to dismantle the Christian calendar altogether. At the end of the *Antichrist*, Nietzsche gave his law against Christianity "on the first day of year one (on 30 September 1888 of the false calendar [Zeitrechnung])."[21] Beijing museums now mark time from the beginning of the common era (an expression which demonstrates a shifting social attitude but not a rethinking of the internal mechanisms of time).

These moves in time will continue to play their role in shaping societal values, but their preeminence will slowly be overshadowed by a new clockmaker; the clockmaker is not the God envisioned by William Paley in the eighteenth century, but a software program embedded in the hardware of the devices we all use. The advent of a novel concept should not be met with too much surprise. Corbin wrote about church bells and villagers in nineteenth-century France, but church bells were once a novelty in France as well; it took a while to adjust to the peals.

Elias rightly pointed out that time is neither an absolute in the world nor a function of an innate consciousness. Yet his cultural assessment of time, an analysis done when cultural histories were extremely popular, cannot tell the story of digital time because it looks at local instantiations of timekeeping. Digital time has a social universality absent in his examples. It transcends the laboratory and the street, and it even impacts the footnotes of the current document, where readers can see when I consulted a specific text. To be sure, one cannot guarantee that every human lives within the digital grid. Individuals can traverse the interstices of digital time and play with those gaps of freedom. In imitation of an earlier generation of anthropologists, postmodernists can search the darkest forests and remotest mountains to discover an individual whose cell phone is used only for games and not connected to a network. These individuals may still exist, but they shouldn't be used as an excuse to ignore the fundamental challenge that digital time offers the humanist.

The challenge is to find the humanism in digital time. Digital time is incremental and, fractured with regularity, reduces subjectivity by drawing all experience into its web. There are, however, ways to keep the humanism of time fluid and engaging. Perhaps the most effective way is through the visual representation of time, for one of digital time's most haunting features is its invisibility. At some point, however, it must reveal itself to make itself meaningful. In the context of Big Data, this most often occurs when data is presented in graphic form. As we take leave of the temporal and enter the visual, it does no harm to emphasize that the best way to experience digital time is too see it.

Notes

1. Elias, *Time: An Essay*, 44.
2. John Markoff, "Time Split to the Nanosecond Is Precisely What Wall Street Wants," accessed July 2, 2018, www.nytimes.com/2018/06/29/technology/computer-networks-speed-nasdaq.html.
3. Bergson, *Duration and Simultaneity*.
4. Bergson, *Duration and Simultaneity*, 50.
5. Bergson, *Duration and Simultaneity*, 52.
6. Alan Robert Lacey, *Bergson* (London and New York: Routledge, 1989), 63.
7. Bergson, *Duration and Simultaneity*, 49.
8. Katrina Navickas, *Protest and the Politics of Space and Place 1789–1848* (Manchester: Manchester University Press, 2016).
9. Till Grallert, "Mapping Ottoman Damascus Through News Reports: A Practical Approach," in *The Digital Humanities and Islamic & Middle East Studies* (Berlin and Boston: De Gruyter, 2016), 175–98.
10. This problem is addressed in Ian Gregory, "Time in Historical GIS Databases," in *Historical GIS: Technologies, Methodologies, and Scholarship*, ed. Ian Gregory and Paul S. Ell, Cambridge Studies in Historical Geography 39 (Cambridge and New York: Cambridge University Press, 2007), 119–44.
11. Walter Benjamin, *Moskauer Tagebuch*, Erstausgabe (Frankfurt am Main: Suhrkamp, 1980).
12. Virgil, *Aeneid 5: Text, Translation and Commentary*, ed. Lee Fratantuono and R. Alden Smith, Mnemosyne. Supplements ; Monographs on Greek and Latin Language and Literature, volume 386 (Leiden and Boston: Brill, 2015), 122.
13. This translation stems from Virgil, *The Aeneid*, trans. C. Day Lewis (London: Hogarth Press, 1961).
14. Virgil, *Aeneid 5*, 442.
15. Walter Benjamin, *The Writer of Modern Life: Essays on Charles Baudelaire* (Cambridge, MA: Harvard University Press, 2006), 84.
16. Walter Benjamin, "Das Kunstwerk im Zeitalter seiner technischen Reproduzierbarkeit," in *Illuminationen: Ausgewählte Schriften 1* (Frankfurt am Main: Suhrkamp Verlag, 1977), 140–1.
17. Corbin, *Village Bells*.
18. Bergson, *Duration and Simultaneity*, 52.

19. Clifford Geertz, "Thick Description: Toward an Interpretive Theory of Culture," in *The Interpretation of Cultures: Selected Essays*, 3rd ed. (New York: Basic Books, 2017).
20. Thomas Boswell, *Why Time Begins on Opening Day* (New York, NY: Penguin Books, 1987).
21. Friedrich Nietzsche, "Der Antichrist," in *Der Fall Wagner; Götzen-Dämmerung; Der Antichrist; Ecce Homo; Dionysos-Dithyramben; Nietzsche Contra Wagner*, ed. Giorgio Colli and Mazzino Montinari, Kritische Studienausgabe, KSA 6 (Berlin: De Gruyter, 1988), 254.

8 Data Visuals

An unexpected consequence of the digital age has been the expansive influence of visual materials, thus tying the digital age to processes that evolved two centuries ago. The invention of photography in the first half of the nineteenth century and the history of film in the twentieth century transformed the visual experience of human beings and ensured the uninterrupted proliferation of images. Television also played a role, whether in the homes of Americans in the Midwest or amongst Nazi officers stationed in Paris during the occupation in the 1940s. The flat screen television as wallpaper in waiting rooms, restaurants, and living rooms has given an air of ubiquity to the moving image. The digital age just added to these possibilities. On mobile devices, whether smart phones or laptops, users can access billions of videos of their own volition or be bombarded by videos of a major corporation's volition.

Despite all the forerunners to the most recent visual revolution, an old German saying from the Reformation still maintains its hold on academic thought: "*Was G'lahrte durch die Schrift verstahn, das lehrt das G'mähl dem g'meinen Mann.*" (What scholars learn from writing, pictures teach the common man.)[1] Except amongst visual specialists within the humanities, images have taken a back seat; when presented in a work, they still generally appear as illustrations rather than as sources in their own right. In *Eyewitnessing*, Peter Burke presents the rather (un)surprising statistic that the journal *Past and Present* did not include any images in articles published from 1952 until 1975.[2] Over time, a cautious acceptance of imagery emerged amongst historians, but illustrations still overwhelmed analytically significant imagery. An even more startling example is hidden within the realm of the philosophy of art. In a seminal work on art, Arthur Danto presented his readers with only two images—the images were identical and represented a rectangle with a line through it.[3] The visuals employed to conceptualize a visual profession were reduced to structural forms (the book has more logical equations than images). The philosopher's sketch, no doubt a reflection of empirical disdain, is hardly unique to Danto—Wittgenstein also liked grids—but when presented in the context of art, the revelation is striking.

Evidently, an abundance of visual stimulus cannot be equated with a wealth of visual analysis. The solution to this dilemma is not to fill books with more images or simply laud the construction of massive video databases because they can provide the historian and sociologist with empirical evidence—quantity is never a replacement for quality. Two alternatives can be recommended. Following Burke, one could justifiably advocate more visual education and increase visual sensitivity in the larger community of humanists; this is already an ongoing project. Alternatively, the emphasis on the digital age creates other avenues to be explored. Big Data, for instance, is not about art or photographs per se, so the traditional concerns evinced by Burke have to be reserved for another day. Rather, the largest question concerning the relationship between Big Data and the visual universe is the translation of the information in a database into visual imagery in such a way that the viewer of that imagery can look into the heart of the data. This represents one of the most significant translations of a quantitative entity into its qualitative equivalent. In this respect, Big Data is as much visual as quantitative, because it has to be presented to readers in as vigorous a way as possible. As Edward R. Tufte wrote, "often the most effective way to describe, explore, and summarize a set of numbers—even a large set—is to look at pictures of those numbers."[4]

Big Data, in an ocular mode, revitalizes the gaze, just a different gaze from the one to which we have become accustomed. Data is experienced through the intermediary of a graphic and impacts the reader's mastery of the information being processed. In this world, graphics are not simple graphs with an X-Y axis and a line that rises and falls like a profile of the Swiss Alps. Franco Moretti encourages "number-crunching" and presents the results in bar charts and scatterplot diagrams; not quite the stuff of artists but an intricate visual representation nonetheless.[5] The complexity of interactive graphics, an art form of its own, has already been well established in fora such as the *New York Times*. Appreciating a graphic is not the same as admiring a photograph or painting, so not all of Peter Burke's hopes will be fulfilled, but a specific style of eyewitnessing is required to appreciate Big Data.

The presentation of information in visual form is by no means new. In the middle of the nineteenth century, Charles Joseph Minard, a civil engineer by training, gained lasting fame with his *Carte Figurative*. This elegant graphic portrayed the fate of the Napoleonic army once it stepped onto the territory of the Russian Empire. The graphic has some numbers, a few dates, and a temperature bar to satisfy viewers with good vision, but the interpretive thrust comes from the visual effect of the conspicuous brown and black stripes, whose thickness corresponds to the size of the army. Really, no more is needed to tell the story. The impact is not just a statistical treat for military buffs because the aesthetic gratification, a pleasing view of Napoleon's demise, can easily overwhelm the numbers. Edward R. Tufte would consider this "beautiful evidence."[6]

Sometimes a picture is the only way to wrap one's head around a massive set of information, whether the information is qualitative or quantitative. Tufte, a great defender and advocate of graphic design, wanted, like Burke, to overcome prejudices against visual representations such as the assumption "that data graphics were mainly devices for showing the obvious to the ignorant." These graphics had a higher standard, which was to tell "the truth about data."[7] Obviously, Tufte never crossed paths with postmodernism and appears unaware that truth-telling has a tainted history. Nevertheless, he recognizes the gravity of visual representations and tirelessly promoted the aesthetic joy of graphic representation. It suggests that data aesthetics can arrive without a postmodern dressing.

Since the link between Big Data and its representation in visual imagery will only intensify, data visuals have to be conceptualized broadly. For example, humanists who engage with Big Data will want to present their results in graphic form, a method traditionally more popular in scientific journals. It is therefore interesting to see how humanists paired data with visual representations before the advent of the digital universe. Since the graphic arts have such powerful representative possibilities, the efforts of these visual artists deserve a moment to understand the array of visual strategies that can transform a bunch of numbers into a work of art. This transformation is essential to grasp the shift from the quantitative world of Big Data to the qualitative experience of the graph. This is perhaps the best instance to see how Big Data requires a craftsperson to make itself intelligible. The arrival of the visual artisan adds a humanist aesthetic to the numbers and suggests that the representation of Big Data should be the subject of more aesthetic debate. The transformation of the individual snippets of data also has to be considered, as was the case with time. The graphics necessarily summarize, average, and consolidate items that were never identical from the start. The quality of this transformation requires exploration to disabuse the notion that the graph is a replica of the original information. This inquiry allows for a few comments about the epistemological status of the data visuals.

Data-oriented humanists have been around for generations, particularly economic historians who bridged a world between statistics and historical analysis. In *The Habsburg Monarchy as a Customs Union*, John Komlos presented graphs on demand for rye, grain shipments, and further economic issues.[8] The graphs are utilitarian, follow standard economic models of the time, and have few if any aesthetic elements; they appeal to a mind envisioning the world mathematically. They are only a weak example of graphical use and hardly make the case that they foreshadow the contemporary increase in graphic design. Nevertheless, they start with visuals and exhibit the potential for improving the graphics.

A few years earlier, Paul E. Johnson published *A Shopkeeper's Millennium*, a history of Rochester, New York, in the first half of the nineteenth century. The frontispiece shows a map of Rochester in 1838, and the table of maps indicates that two more maps depicting Rochester neighborhoods in 1827 and 1834, can be found later in the book. In contrast to the frontispiece, which is a fairly traditional period map, the next two are schematic, more geometric, and abstract—geographic names and other details have been removed, and all one sees are rectangular shapes in different shades. This reflects a late twentieth-century design intended to quickly indicate functional and social divisions within the city.[9] The two depictions from 1827 and 1834 are on back-to-back pages, so one can think of them as components of an incredibly small flipbook because the viewer is meant to see how the city changes over time (the flipbook was not the original intent but this exaggeration allows one to think of the images dynamically). The data was culled from directories and tax lists, and maps were designed to visualize a process through which a city with "no distinct commercial and residential zones, no residential areas based upon social class" was quickly segregated, resulting in the "estrangement of master from wage earner."[10] In a similar spirit, Kenneth T. Jackson's *Crabgrass Frontier*, which looked at zoning in the United States almost one hundred years later, paid specific attention to federal zoning strategies that disadvantaged African Americans who wanted to purchase homes with financial aid.[11] These zoning practices are ripe for data visuals, especially since Jackson, unlike Johnson, had masses of available statistics.

These are cases where standard historical works would have profited immensely from dynamic data visuals. In Johnson's case, the sample would not have to be limited to two years and a map that moved in time could show change dramatically and effectively. With colors, the map could pay more attention to different professions and avoid the standard categorizations of middle class and working class. The graphic would then undermine (or reinforce) interpretations that required these two Marxist categories. The assembling of data from Rochester has a positivist inclination that goes hand in hand with the visuals. The mode of representation and the choice of colors will have aesthetic content, but the underlying information is deeply empirical. Most recently, Peter Selb and Simon Munzert have tabulated and visually represented Hitler's election results from the 1920s and early 1930s to demonstrate that his charismatic speeches did not have a major impact on voting habits. In the appendix, the county maps of Germany are presented in full color with tonal choices in the online version, and dramatically convey the electoral landscape. In contrast to Minard's representation of Napoleon's invasion, these visuals require a little more attention to understand their full weight.[12]

Data does not always have to be collected to satisfy the empirical curiosity of historians and political scientists, nor does it have to be transformed into data graphics. Artists, with their inclination towards creative play, can pull together data and transform survey information into oil paintings. In an effort to define and come to terms with popular definitions of beauty, Vitaly Komar and Alexander Melamid produced a series of paintings called *America's Most Wanted* (1994–1997). Although the title suggests something linked to a criminal fugitive, the artists painted a serene pastoral landscape. The painting was not a function of their own imagination, but a visual translation from data they had collected in a survey. Respondents had been asked a series of questions to reveal what they most wanted to see in a painting. The surveys, done in a number of countries, were conducted by polling companies and thus had a formal and methodological element to them. Although the Russian artists originally designed the art project to allow viewers a greater amount of democratic decision-making in the artistic process, the project can be inserted into a debate on Big Data. It shows how data samples can be translated into beautiful imagery. In this case, beauty is defined by those who answered the survey and produced the data set, a situation which is not often the case. The project makes the case that (data) visuals are the skin that beautifies the skeleton.

Nowadays the last assertion is self-evident because these visuals are already standard practice in online publications such as the *New York Times*. On April 19, 2016, the newspaper printed a map of New York City demonstrating how each neighborhood voted in the Republican primary.[13] The colors of the map were matched to the candidate, and the viewer-reader could choose to look at all precincts or just those with either a white, black, Hispanic, or Asian population of at least 50%. The visuals tell an irresistible story about voter distribution. This is just a Big Data version of what Johnson was attempting.

About ten days later, the same newspaper published a data visual showing the level of advancement of sixth graders in the richest school districts versus their counterparts in poorer areas—data taken from across the United States was mapped onto an X-axis that highlighted the socioeconomic standing of parents and a Y-axis pertaining to the level of advancement.[14] The rather messy graph showed the expected conclusion that wealthier kids performed better. Of greater import, the graph allowed the viewer to look at her own school district and race-based performance in that district. Pink circles showed white children, blue for Hispanic, and green for black children. The visual trend within the colors showed the discrepancies. When a specific county was selected, say Duval County, Florida, it immediately highlighted where the races stood within that same district; the discrepancies are immediate as one graphic color occupied the upper right whereas the other two were lower and to the left. The only way to truly grasp the power of the data visual is to look at it—this textual description pales in comparison.

Not all contemporary data visuals are from ready-at-hand data sets; many assemble historical information and cobble it together just as Johnson did. Migration visuals, for example, dramatize human movement over the centuries. In the exhibition *Axé Bahia* at the Fowler Museum at

UCLA, a video demonstrated the flow of slaves from Africa to the New World from the first crossing until the end of the slave trade. The viewer sees little dots emerging in a specific part of Africa, crossing the Atlantic, and then ending at a destination in South America, the Caribbean, and North America. The visual moves forward chronologically, and as more slaves were forced across the ocean, more dots can be seen as they merge into a thicker stream of black. Amongst other things, it quickly becomes apparent that most slaves went to the Caribbean and South America and not to the United States.

The visual appears within the context of other art works, so the visitor to the gallery sees it in a unique context, where visual impulses are prioritized over the data. While the graphic conveys historical information, the visual creativity is its reason for being in the show. Had the curators just wanted to provide some useful data as historical context, they could just as easily have presented utilitarian charts and graphs. The design element is the critical component and, like Minard's *Carte Figurative*, achieves the status of beautiful evidence, despite the absence of beauty in the historical events being portrayed.

Migration visuals don't have to focus on a haunted past. Metrocosm presents a visual of "Everyone Who's Immigrated to the U.S. since 1820."[15] Based on available data from the Department of Homeland Security's Office of Immigration Statistics, this beautiful visual pays no attention to slavery and instead focuses on "legal" immigration. Colored dots can be seen flowing from one part of the world to the United States, and here the viewer can identify how migration patterns have changed dramatically over time. The map highlights which countries provided the most immigrants, so it quickly becomes clear how the original flow from Europe slowed down towards the early part of the twentieth century. By the start of the twenty-first century, the dots are arriving from Central America and Asia. If all the statistics were incorrect, the visual would still be compelling because of its aesthetics.

With such an abundance of visual stimulus, why should we look at the graphics with downcast eyes? The French anti-ocular tradition, of which Martin Jay wrote, did not have data visuals in mind (though it understood the power of computers), but the concept of an anti-ocular position needs rethinking with the current abundance of artistically designed visuals. Data visuals don't neatly fit into a philosophical debate about empiricism and sense data, an original foil of the anti-ocular tradition, but they have relevance in postmodern debates and cannot be dismissed with sweeping critiques of technologies. Gilles Deleuze had issues with computers and posited that computer surveillance was usurping the surveillance role of vision. He writes of a computer "whose passive danger is jamming and whose active one is piracy and the introduction of viruses."[16] These comments precede the world of massive databases and, hardly prescient, push away from the immense visual dimension of computer technologies. The penetrating critique leaves data visuals untouched, though it stands to reason that the advent of these graphics has something to do with the French *veiller*, if not exactly surveillance.

Postmodern critiques of vision don't neatly apply to data visuals because the computer screen does not look at and observe the viewer; the act of viewing is critically different. The viewer cannot penetrate into the depth of what she is looking at; she cannot focus on a data visual as one would a photograph or film. The qualities of data visuals relate to a numerical gaze, albeit numbers transformed into an aesthetic message. This visual experience therefore cannot be disassociated from numbers, equations, and algorithms. Furthermore, the depth of the empirical experience only goes so far; the user never really knows what lies within it. A viewer might remain ignorant of the level of exactitude that went into the visuals, much like a science textbook never tells its readers what degree of "reasonable agreement" went into successfully completing the experiment.[17] The resulting visual representation is slightly divergent from the original data because the apparently exact data has been translated into looser and rounded visuals. Frequently, one cannot apprehend any of the original numbers but is staring at a translation from those numbers (there can be multiple levels of translation). When the graphic is done effectively, one does not have to be aware of the unique quantities in the background to be influenced by its makeup. Therefore a funny type of blindness is operative here.

The visual experience also pulls the humanist a little deeper into the world of the scientist because a comparison can be made with older generations of scientists who spent hours looking at oscilloscopes. Humanists, many of whom will become dependent on data visuals, will comb them for trending clues and adopt the same visual techniques as the scientist. Contemporary data visuals are more sophisticated than those grainy waves that showed up on oscilloscopes, but the parallel in visual practice is noteworthy. If visuals are gaining momentum, and scientists and humanists learn to see with similar, sophisticated tools, what then separates the scientist from the humanist?

The separation can be maintained only if the humanist recognizes the complex conceptualization of the data visual. The numbers have to be apparent through graphic design and its methodologies. This is an ideal opportunity for humanists to seek out new interdisciplinary partners and move away from the familiar ones found in literary criticism and anthropology, the standard bearers for postmodern ideas. With only a finite sum of intellectual energy, space made for new intellectual partners will reduce the space for the older ones. Earlier chapters suggested a greater need in the humanities to understand algorithms. In this visual environment, learning more about the graphic arts will be a little like the scholar working on improving her grammatical style because she recognizes the importance of the medium that conveys her ideas.

154   *Data Visuals*

In 1976, Jacques Bertin published his *Sémiologie graphique*, a seminal work that, in over 400 pages, explained the basic principles behind presenting information graphically—the viewer will quickly realize the complexity of the enterprise.[18] Bertin's work is replete with regular graphs, standard axes, and ratios determining the size and positioning of graphic elements. To the delight of Moretti's distant readers, Bertin also has a graph based on a French dissertation from 1949 that counted the frequency of words from a selection of seventeenth-century authors—the word frequency is represented as an approximation ("non-quantitatively"). Bertin demonstrates how the visuals differ when, for example, the authors are ordered in a grid either according to the vocabulary they use or according to their birth. In a second graph, one visually sees how the status of words rises and falls with their frequency of usage.[19] Bertin also comments on the strengths and weaknesses of cartographic representations. A map indicating the growth of Protestantism has concentric circles radiating out from the centers of influence—the circles quickly show where the Reformation had its origins (Wittenberg, Geneva) but, according to Bertin, the concentric circles exaggerated the even spread of the Reformation, where a topographic map would have been better suited to encapsulate the irregularities. In neither of the above cases would the viewer be exposed to direct quantification; the visuals imply quantity but in a general sense.[20]

An abstract map of France illuminates interdepartmental migration from 1954. Embodying two pieces of quantitative information in a single graphic, the visual craftily uses arrowheads to show the size and flow of all the moving people. The area of the arrows relates to the absolute number of migrants, and the length of the arrow is "proportional to the migratory tendency (percentage of migrants)" from the specific departments. Despite these parameters, no visual exactitude emanates from the representation. Rather, it has a 'look and feel' quality which reduces the importance of a detailed quantification. Not only does the map confirm the saying that not all graphics are graphs, but it also requires an able eye, sensitive to colors, slopes, and perspectives.

Bertin's course on graphic design has a strong numerical component, yet it pays ample attention to the skills required to decode an image and hints at how these skills can be exported into the world of the humanist. First, the humanist cannot settle for oversimplified representations using mundane axes or block diagrams of yesteryear. Similar to the architects who build our libraries, graphic designers have to be pulled into the process. Interestingly, this will stimulate further debates on the adequate representation of data, since competing graphic schools will make their own choices. For those inclined to support the notion of primary colors, specific hues and tones will take precedence over others because they are more appropriate as sense data. In contrast, colors could be chosen according to cultural habits and shapes from unique human environments. The selection of data visuals is thus no less important than the selection of words and the development of prose in any work—they stand at the same elevation. Scholars have long debated word choices, gerunds, and verb tenses; the same pattern of interpretation emerges with the selection of data visuals.

These thoughts are in vivid action in the work of Jer Thorp, who designed the algorithm to place the names on the 9/11 memorial in Manhattan. Thorp was the *New York Times*' first Data Artist-in-Residence and has therefore seized the opportunity to visually articulate and transform data from the influential newspaper. In a series from 2009 called 365/360, Thorp visualized years of news in the *New York Times* to create beautiful and stimulating graphics that indicate the top organizations and personalities from 1985 to 2001.[21] The images show lines dancing in and out of the center in helical forms; text helps the viewer identify the news item as the line pulls into a thicket before reemerging mysteriously somewhere towards the periphery. Thorp has also created a video that draws from Twitter and, using a three-dimensional globe, shows over ten thousand tweets of people saying "Good Morning" over a twenty-four-hour period. The tweets are mostly in English but include foreign languages as well. This last graphic representation might be a prime example of the aesthetic potential of graphic visuals because the good mornings as data might not be of great interest to everyone. In contrast to a free artist, Thorp is bound by the data and thus creates with restraints, one of which is the necessary symmetry that lurks in small pieces throughout the work.

Edward Tufte was also acutely aware that visual techniques were not self-explanatory and required techniques of their own to read them. In *Visual Explanations*, his pedagogy begins with an analysis of a photograph of Prague from 1968 to introduce the viewer to the familiar medium of photography before delving into the less familiar territory of graphic design. Yet the approach easily drifts from aesthetics: a photograph of a visible watch "documents the hour."[22]

For the humanist, Tufte's analysis goes in the wrong direction. We should not be reading a photograph like a statistical graph but rather the other way around—the trained eye of the art historian or visual thinker is the prerequisite for understanding the data visual since data visuals have strong aesthetic and artistic components (Tufte would actually agree with this). If we accepted this last sentence as a maxim, the humanities could move away from bar charts and scattergrams and insist that data be represented in a sufficiently sophisticated aesthetic fashion. Accepting the maxim is a simple and necessary step indeed, especially with all the concerns about the humanities succumbing to data.

Data visuals have to be considered qualitatively, but the moment one does a new set of issues arises. The qualitative emphasis quickly reveals the imperfections of the graph because a data visual cannot, following Ranke, represent the data exactly as it is, and therefore a relativist has

156 *Data Visuals*

reason to question its objectivity and return it back onto a postmodern track. Of course, the data visual can only be an approximation because its job is to represent massive amounts of information as concisely and effectively as possible; this should not, however, be used as an excuse to adjust its meaning to fit older ideas. In recognizing that it is but an approximation, one must accept that the approximation is built upon a unique foundation.

Framing the issue in concise philosophical terms is not easy because the link between the qualitative and the quantitative evokes complex questions: what happens to the original data or numbers or facts once they are portrayed? Do they disappear into the data visual and lose their identity, or do they preserve their individualism, though this might no longer be perceptible? The aesthetic component of the visual also has a role to play. If the data visual evolves into a beautiful form of art, does the data cease to play a role as it cedes to the imagery? Can one contemplate the aesthetic impulses of the data visual while completely ignoring the quantitative component? These posits simply reiterate the earlier point that the quantitative and the qualitative cannot be extricated from each other.

A parallel surfaces with the theme of layering from other chapters. In an earlier discussion on language, an assertion was made to the effect that the language in the algorithmic layer was fundamentally different in structure from the language that the algorithm sought to translate—a strict barrier separated the two, though they operated simultaneously. In contrast, digital time on the digital surface descended deep into the depths of digital experience for the boundary present in language had disappeared. In the current visual instance, one cannot identify either an impassable boundary or a completely uninhibited flow. Data visuals do a remarkably effective job at amalgamating the quantitative layer into a digestible qualitative experience. That being said, the data does not disappear. A larger circle, a thicker line, or even a photograph retouched to incorporate quantities hides the quantities by performing an act of translation. The translation is irreversible in the immediate sense that the user cannot keep zooming in on the visual with the hope of finding the singular data bits upon closer inspection. The data does not cease to exist, it just exists at another address. This address is the foundational base for the data visual. The qualitative and quantitative freely interact but without losing their distinguishing properties. The layering is more akin to a soft resistance on both sides; they leach into each other without eliminating each other.

The foundation of the data visual is significant because as much as the artist is free to choose any visual representation—by color, by size—the choice of foundation cannot be made. This is not to say that the original data represents a foundational truth (this is not at issue here), but that the data visual has a readily identifiable source to be dealt with qualitatively. With this in mind, the creator of a data visual can choose any number of representations. Someone like Edward Tufte would argue that there is a most beautiful way to represent the data, but this does not have to be accepted at face value. Because so many options avail themselves, the representation will have to be an approximation of the data (though this is not the only reason there are approximations).

The approximation should not be of major concern. If we remember, Wittgenstein made every effort to deny that exactitude was a standard worth pursuing. He did not suggest that the absence of exactitude was an opportunity for an epistemological free-for-all. Rather, a looser standard was more effective. Wittgenstein gave examples of the effectiveness of inexact language. If someone utters "stand over there," we neither are baffled by the absence of an exact location nor take this as an opportunity to stand wherever we want. Despite his obsession with language, Wittgenstein also had a few visuals in mind: a blurred photograph of a human being is no less a photograph of a human being. These were concentrated efforts to overcome the objections of a pedantic and nitpicky skeptic. All you can ask is that a good data visual approximates the foundation it is responsible to.

Since the original data is available, the potency of the representation can always be checked (if the data were to disappear and all one had was a screen shot of the visual, a whole different set of questions would have to be asked). The representation could lie—just like a map can lie, and statistics lie in their own way—but this could be double checked against the original data to see where the visual veered from its base. One cannot begin to promote epistemological doubt without first exploring how the data intersects with the visual. This investigation does not test the data itself, only its link with the graphic; the examination occurs at this layer.

In this way, the data always remains below the surface as a tangible source. The fact that its individual components retain their original presence is crucial. At the same time, the viewer does not necessarily see this layer—you can look at a human being and not know that a skeleton lies beneath. The viewer cannot individuate the amalgamated information unless specifics are presented in another, more linguistic form, a process similar to the ambiguous nature of time in verbs; if you want more exact time, you have to write it out in numbers. It takes an inquisitive mind to understand that the visual represents a source of information but does not contain the information per se.

The aesthetic representation is another thing altogether. A comparison can be made with a paint by numbers set for the amateur artist; the numbers disappear when complete and the beautiful imagery leaves its lasting mark. This parallel has its merits but works only insofar as the artists are beholden to something (if beauty is in the eye of the beholder, then the data visual might be said to be beholden to data). This trivializes the graphic efforts because representing the data is nowhere nearly as restrictive as paint by numbers. Minard's representation of Napoleon's failed invasion has an aesthetic that is independent of any specific quantitative information; the visual impulse transcends the quantitative representation of fallen soldiers and hoary winter days.

What, then, is the hidden quality that gives the graphic its aesthetic appeal? Here one has to grasp the balance between visual attraction and the conveyance of information. Over the years, the New York Subway has commissioned artists to create transit maps, and some have been more effective than others. More philosophically, these visual representations can be inserted into the framework of traditional debates. For example, beauty as a standard of art was challenged in the early twentieth century by Marcel Duchamp's readymades: why should a data visual be judged for abstract beauty rather than on its aesthetic impact? In the same vein, art has long since ceased to be the privileged domain of sculptors and painters. Throughout the twentieth century and still today, more and more art domains have gained respect in traditional cultural venues. Fashion photography, an outlier because it was both photographic and commercial, has only recently been given serious attention. Data visuals, with their own aesthetic charm, are within this sphere of cultural activity. This recognizes the futility of conceptualizing the data visual without an aesthetic component; the lack of aesthetic for the data visual is inconceivable. The data visual can therefore be philosophized just like any other piece of art. It can be philosophized well beyond any talk of accuracy or effectiveness, and even independently of the quantities it embodies.

In his postmodern work on film, Christian Metz made familiar dismissive claims about visual experience. He wrote, "the only principle of relevancy capable of defining, at present, the semiotics of the film is . . . the desire to treat films as texts, as units of discourse."[23] The film, an apparent source of accurate information, offers viewers a fantasy: "the notion of 'visual,' in the totalitarian and monolithic sense that it has taken on in certain recent discussions is a fantasy or an ideology and the image (at least in this sense) is something which does not exist."[24] Metz was arguing against a "cult of the 'visual'" that bordered "upon the irrational."[25] His words were clearly directed at film but reflect a general postmodern impulse that linked vision with empiricism and thus a suspicion of the visual.

Given the specific nature of the data visual, one would be hard pressed to continue his line of thinking. Nowhere in this discussion has the data visual been linked to discourse. On the one hand, the foundational data is simply too complex and mysterious to be conceptualized as discourse. On the other hand, the efforts of the graphic artists, linked to data and aesthetics, would be trivialized if reduced to vague comments on discourse. As the presence of visual material increases, the textual temptation will diminish and become less of a diversion. One might assert that the viewer *reads* the data visual, but the presentation has no characteristics that can be mapped to language; translation in any conventional sense does not apply. Similarly, if we insisted on referring to the "vernacular syntax" of the data visual, we would misrepresent how the data visual functioned. Data visuals have already started to challenge purely textual analysis in a way basic imagery, such as photographs and film stills, never did. The impact of words will be more fleeting as an eyeball trained on visuals will find more common cause with moving images and shifting displays. The humanist will be drawn into this process.

Just like the archaeologist needs to know how to set up a dig and the historian of Spain Spanish, the new humanist will require more substantive visual training. For example, colors will have to be studied to situate their meaning.[26] Geometric shapes can be assessed, and learning basic graphic techniques can be advocated. The depth of required knowledge can be evaluated, and not all humanists will choose this route. Some, however, will and, for the health of humanists, must. Closer attention to data visuals represents a golden opportunity to vitalize data and avoid being swept aside by a quantitative wave. Since the quantitative and the qualitative interact regularly, the data visuals contain a sampling of positivism in the form of ordered empiricals as well as a taste of aesthetic wonder.

Notes

1. Quoted in Grete de Francesco, *The Power of the Charlatan*, trans. Miriam Beard (New Haven: Yale University Press, 1939), 105.
2. Burke, *Eyewitnessing*, 12.
3. Danto, *The Transfiguration of the Commonplace*.
4. Edward R. Tufte, *The Visual Display of Quantitative Information*, 2nd ed. (Cheshire, CT: Graphics Press, 2001), 9.
5. Jennifer Schuessler, "Reading by the Numbers: When Big Data Meets Literature," accessed April 5, 2018, www.nytimes.com/2017/10/30/arts/franco-moretti-stanford-literary-lab-big-data.html.
6. Tufte, *Beautiful Evidence*.
7. Tufte, *The Visual Display of Quantitative Information*, 53.
8. John Komlos, *The Habsburg Monarchy as a Customs Union: Economic Development in Austria-Hungary in the Nineteenth Century* (Princeton, NJ: Princeton University Press, 1983).
9. Paul E. Johnson, *A Shopkeeper's Millennium: Society and Revivals in Rochester, New York, 1815–1837*, American Century Series (New York: Hill and Wang, 1978).
10. Johnson, *A Shopkeeper's Millennium*, 48–50.
11. Kenneth T. Jackson, *Crabgrass Frontier: The Suburbanization of the United States* (New York: Oxford University Press, 1985).
12. See Peter Selb and Simon Munzert, "Examining a Most Likely Case for Strong Campaign Effects: Hitler's Speeches and the Rise of the Nazi Party, 1927–1933," *American Political Science Review, 112*(4), (November 2018): 1050–1066. These authors, whose background in political science explains the extensive quantitative analysis, build upon the qualitative work in Ludolf Herbst, *Hitlers Charisma: Die Erfindung eines deutschen Messias* (Frankfurt am Main: S. Fischer, 2010). See also Claudia Schwartz, "Der Mythos von Hitlers Charisma |

NZZ," *Neue Zürcher Zeitung*, August 10, 2018, www.nzz.ch/feuilleton/der-mythos-von-hitlers-charisma-ld.1409935.
13. Matthew Bloch and Wilson Andrews, "How Every New York City Neighborhood Voted in the Republican Primary," accessed April 4, 2018, www.nytimes.com/interactive/2016/04/19/us/elections/new-york-city-republican-primary-results.html.
14. Motoko Rich, Amanda Cox, and Matthew Bloch, "Money, Race and Success: How Your School District Compares," accessed April 4, 2018, www.nytimes.com/interactive/2016/04/29/upshot/money-race-and-success-how-your-school-district-compares.html.
15. Max Galka, "Here's Everyone Who's Immigrated to the U.S. Since 1820," *Metrocosm* (blog), May 3, 2016, http://metrocosm.com/animated-immigration-map/.
16. Deleuze, "Postscript on the Societies of Control."
17. Kuhn, "The Function of Measurement in Modern Physical Science."
18. Jacques Bertin, *Sémiologie graphique: Les diagrammes, les réseaux, les cartes* (Paris: Gauthier-Villars, 1967).
19. Bertin, *Sémiologie graphique*, 220–1.
20. Bertin, *Sémiologie graphique*, 352.
21. They can be seen at www.jerthorp.com/365.
22. Edward R. Tufte, *Visual Explanations: Images and Quantities, Evidence and Narrative* (Cheshire, CT: Graphics Press, 1997), 13.
23. Metz, *Language and Cinema*, 21.
24. Metz, *Language and Cinema*, 35.
25. Metz, *Language and Cinema*, 34.
26. C. L. Hardin, *Color for Philosophers: Unweaving the Rainbow* (Indianapolis: Hackett Pub. Co, 1988).

9   Digital Forgeries

The beauty of visual graphics presented in the last chapter aimed to inspire aesthetic hope in the world of Big Data. But what if we suddenly learned that the graphics had been faked? The stunning colors and composition of the graph would not change, but the beauty would fade and our eyes would turn away. Barring willful ignorance, it would be impossible to look at the tainted image in the same way. Those who initially fawned over a Han van Meegeren forgery in the 1930s could no longer be moved once they were convinced it was not the Vermeer they had believed it to be.

Earlier efforts at forgery seem almost quaint when compared to the fakes and forgeries that speed through the digital atmosphere. Everyone is familiar with photoshopping and videos that swap one person's head with another person's body. Yet identifying the simple truthfulness of a photographed image or a sewn video is not at the crux of digital forgeries. In a narrow sense, photoshopping and related phenomena such as counterfeiting precede the digital age and, on the surface, digital manipulations differ only in form and not in kind. In a broader sense, digital forgeries are much more complicated. With respect to data visuals, it naturally follows that the forgery can be accomplished at a number of different levels—the data but not the graphic, and the graphic but not data, are both possible complications. The purpose of the following discussion is to disentangle these complexities to position the layers of digital forgeries relative to earlier themes.

Exploring the act of forging is not a mere curiosity because forgery is a fundamental component of the postmodern project. Any aspect of experience that has us questioning the facts of the matter was supported and promoted by postmodernists. In response, other scholars who studied forgeries took issue with these claims and cautioned against a zealous relativism. In the 1980s, Rudolf Arnheim wrote an essay called "On Duplication" (not *On Duplicity*) in which he addressed the particular problem of making copies. Arnheim was concerned that "[m]ore broadly, fakes are cited to show that facts do not exist objectively and that their evaluation is not based on understanding. Facts are nothing but products of convention."[1] Arnheim's fears were not unfounded. In 1981, Sherrie Levine presented her series of photographs, *After Walker Evans*, in a New York Art Gallery; the photographs were taken from a Walker Evans catalog but attributed to Levine. The series, which questioned authorship and invention, represented a quintessential postmodern moment. In this vision, the presence of doubt in terms of identifying a copy versus an original, no matter how small, gives an impulse to various forms of skepticism. This habit persists to this day. In a recent work on forgery in the world of art, Thierry Lenain writes that when it comes to forgery, "the only evidence we may rely on is made of discourses."[2] This confirms Arnheim's suspicion, but it also shows the persistent influence of the linguistic turn because it reduces the visual to the linguistic. This linguistic assertion is worn in the heel, but it ascertains how quickly forgeries get sucked into postmodern explanations. In assessing the impact of digital technologies on postmodernism, forgery puts the discussion in the trickiest of circumstances because of its essentially hidden qualities.

Digital forgeries cannot fall back on older approaches and have to be considered with a new set of questions that take digital peculiarities as a starting point; the result will be a better characterization of forgeries designed to put those peculiarities in greater focus and allow the humanist to move on from there. For example, the traditional forger of a painting had to make sure the materials, such as the oil and canvas, bore a close enough resemblance to the original painting, though the materials did not determine what the forged painting would represent. In a digital forgery, there is a much closer link between the materials (the bits and bytes) and the forged object. This has to do with the layered nature of digital experience and needs elucidation to be made effective. Another component is the visual detection of the forgery. Carlo Ginzburg stressed how the nineteenth-century art expert and connoisseur Giovanni Morelli painstakingly examined earlobes and fingertips to ensure authenticity; in another domain, Sherlock Holmes used his magnifying glass. But is there a digital equivalent to this activity? Can the zoom function be used to detect forgeries, or is it better employed as a heuristic device to explain why digital forgeries are so different? How can we even determine if the elements of a data set have been forged?

With the forgery of paintings, there is a general understanding that the forger is a talented individual but lacks the skill of visual innovation that made the original work special.[3] It is hard to see how this translates in the digital world. Instead of comparing the talents of the original artist with the forger, it would make more sense to distinguish between the artist and the computer programmer. Both skilled individuals are involved in the process and therefore one might be more talented than the other. This thought introduces the next dilemma, which is closely associated with authorship. In the digital world, is it possible for a single individual to forge something, or is digital forgery necessarily a group project because it has a technical and humanistic layer? In looking ahead to possible responses, these questions demonstrate that understanding the digital forgery is as much a relational as a philosophical issue.

The most common cases of forgery, traditionally speaking, pertain to painting. Han van Meegeren, the talented artist, is common fare not only because he fooled so many people but also because his actions became a reference point for discussions on connoisseurship, the art of critically evaluating aesthetics and authenticity in paintings. Yet not all famous forgeries appear on a canvas. In the early twentieth century, Russian anti-Semites published the *Protocols of the Elders of Zion*, falsely ascribing this conspiratorial text to the Jewish community.[4] Written forgeries are of a different quality from that of painted ones. The authors did not model the text on an existing work of late nineteenth-century Zionists (it was modeled after something completely different), and it did not attempt to reproduce the style of a single author or anything similar to the efforts of van Meegeren.[5] Rather, the Protocols made statements in the name of someone else without properly identifying the originals. The reproduction of the Protocols into numerous different languages had nothing to do with forgery at all. The contemporary equivalent of the Protocols would be no more than a falsely ascribed document that began to circulate throughout the Internet. The Protocols did more harm than the forged Vermeer, but they are not of the same category because their status does not depend on the medium of production.

A more perplexing, if quirky, commentary on the forging of writing is invoked by a great Argentinian librarian. Jorge Luis Borges told the fictional story of Pierre Menard, a symbolist poet who copied sections of Don Quixote word for word. Borges diligently provided excerpts from Cervantes and Menard to show they were exactly the same. Despite looking at two identical twins, Borges insisted their meanings were unique, for even "the contrast in style was striking."[6] His examples appear convoluted because it makes no immediate sense to say that an exact copy of a written text could be different. A reader can read Cervantes at a library and then return home to read her own copy without thinking the content is any different, though the physical books are. Yet Borges was making the point that innovation and creation are not mere empirical activities of an individual but are tied to other factors such as the environment in which one finds oneself.

All these concerns reappear in the digital world, and basic digital forgery already exists in a variety of formats. The fingerprint, a mid-nineteenth-century innovation in biotagging, has become an alternative for the password as a means to unlock an iPhone (apparently, the fingerprint of a corpse can still be used to unlock the phone), but this means of security is easy to copy. A savvy techie can take a high-resolution photograph of your thumb and put it to good use on the owner's iPhone; this represents a form of impersonation without the personality of the owner.

Unlike a forgery by van Meegeren, this process resembles the act of photocopying because it is making an accurate reproduction of an existing fingerprint; the method does not create an additional, say sixth, finger and pass it off as someone else's. The digital forgery of a fingerprint is more closely tied to a mere physical trait of an individual, not their specific artistic or cultural talents, which, as Borges emphasized, cannot be found in physicality alone.

A more effective entryway into digital forgery can be made by considering what would be involved in forging a variant of the graphic of Jer Thorp mentioned in Chapter 8. The current author could, for instance, have claimed the graphic as his own after having made minor edits and touch ups to a screen shot and presented it here. If the presented image had been no more than a screen shot, the visual impulse would have no link to data; the image has been severed from the original data, and the underlying digital codes that constructed the screen shot have nothing in common with the codes that produced the graphic. The viewer could easily recognize this lacuna because the viewer expects a connection between Thorp's artistry and the data. The absence of data would be easy to demonstrate. The appreciation of Thorp's work is necessarily tied to the understanding that data has a generative quality; Thorp's efforts would lose much of their charm if he admitted they had simply been drawn and had no attachment to data whatsoever. Therefore, the forger would have to deal with a data set to construct a forgery; the visual and the data both have to be taken into consideration in the process.

What would it then require to expose a forgery of Thorp, and, though the imagery is based upon data, would an old-fashioned connoisseur have a role to play? Since the curves in the display are based on data, how could one perform an effective visual autopsy? A connoisseur could not scrape paint from the surface of a Thorp image to examine a sample but could identify irregularities in the color palate and sense stylistic elements that would not be in harmony with Thorp. If the examiner noticed minor color variations or unnecessarily thick curves, she could raise the shadow of doubt necessary to link the work with forgery.

As mentioned, Carlo Ginzburg celebrated the nineteenth-century art connoisseur Morelli because he did not look at a painting in a holistic fashion.[7] Instead, he sought to identify traces the artist left behind. In these moments of detail, the artist revealed himself, and this was Morelli's way of testing authenticity and uncovering forgery. Ginzburg transformed the references to Morelli into a parable about the humanistic method—Morelli was a humanist because he looked for individualistic traits or traces rather than the generalizations which fascinated scientists. In describing the process, Ginzburg promoted the idea of traces, like the footprint left by an animal or, to add an example, the little irregularities left by the abandoned railways of the American West so beautifully depicted in the photographs of Mark Ruwedel.[8] Ginzburg was looking

Digital Forgeries 165

for a way to individualize the search for experience and estrange it from Galileo Galilei, whose laboratory experiments transformed everything into a general law. Would Morelli's method have a place in solving a thorny Thorpian fraud, or would the data underlying the image negate the humanist's pursuit of individualism?

Since the visual projection has a link to the data itself, one has to assume that the data plays an actual role in the graphic; Thorp is not completely free creatively, and therefore the visual is not the best place to identify a trace. Just looking at the data itself compares to examining the selection of paints an artist used without recognizing that the paints themselves could be applied to any painting. Unless Thorp manipulated the data, the data are provided to him as immutable; he can then mix them in the visual representation, but the underlying data set is supplied to the artist. The data set may contain falsehoods or have been artificially created, but for the moment, this represents a separate problem. The authenticity of the artwork could not be verified just by looking at the bits and bytes of the data set, though one could determine he never had access to specific data.

The more effective manner would be to look at the tools Thorp accessed to construct the visual, that is, the software and other interfaces that generated the imagery for his manipulation. By mastering the computer techniques, the connoisseur would discover the subtle skills required to transform bland data into piebald expositions. She would be investigating an intermediary because the intermediary formed the core of Thorp's mastery. Thorp superimposed his aesthetic inspiration onto the software; the software was the brush, and the connoisseur could still explore how this digital brush left traces throughout the work.

Digital traces won't leave a mark in our physical world, but they exist in a substrate of bits and bytes, regulated by a rule that puts those bits and bytes into a form we experience. Below the surface, a programmer can identify the rivers and valleys that make up this digital landscape. Access to these layers is not immediate and needs cooperation with the computer scientist (Thorp is an algorithmist). If the connoisseur persists with efforts of verification, these exertions have a scientific component to them, foreign to the initiative undertaken by Morelli. The traces are not eliminated, they just have a digital form and require other skills to be revealed.

Traditionally, one could expect the art connoisseur to take out a magnifying glass to take a closer look at Thorp's artwork. Sherlock Holmes had a lens that appeared in numerous stories and inevitably propelled the narrative towards its conclusion. In *The Speckled Band*, Holmes examined a chair with the lens to conclude that its owner had been standing on it.[9] In *The Sign of Four*, Holmes explained to Watson, the narrator, that the lens was powerful enough to reveal numbers that had been scratched with a pin-point on the inside of a watch case.[10] The magnifying glass moves towards a fixed object and is situated between the object and the eyeball.[11] In a digital world, a connoisseur can still identify suspicious traits by *zooming* in on imagery, but the trajectory of the magnifying glass and the zoom function flow in opposite directions. In effect, the magnifying glass brings the viewer to the object, whereas the zoom brings an object to the viewer.

Zooming would seem to be the digital equivalent of the magnifying glass, yet zooming and magnifying are not synonymous. Zooming in either direction does not allow one to get closer to a fixed object. It just asks the computer to present the digital information in a different way; the object was never fixed for it keeps changing beneath the screens, although one thinks of the zoom as the equivalent of a magnifying glass. The digital process has a magical quality not so different from a kaleidoscope; the digital zoom is a little bit like shaking a kaleidoscope. The parallel is extravagant but conceptualizes each layer of the zoom process as a refreshed or entirely new image based on an original set of building blocks. The most detailed image already inheres in the data stored in electronic format, and the zoom function calls upon it to be presented in a specific way (this is another case of spacelessness). Visually, it is quite true that you can take a closer look with each step, but there is a sense that you are not getting closer at all—for you continue to look at completely new images (and not a 'closer' version of the old one). Therefore, the visual information at the surface can say only so much. To be sure, the zoomer has control of the mouse, but not the manner in which the object comes to be seen.

The kaleidoscopic metaphor chips away at Nelson Goodman's distinction between autographic and allographic. Goodman developed these two categories because he wanted to distinguish between art forms such as painting, which had a specific object at their root, and writing, which could be reproduced at will with special fonts and in varying formats. The painting, autographic in nature, was the greater challenge because it required a higher degree of uniqueness. The kaleidoscopic metaphor merges the autographic and allographic. The digital art can be enlarged or minimized at will, much like the publisher of the Protocols of Zion could opt for larger or smaller fonts, and the graphic could be presented in almost any format as long as the aspects or ratios within the graph adhered to the original (changing the size of the work is no longer an activity reserved for a magnifying glass). With respect to identifying an original or authentic work, it would make no difference where the zoom stood or what size the font was; originality lies on another layer. A text has its own substrate resembling that of the graphic; the difference between paper and canvas comes close to being eliminated.

The ability to perceive the visual arts in any size depending upon one's own chosen environment would seem to elevate Arnheim's fears about facts being conventions because "they vary with the setting."[12] Larger or smaller, in a car or in a library, the setting can never be the same; therefore, what appears as a constant set of facts continues to change, and this pluralism of representational possibilities accommodates the postmodern thesis. Counterintuitively, the truly infinite representational possibilities guarantee the opposite conclusion and assist in alleviating Arnheim's anxieties. Because we can never expect the visual presentation of a Thorpian work to be identical on a computer screen in Moscow and an iPhone in San Diego, we cannot draw meaningful conclusions about duplication. One must, therefore, look elsewhere for conceptual inspiration. The most likely candidate is found in a digital location that produces the imagery. If the question of convention still has to be solved, it cannot be solved based on visual impressions alone.

Borges's Menard, the copyist who wasn't, deserves reconsideration because Borges essentially wanted to undermine the notion that evaluating the content of a forgery or the work of a plagiarist did not extend beyond the allographic letters on the page as Goodman suggested. In the digital copy, the duplication is irrelevant because it is a necessary function of the digital world that everything can be repeated *ad nauseam*. An author who carefully rewrote the work of a predecessor would be in limbo if that predecessor had written a digitally born work; he could not be said to copy the original because the digital substrate was designed to do this already. The digital repetition would already be taking place in any number of social contexts, so Menard's activity would be redundant. The digital Menard would have to find another way to manipulate the original text, and this other way might involve looking below the visual surface and then exploring the digital substrate where the manipulation happened.

Much of the current complexity is a function of the digital world being dependent upon reproduction, or better said repetition (and not in Walter Benjamin's way, where reproduction was a matter of choice, not design). If Arnheim casts duplication in a web of philosophical problems, reproduction/repetition is a form of oxygen for the digital world; it cannot live without continually reproducing whatever it comes across. This is not a matter of convention because it underlies the actual creation of the object, rather than the social circumstances of those who evaluate the object for its authenticity or originality. The digital duplication is an essential act of survival. Our understanding of forgery has to be done with an appreciation of this transition. Therefore, Goodman's and Borges's examples have to adjust.

Repetition helps to disclose artistic traits in a digital piece. Not all digital works will necessarily reveal the repetition at the surface, but when they do, the expert can explore the context of these emergent symmetries that are associated with repetition. This notion is compelling because the repetition one can visually identify, such as in Thorp's piece, is the structure of the digital substrate forcing itself into view. It reflects a methodological rather than substantive correspondence insofar as one will never see bytes or even traces of a programming language, but the principle of repetition, common to both the programming language and the picture, can be recognized. Again, this does not imply that both operate on the same layer, as was seen with digital time, but for a moment one gains a sense of where they overlap. In this bitty world, the specialist must be able to recognize symmetries that come from repetition as well as the irregularities that so fascinated Morelli.

Of course, if the connoisseur managed to get below all these levels, what would she be hoping to demonstrate? Morelli wanted a method to prove that he could identify authorship of a painting and prevent any potential van Meegeren from duping the professional community. But would a digital connoisseur have the same concern? Walter Benjamin, whose ideas on authenticity appeared earlier, made light of the idea of the original and deemed it little more than the quirkish fascination of a commodity-based society. With a digital forgery, the process of identification deals with fixing the original spot, the coordinates, from whence the artwork came in the digital world; thereafter one can look below the surface for digital stylistic traits. The identification of an actual author associated with the original is not always necessary.

The most complicated identification techniques come from algorithms designed to detect modification in digital sources; they might not find the original but they can tell whether an image has been manipulated. Since an algorithm does not have eyes, the techniques do not involve looking (for example, it would not reduce a pointillist painting to the tiny individual points; it would never *see* the points). This is not anti-ocularism but a natural outcome of the algorithm's tendency towards mathematics. Techniques to analyze forged digital imagery differ, and this pluralism is reflected in the chosen mathematical modeling. In general, they pull the image apart into smaller pieces and then search for irregularities in the arrangement of pixels. The program can detect where the image has been altered. The process sounds easy, but, as expected, there is a running battle between sophisticated forgers and the programmers trying to catch them.

The sophistication of these efforts has also tempted researchers to develop programs that identify aesthetic originality in art; these efforts ask questions about traditional artworks but lead into digital questions. The Digital Humanities Laboratory at Rutgers University has a project to link Art and Artificial Intelligence (this laboratory is digital first and humanities second).[13] Forgeries do not sit at the heart of its enterprise, but in trying to identify originality, it addresses analogous issues. Computer scientists ran an analysis on 1,700 paintings that had been entered into a database using computer vision. The computer scientists wanted to evaluate which paintings were the most creative in their time because creativity emphasizes "the originality of the product."[14] They ran an algorithm and tested how their results lined up with the general consensus of art historians, hoping to make the point that Artificial Intelligence had a valid role to play in judging artistic production. Not surprisingly, art historians either objected to or completely ignored the findings.[15]

Alternatively, the leaders of the project could have applied the program to 1,700 known forgeries without instructing the algorithm that they were looking at forgeries—would the algorithm still make claims about forgeries? If the van Meegeren was thrown in amongst the Vermeers, would it have a way to distinguish between the two? Or would it, contrary to the generally accepted view of art historians, claim that they both embodied originality? If it had no way of discerning the original from a forgery, it would gain the reputation of a duped connoisseur.

The laboratory's search for originality has been designed with traditional media in mind, but what would it mean for their software programs to identify a forgery with digitally born materials? The methods are intriguing because they show how a computer scientist can dissect a painting, but the traditional process is easier to conceptualize because the forgery of paintings has such a long history. In the digitally born case, the program could identify originality (and the consequent ability to identify a forgery) with respect to the public reception of a digitally born graphic; but at some point, it would have to turn to its own methods, that is the world of software, to evaluate the artist's creative capabilities. The expert evaluation would depend not just upon key clues from art historians; it would need individuals familiar with the software artists used to create the artwork. In essence, it pulls the actual evaluation deeper into the digital laboratory because the artists' tools are technological in a way the paintbrush was not.

Once the laboratory decided to examine the authenticity of a work (even if the work was aesthetically original), it would have to evaluate digital conventions so that it understood how these conventions had been manipulated to produce a digital artwork that had been falsely attributed. The exercise is essential but hard to grasp, because it seems too obvious yet too far removed from the visual stimulus of the work itself, whose aesthetic appeal should have the final say. The digital forgery has a layer that lies beyond the experiential, and the layer plays its own critical role because it demonstrates how the act of forging in the digital world requires tools other than a trained aesthetic eye.

For at least a century, connoisseurship has been more than just an autopsy in the Greek sense of *autoptes* or eyewitness. The artistry of identification did not stop with Morelli's sophisticated visual evaluation; it came to include all sorts of scientific assistants. The most obvious instances involve an appeal to chemists who could evaluate the chemical composition of paintings and sculptures to date them more accurately and match them with the materials of known originals. The digital appeal to the hard sciences as a testing partner is no different in this regard, but the invitation is to a specific branch of the hard sciences, namely mathematics. If we remember, when Auguste Comte developed his hierarchy of positive knowledge, mathematics was at the top of his program. In other words, the digital partners called upon to solve mysteries of forgery, to ensure the preservation of artistic truth, will be steeped in the skills of nineteenth-century positivists. This transition does not have to be accepted, but it does have to be recognized, since it is a natural outcome of the production of artistry and graphics in the digital universe.

At some point, one might even begin to question whether forgery in a digital context makes any sense at all. Since the digital world is a little unreal, it would be easy to claim that in a digital world premised on repetition, the false recreation of an existing reality is an oxymoron. The more substantive objection concerns the ability of digital procedures to eradicate the aesthetic component in the construction of the artwork. The forger has no aesthetic input into the artificial masterpiece and simply has the good sense to arrange a series of bits and bytes to recreate the original visual stimulus. If the forger did no more than play with the software as did the original artist with the computer-produced image, then that is all it takes to make the forgery successful.

The process is fundamentally different from van Meegeren's. Van Meegeren was an effective forger because he had extensive experience with painting in an older style and understood the paints with which he worked. When van Meegeren set out to copy the Vermeers, he first had to study the composition of seventeenth-century paintings and develop formulas for the paint that were based on raw materials of the age. He understood that the texture, odor, and aging process inherent in these materials would be looked at closely by anyone testing the painting's authenticity. Van Meegeren had to paint a painting that looked like a Vermeer because he could have used the same materials to create a Paulus Potter or a Dirck Hals (in the 1920s, art critics had already commented that his honestly self-identified paintings resembled those of the old masters).

In a comparative perspective, the software is the paint, the texture and the odor of which the forger has to be aware. The forger could be said to understand the conventions of software design as the effective source of the forgery. This has a parallel with Borges's example insofar as the discernible and external aspects of the work of art do not constitute its entire meaning. Borges showed how Menard maintained his originality although he copied Cervantes word for word. Borges was telling his readers that before we passed judgment on Menard, we needed to look at his typewriter, his desk, his stool, his studio, and the windows to the outside. The same applies to the process of digital forgery. Before fixating on the imagery, more needs to be known of the computer, of the software, of the keypad, and of the math that helped create the symmetries that pour onto the screen. Menard and the digital forger have something in common, though they might seem worlds apart.

The example can be pushed a step further because the digital piece can exist without it ever being looked upon; a copy could be made that sits latently below the surface. Its component parts can be in place and readily available without it ever being called upon to manifest itself. This represents an awkward circumstance because it depends upon a potential realization rather than an actual sighting; yet once its footprint is clear in the digital world, it would make no sense to say it does not exist. The Thorp imagery may never be called up again, and yet it would linger, waiting to be recomposed (almost like a microbe waiting to find a host). The same cannot be said of an oil painting, which does not exist as anything but the sum of materials and human actions that went to compose it. Furthermore, there will never be an exact latent state for the digital image because it does not have to be preserved in an exact format to emerge as that exact image.

For all these recent innovations and discombobulations, traditional problems have not disappeared. The distinction between digitized and digitally born forgeries can render more clarity. For example, one might have a digital photograph extracted from a traditional negative of a Parisian street scene from the 1840s. A responsible curator would demand to see the original rather than accept the scanned version as evidence. But what would happen if all the negatives had burned and the curator had no more than the digital scan? In this instance, the connoisseur could evaluate the visual clues of the digital remnant, just like Morelli did in the nineteenth century. They could identify both objects in the photograph as well as the style of the photographer to the degree that both these elements could be evaluated. This process could also check the timing, location, and composition of the digital scan to determine its position in the digital universe. All these tags would pinpoint its production to a unique digital time and place from whence one could draw more conclusions about irregularities in its potential creation. Here the digital process is more of a tool than anything else.

A situation can be also imagined in which the digital record disappears and researchers are left with only a few scattered printouts. For example, online dating services such as Yahoo! Personals allowed strangers to establish digital connections and build an extensive e-mail correspondence. As a memento, the digital correspondence could have been printed out in two thick volumes to celebrate a first anniversary only to have the digital version lost forever as Yahoo! changed conditions, servers disappeared, or passwords were lost. Only the printout of the digital record could now be identified; all the digital encoding and tags were no longer available, and one only had recourse to traditional methods—how could future generations be sure that a letter had not been inserted by a lover to shift researchers' interpretation of that famous correspondence? Traditional methods would suffice in this instance.

The photographic and textual forgery examples should not be confused with the contemporary fake news phenomenon. The digital world has played an instrumental role in spreading fake news, but the digital underworld is rarely the source of these stories. Most incidents of fake news involve flesh-and-blood characters whose actions have been cast in doubt. When the Russian Ministry of Foreign Affairs stamps a document with "Fake News" and uploads it to its website, they are contesting the account of events of something that first happened in the analog world. The veracity of the story is not lodged in bits and bytes, and the doubt manufactured by the stamp is akin to the doubt bred by eyewitnesses of a car crash giving contradictory stories.

Obviously, permutations and combinations could be made endlessly, and then they would amount to little more than imaginative distractions. The focus should pull all these examples together to better understand where postmodern premises intersect with a meaningful handful of transformations. At the outset, it was clear that the inability to identify a forgery could promote postmodern claims about conventional knowledge, but, as seen, the identification of a digital forgery transcends the human activities envisioned at the time of Arnheim and his contemporaries. Digital forgeries do not eliminate talk of conventions since the uniformity of the digital world should not be exaggerated; yet the conventions are active on an altogether different platform and therefore the mere mention of convention does not in and of itself resuscitate postmodern theses. Instead, these conventions operate at another layer, a layer asynchronous with the aesthetics of the graphic but interlocked with it nonetheless.

The nature of these conventions is the central component because so much has changed since Levine 'copied' Walker Evans's photographs; a similar performance in a digital environment where copies are taken for granted would be met with skepticism. Since the digital world is premised upon endless copies generated anywhere out of nothing, toying with a copy has lost its conceptual edge. Levine, the artist, would be expected to do much more than just photograph a photograph. Taking a screen shot of a digital work and casting it off as her own would impress no one. The casual viewer would not see the point, and the philosopher of art would not recognize a challenge to established norms. Levine's exhibition was meant to challenge accepted definitions about beauty and the artistic process. The screen shot could disrupt visual etiquette, yet it would still say nothing about the digital conventions that lay underneath. As long as one left those conventions alone, one could not afford a bold conceptual statement. But to ignore the digital conventions would undermine Levine's own method, which was to say the value of art lies not just in the physical art itself (this was Borges's point as well). One would thus have an obligation to pursue a deeper investigation into the digital conventions.

The point has already been made that these conventions are steeped in a world of mathematics foreign to the traditions of the art world. The mathematical convention does not parallel the visual or artistic convention and has its own foundation. One could recreate a Walker Evans photograph without ever having seen it, if all one had was the digital file based upon a scan; the philosophical outcome would be completely different and could more easily be used to elaborate on positivist rather than postmodern principles. The essential point, however, is not the existence of a convention but the establishment of a relationship between the digital convention and the output as a graphic or other stimulus on the screen. Similar to the comparison between the algorithmic and common language, the two conventions operate separately and therefore do not influence each other on a one-to-one basis, though the visual representation has its fate tied to the digital world below. The pluralism inherent in digital reproductions and repetitions therefore should not be seen as a postmodern victory because the digital reproduction relies on the binaries discussed in previous chapters. This repeats the paradox apparent in so many discussions: the surface of the digital world embodies pluralism, whereas its substrate has a strange uniformity to it.

After all that has been said, the skeptic might well argue that little is to be learned from digital forgeries. On the one hand, the inherent repetitive capacity of digital technologies places us squarely in a post-forgery age. The connoisseur is unnecessary not because the creative means of artistic production have changed, but because identifying forgeries serves no purpose. On the other hand, if we were to continue to accept the persistence of forgeries, they have become so mired in a sea of conflicting conventions, we would hardly make a step forward by trying to disentangle this web. This chapter serves as appropriate evidence because it does more to define the peculiarities of digital forgeries than it does to establish a recipe for identifying them should one pop up.

Yet the potential of digital forgeries does so much more than separate true genius from the copyist. The investigation of forgery ceases to be a mere philosophical exercise, because it has added a mathematical dimension; somewhere within all that math lie hidden keys to the question of forgery. Humanists who might be seeking a return to the days of Morelli should not be alarmed, because in the days of Morelli, art connoisseurs had access to scientists and did not resist their input. Consulting a programmer follows in this tradition. The study of digital forgeries should be considered a boon rather than a burden for the curious mind because it transcends single disciplines. So many of the forgery examples developed by analytic philosophers depend upon logical analogies; the analogies have imaginative scenarios, but they reduce visual or literary aesthetics to an afterthought. Borges's story of Menard is fascinating, but it bypasses literary alternatives with its focus on identity. Levine did not establish a logical parallel in the spirit of analytic philosophy, but the simple act of photographing the original reduced the issue of forgery to identity politics; it could not go beyond the question of comparing two identical things. In contrast, digital forgeries have separate layers, so the ultimate question of forgery cannot be reduced to comparing two identical visual and textual representations and then using the comparison to make statements about truths and conventions; it requires the mastery of skills that might seem unusual for the humanist. It adds a devilish challenge, to be sure, but one which humanists should welcome. Coming to terms with digital forgery requires incredibly creative activity, though the creativity might be just a touch less than in the original.

Notes

1. Rudolf Arnheim, "On Duplication," in *The Forger's Art: Forgery and the Philosophy of Art*, ed. Denis Dutton (Berkeley: University of California Press, 1983), 234.
2. Thierry Lenain, *Art Forgery: The History of a Modern Obsession* (London: Reaktion Books, 2011), 8.
3. See Arthur C. Danto, *After the End of Art: Contemporary Art and the Pale of History*, The A.W. Mellon Lectures in the Fine Arts 1995 (Princeton, NJ: Princeton University Press, 1997), 209–10.
4. Stephen Eric Bronner, *A Rumor About the Jews: Antisemitism, Conspiracy, and the Protocols of Zion* (Oxford and New York: Oxford University Press, 2003).
5. Nelson Goodman differentiates between forgery in the different arts. See Nelson Goodman, "Art and Authenticity," in *The Forger's Art: Forgery and the Philosophy of Art*, ed. Denis Dutton (Berkeley: University of California Press, 1983).
6. Jorge Luis Borges, "Pierre Menard, Author of the Quixote," in *Collected Fictions* (New York, NY: Viking, 1998). This is taken up in Danto, *The Transfiguration of the Commonplace*, 33–36. See also Monroe C. Beardsley, "Notes on Forgery," in *The Forger's Art: Forgery and the Philosophy of Art*, ed. Denis Dutton (Berkeley: University of California Press, 1983).
7. Ginzburg, "Clues: Roots of an Evidential Paradigm."
8. See Mark Ruwedel, *Westward: The Course of Empire* (New Haven, CT: Yale University Art Gallery: Distributed by Yale University Press, 2008).
9. Arthur Conan Doyle, "Speckled Band," in *Sherlock Holmes: The Major Stories With Contemporary Critical Essays*, ed. John A. Hodgson (Boston: Bedford Books of St. Martin Press, 1994), 152–73.
10. Arthur Conan Doyle, *The Sign of Four* (New York: Quality Paperback Book Club, 1994), 10.
11. In the 1980s and 1990s, any intermediary was accused of being designed to return the appropriate measurement; a measurement device such as a microscope was not merely an objective eyeball. The magnifying glass in this version skews reality.
12. Rudolf Arnheim, "On Duplication," in *The Forger's Art: Forgery and the Philosophy of Art*, ed. Denis Dutton (Berkeley: University of California Press, 1983), 234.

13. https://sites.google.com/site/digihumanlab/home.
14. Ahmed Elgammal, "Which Paintings Were the Most Creative of Their Time? An Algorithm May Hold the Answers," *The Conversation*, July 30, 2015, https://theconversation.com/which-paintings-were-the-most-creative-of-their-time-an-algorithm-may-hold-the-answers-43157.
15. Ahmed Elgammal, "Computer Science Can Only Help—Not Hurt—Art Historians," *The Conversation*, December 4, 2014, https://theconversation.com/computer-science-can-only-help-not-hurt-art-historians-33780.

10 Conclusion

A primary goal of this entire narrative has been to identify the weaknesses of two contemporary tendencies, the first silently leading into the next. Underlying each and every example has been the premise that digital technologies cannot be treated as mere tools or nothing more than advanced research assistants. Digital techniques cannot be drawn from a toolbox, help with a task, and then thrown back in the toolbox to be forgotten until needed again; they have a fundamental interpretive impulse. Since they can change the interpretive heading in the humanities, they necessarily impact common assumptions about postmodernism. Many commentators have insisted on presenting postmodernism as a viable and static alternative to digital techniques precisely because they look upon these techniques as mere tools. They do not take the time to explore how the building blocks of these technologies challenge the reliability of traditional postmodern theses.

The humanities have grappled with technological change for centuries; the current dilemma thus echoes the past. Over the years, humanists have embraced technologies for their functional qualities, whereas others have found deeper philosophical meaning in them. The Gutenberg printing press of the fifteenth century has been celebrated as a functional achievement because it allowed Protestants to publish unheard-of quantities of pamphlets, but the moveable type press had a direct impact on the content of writing and hence of worldviews. In nineteenth-century Europe, the train became a living metaphor for the hustle and bustle of industrial society, but for Einstein, it had a theoretical quality. In his accessible writings on relativity, he explained time frames based upon the experience of train travel. The functional engineering of the train faded in face of the relationship between the train voyager and the passage of time. Postmodernists probably paid less attention to the train, but they were influenced by Einstein and thus, if only indirectly, transformed a technological and scientific advancement into a philosophical idea that transcended the specific functionality of that achievement. These are the most innocent ways to say, with little fanfare, that one cannot treat digital aids as mere tools, for the impact is far deeper.

The moment one accepts that technology is more than a tool, one must be ready to re-evaluate basic premises, for otherwise stagnation is the only option. The optimist has an opportunity because she can take advantage of this unexpected consequence to emphasize more methodological diversity. The advent of digital technologies did not expressly target postmodern belief, like Copernicus's heliocentric model did not target the Catholic Church, but it introduced a methodological shift that cannot be dismissed simply because it is perceived as a peripheral tool. Since these unprecedented technologies emerged so unexpectedly, one can be forgiven for not having anticipated all the changes they bring with them. Time will, of course, be less forgiving to those who ignore them.

A fundamental shift in attitude affects not only postmodernism. Other candidates across the spectrum are ripe for change. Within the sciences, entire sub-disciplines might disappear to make way for new pursuits; academic disciplines might start to look like the Mos Eisley cantina in the first Star Wars film with its mix of ill-defined characters. Who can possibly tell what lies around the corner? The real hope expressed in this work is that we embrace the novelty. There is no shame in recognizing the inevitability of change.

No movement needs greater change to be awoken from its torpor than the linguistic turn. Generation upon generation of scholars have done its bidding, and it would run out of energy even without digital technologies. It originally functioned to free scholars from a universalizing metaphysics but then evolved into its own universalizing force. Martin Jay's recent assertion about needing a new language to describe the senses, nothing more than an academic conceit, shows how difficult it is to free ourselves from that turn. Jay's assertion is just a modified version of the question 'Does a tree make noise if no one is there to hear it?' His Derridaean version is something like 'Does a fart smell only if an academic writes about it?' This does not make complete sense.

Over time, plenty of alternatives have surfaced. As evident in the chapter on language, it should be clear that choices can be made. From within the philosophy of language, Wittgenstein posited examples that had no purchase on language. From without, R. Murray Schafer stressed the independence of sounds. These claims were made by individuals unconnected to the digital world. They stress the point that there resolutely is an *hors texte* and life outside of grammar. This message should be heeded even by those who have no interest in gazing over the digital landscape.

Once one takes the digital world into consideration, the changes become more dramatic. Whether the lessons are drawn from algorithms, time or data visuals, the linguistic turn cannot remain the same. Algorithms and their kin will not wipe out French grammar, but they act with such forceful independence, their fates are not tied to language. Erwig's introduction to algorithms highlights the tortured path one takes when one insists on linking the two; irregularities pop up all along the way. The 'grammar' of the algorithmic language has no match in the tenses and aspects of the grammar in this sentence. As such, the grammar of this sentence cannot limit the algorithm. In contrast, the algorithmic language can reflect the structure of the ordinary language over time. It can steer translation to favor certain locutions and indirectly enter into the vernacular; it is not just a word or phrase, but it includes a logic born within the algorithm. This is a complex environment with a massive impact that transcends the ambitions of twentieth-century discourse theorists. None of this implies that language is unworthy of investigation; it still is, but not in the way we thought.

Linguistic limitations were seen elsewhere as well. Timekeeping in the digital world has no relationship with grammatical time yet exerts an influence every bit as large. Verb tenses and aspect, a subject that received quite a bit of attention, are absent in digital time. Although most proponents of the linguistic turn have conveniently ignored verb tenses in favor of individual words, this omission cannot be used as an excuse to dismiss their absence in digital time. Their absence disengages digital time from the linguistic turn, though this may have been a completely unintentional consequence.

Data visuals exist in the same category; the emergence of this digital tool was not designed to impact the linguistic turn but, because of its dominant role, cannot do otherwise. Scholars can choose to revive an age-old debate about the relationship between words and images, but data visuals are so much more complex than a label on a photograph. They represent a vast world of secondary materials and are able to intertwine this data with aesthetic perspectives that don't go anywhere near linguistic representations. Although data visuals combine letters to make words and expressions, these hardly limit its expressive possibilities. Instead, they are visual treats worthy of ocular celebration and highlight the futility of subjecting all experience to linguistic analysis.

The shifting nature of theory in the data world is no less significant. The building blocks of conceptualization are distinct from the postmodern period, when the concepts were drawn not from data but from fragmentary sources and designed to undermine empirical claims. Now the situation has changed at two levels. First, the theories will emerge in relation to large data sets. The rather casual dismissal of these empirical sources will become increasingly difficult, thus theories will be tied to information generated in large quantities. Second, the human role in theorizing will continue to be debated as scholars vacillate between the simple identification of data trends and a continued insistence on a pure, human-based conceptualization.

These debates have an ongoing impact across all fields of critical inquiry. It is ill-advised to return to the linguistic turn of the 1960s, but one cannot return to the positivism of the 1840s. A modified positivism (and positivism has been modified since its inception) is clearly on the agenda and gaining momentum, though not necessarily with that name. As the discussion which began with Comte suggested, the data world has many commonalities with the Frenchman's aspirations: its subtle disdain of abstraction and the pursuit of general but not universal laws. It undermines the ambition of scholars from Dilthey to Derrida who made passionate pleas to see beyond what they portrayed as straightforward observational analyses.

These post-positivists could not envision the diversity and dynamism of the new empirical world and, in fact, neither could Comte. The data is not just about numbers and quantities, nor is it necessarily observational; as the example with Google Maps indicated, even though one is seeing something, vision is not at the core of the problem. The emergence of all this data will not end theory for all time, as might have been hinted at the outset. It must, however, end theory in the constricted form in which it survives today. Theory has been surrounded by such a cloud of relativism that its definition has become increasingly narrow. The restricted field of operation is an issue but, fortunately, the digital creation of data will be instrumental in expanding that field. It is unavoidable that the expansion will contain positivist elements, but it will encompass a liberating moment that lurches forward.

The digital world introduces many aspects that resist qualification with traditional theories. In the data world, repetition is also a novelty because it transcends the single user, is the lifeline of any data analysis, and generates complex composite images that cannot always be reduced to their parts. Developing an approach that befriends repetition has to be contemplated. In the spirit of Comte, theorists will be able to leave the fine-tuned technical work to sub-disciplines while they seek out laws that link separate fields. These theorists will accept postulations supervalent upon the data world and will, as time moves on, have to define how they interact with the data without seeking to undermine it.

None of this suggests that a theory based on massive data cannot be criticized. As mentioned, the senses have an awkward position in this world, though no more awkward than when they were treated as discursive phenomena; here a corrective is required that extends well beyond digital concerns. One will always have the feeling that the data world lacks a real third dimension to give it body, but then most traditional scholarly interactions were textual and lacked the third dimension as well. The moment a lack or gap is mentioned, the relativist can peddle uncertainty. As long as this uncertainty guards against technological hubris, it can play a healthy role because it will ensure that the wealth of data will neither constrain interpretation nor serve up uncontestable conclusions. If it just takes us back to where we began, either an antiquated positivism or a dilapidated postmodernism, then it serves no proper purpose. Theory will only run into a bottleneck if it insists on preserving the purity of either side. Otherwise, it can comfortably become the herald of versatility.

The diversity of digital experience will not come from standard postmodern theories or attitudes. The diversity will be much more closely aligned with the layered quality of the digital structure, an explanatory means that has popped up over and over again. These layers are an unexpected consequence of sorting out the different functional areas of the digital world. Once algorithms are looked at separately from digital time, the layers slowly start to crystallize. It becomes important to understand how they operate and how they intersect with each other. The layer of the algorithmic language has no immediate connection with the outside layer of the common language it produces, but the layer of time in the algorithmic language often shares the layer of an external digital time. The traits of each layer have to be clearly understood, for otherwise they will be quickly mixed together and their characteristics lost.

The layering is a fascinating phenomenon because it allows a look at the data world through a different lens, like choosing to explain the composition of the world from the perspective of a chemist, physicist, or biologist. It takes the pure functionality out of the discussion, a real concern in the humanities, and stresses diversity without doing so on a scientific level. That is to say, rather than explaining the algorithm and data storage with increasingly complex mathematics, the complexity can be appreciated through the discovery of the relationship between all these layers. The humanist can then position the layers relative to each other and add to analyses that most often adhere to the functionality of algorithms, data, or whatever digital capacity has been discovered. All the single segments in which Big Data played a role made an effort to define the nature of those layers. With the data visuals, the aesthetic came as a function of representation built upon the data that also had its own algorithmic and time layers.

Talk of layers should not be used to induce a discussion on new epistemologies; a fundamental tenet of postmodernism was to cast any additional knowledge as an epistemology, and thus the word frequently appeared in the plural. The plural of the digital layer does not create new networks of knowledge because it is a relationship between pieces of data rather than a statement about the data itself. The layer is not the knowledge (and it would be a step backward to force the layers into a postmodern knowledge template) but a section of the digital world that is at an angle with other sections. Each layer contributes to our perception of the digital output, but it is not a knowledge producer. A layer can determine the position of time, but this does not yet tell us what we know. The best approach is to put aside the term epistemological, an act of practical and linguistic freedom, and seek out other layers that can be said to be the building blocks of the digital world.

This rings especially true with algorithms. An algorithm is not another epistemology, especially since it is composed in mathematical languages few humanists can understand. This sweeping generalization would obscure the component parts of the algorithm of interest to humanists. Exploring the layer at which decisions are made confronts this tendency towards generalization. It had become a mantra of the postmodern movement to reveal binaries in the real world; the impetus became so strong that scholars occasionally had to force historical and social actors into a binary to prove the degenerative effect of painting the world in binary terms. With the algorithms, the quest for binaries has no purpose because binaries are at the core of the decision-making process; they are there and make a real and immediate impact. This does not mean that our decisions, such as buying bread or searching for a book, are based solely on binary principles; but that these decision-makers, all around us, play a part in our own selections. Humanists will have to reference binaries but not in the epistemological format of yesteryear. Not only will we come to a better understanding of a tool that is regularly used, but it will also force a dramatic reassessment of a term that lies at the foundation of an older generation of philosophy.

Another layer involves the intersection, or lack thereof, between the language of the algorithm and natural languages. In a continued effort to eliminate the universalizing aspects of the linguistic turn, the rather rigid border between the language of the algorithm and of a natural language was brought to the fore. The two sides cannot be translated back and forth between each other without something giving. With Google Translate, a third party in an awkward discussion, the situation is even more complicated since standard attitudes to translation are disrupted. Revealing these linguistic layers prevented facile references to metaphors and other classic grammatical components, thus offering the algorithm much greater independence. Exploring this power of binary decision-making and its impact on language will guarantee that we can reissue anniversary volumes of the postmodernists without pretending they were published yesterday. When done properly, the binary investigation won't recreate the artificial oppositions postmodernists did so much to expose. Instead, it encourages reconciliation with ideas that seem hopelessly opposed: how can an on/off switch be the source of such diversity? We have been taught to answer "it can't," but it actually does.

The broader investigation on algorithms permitted an exploration of an environment in which the linguistic turn did not dominate. When the discussion shifted away from the linguistic turn, comments on postmodernism naturally became sparser as digital issues loomed larger. In particular, a series of topics associated with the production of massive amounts of well-ordered data took center stage. Digital space was a natural launching point because Big Data is so immense and yet seems to occupy no space at all, a rather compelling philosophical conundrum. Exploring the intricacies of this riddle led the discussion beyond the quantitative aspects of Big Data and immersed all this information into a framework close to the hearts of humanists.

The Wayback Machine embodies the conundrum because it hovers between the real and the digital worlds. This practical search engine brought two important qualities of Big Data to the fore. Although all digital information has to be stored somewhere, the Wayback Machine had the task of storing information that had never occupied any space. Focused on websites stuck in two dimensions, it did not touch upon objects outside the screen. A corollary to its spacelessness was the lack of aging associated with the stored information. Unlike museum objects, the digital information captured by the Wayback Machine could be refreshed *ad nauseam*; it would not experience the process of decay familiar to mere mortals. Technologies can change, the information may become inaccessible and disappear over time, but it could not be said to decay. For this reason, the Wayback Machine is an ideal vehicle for explaining why Big Data necessarily evokes new conceptualizations of space and objects in space.

The emergence of Big Data gives credence to the idea that the nature of factuality is always changing; the immutable fact is mutable because it can be broken down, reconstructed, and then repurposed at will. The fact has more flexibility than ever, but the facts are not simply social constructions because a large portion of this knowledge production never intersects with society at all. It is quietly collected, processed, and on occasion manifests itself at a visible surface. The asocial component of Big Data has to do with its spatial limitations; for the most part, it occupies hardly any space at all, and therefore its reconstruction depends upon less familiar factors. As it grows in size and becomes the dominant form of knowledge, philosophers will have to reassess the precise relationship with this dynamic digital knowledge.

The philosophical challenge was to understand Big Data without losing sight of its inherent incompleteness. In addition to the Wayback Machine, the discussion explored the relationship between Big Data and Little Data. Little Data, as a concept, was introduced to preserve a place for traditional materials and then explore their interaction with Big Data. The mere recognition that Little Data will persist does not define how it will persist in this digital environment. A strategy was developed to avoid falling in a trap in which all alternatives to Big Data were considered local knowledge. The GIS approach to mapping had to be scrutinized because it tends to insist on positioning the local against the universal pretensions of a quantitative method. Since the GIS examples isolated two sides, it necessarily equated Little Data with local knowledge and was unable to qualify the interaction between Little Data and Big Data. In contrast, recognizing the interaction allowed a sober perspective on the nature of the digital substrate. The spaceless digital world impinged on experience in ways that cannot be explained with a hammer and hoe; more work has to be invested to clarify that relationship. The humanist, who is ideally positioned to assert the relevance of Little Data in all the non-digital worlds of experience, must continue to make every effort to define the relationship between Big and Little Data. This endeavor will take time, but a successful solution can accommodate a more rugged position for the humanities in a technological world; it will permit humanists to set terms for the debate that keep pace with technologies.

Big Data is perceived as the collection of facts or statistics, but it also carries a significant temporal component, referred to previously as digital time. Digital time deserved its own discussion to prevent it, like so many other things, from being overwhelmed by Big Data, but also because it can be extracted as an identifiable and independent component of Big Data. Digital time is clearly a social phenomenon insofar as it was born in a digital age. Yet digital time transcends particularism and has no effective room for temporal islands. Consequently, one has to treat digital time as more than a marker or a reading from a stopwatch; it is no mere functional tool to tell historians the exact order of events. At times invisible, it moves smoothly from one layer of the digital world to another. It also pulls words or experiences from one temporal environment into the next, tagging actions with time markers situated in the same grid. Each item can therefore carry an infinite number of time experiences on its back, though the clockmaker for all those experiences remains the same.

Herein lies the circle for the humanist to square. Digital time presents a departure from a smooth Bergsonian duration and Elias's concept of time as a series of social relationships. Instead, it has a regulated and scientific component in keeping with the structure of the databases and the algorithms. It also transforms time into discrete fragmented elements because fragmentation in the form of tagging is at the heart of its enterprise. Intuitively, the humanist would prefer a world of duration; but time is increasingly experienced according to digital rules, and humanists will not be able to superimpose a twentieth-century understanding of time on human subjects of the twenty-first century whose actions occur within a digital time grid. The digital flâneur is a temporal concept unique to our own age. Humanists have to understand how the placement of an item in the digital world has a direct temporal impact on that item. The impact is determined by parameters of digital time, which will often appear too rigid and scientific.

Does digital time put all the ebb and flow of humanistic experience at risk? Fortunately, not all experience will be reduced to digital time. It will always be possible to read the *Aeneid* in a paperback or leave the device at home and take a stroll through the streets of Paris. Alternatives will persist, though these alternatives should not be used as an excuse to ignore digital time altogether; it now plays a significant role in experience.

It has to be analyzed with a spirit that looks beyond weak attempts to emasculate it with references to social construction. Since digital time will not eliminate a raw experiential time, humanists can explore the border zones where the two meet and seek to understand what happens at these rupture points. Close attention to these intersections will give further clarity to conceptions of digital time, while comforting humanists that scientific models have not usurped time and done away with a topsy-turvy temporal existence. Yet to fully understand these border zones, no effort can be spared to conceptualize the significance of digital time; this task cannot be left to others outside the humanities.

It will come as no surprise that the data visuals follow a recognizable pattern: the data world comes into contact with the aesthetic aspirations of a force that lies outside it yet must work with it. The data visuals therefore awaken a potential for the humanist to perform as a craftsman in the digital world. The data visuals are clearly dependent on information designed according to the principles of Big Data and would be completely ineffective if they simply dismissed the data they were supposed to represent—the data visuals cannot escape the logic of the algorithm in this sense. They can, however, build upon that foundation and establish aesthetic rules worthy of philosophical investigation. The humanist will find himself tied to the data, can use the data for interpretation, but can also add unique color and style elements that don't come from the data world. The interplay of the two establishes pathways for unexpected discoveries without falling into the trap of having to undermine the facticity of the original data to assert the effectiveness of the aesthetic.

In contrast to digital time, data visuals are not unique to the digital environment. They build on traditions that go back to at least the nineteenth century, and these traditions will continue to shape the imagery we use to understand Big Data. The novelty of the digital environment rests more in the size of the data, the ability of users to customize graphics, and the kinetic or moving qualities of the visualizations. They do not need to stay put and, rather than resting static, can move and adapt. This movement satisfies a basic premise of postmodernism, a world in flux, but the movement draws from a constant source, one that adheres to the parameters that define Big Data.

If there is another novelty to data visuals, it is their growing ubiquity. As noted, Peter Burke lamented the lack of imagery in historical writing, but when he published his thoughts he could not have foreseen that the inclusion of imagery would be based on data. He was thinking more of photographs and paintings rather than the data visuals discussed earlier. But as postmodernism opened ways to conceptualize art independent of scholastic and studio definitions of the nineteenth century, it should not be a problem to accept data visuals as an art form. And here is an example where scholars can use postmodernism as a powerful springboard to jump into a domain that does not follow in the postmodern tradition.

Moreover, data visuals have to be seen within the context of the recent visual revolution. The work at hand had to focus on data visuals because of their relation to databases, but they also belong in a discussion about the expanding role of visuals embodied in platforms such as YouTube. All the recent forms of mass visual stimuli, building on the tradition of film, photography, and television, have changed our acquisition of information. The act of reading language has been dramatically reduced as the visual format has become the first line of interaction.

The penultimate chapter in this volume looked at a more awkward topic, that of digital forgery, to provide a point of contrast with traditional experience in the real world. It was probably the most elusive discussion because characterizing the nature of digital forgery is more complex than showing how to lie with maps. The layer at which the digital forgery operates is different from the thin layer of a Soviet agent retouching a photograph. Furthermore, digital forgeries do not emanate directly from the world of experience, where the issues of originality can be more easily resolved. The means of identification rests in a non-visual layer akin to the carbon dating and the chemical tests used to identify photographic processes in older images. A holistic appreciation of digital forgeries can be accomplished only with a greater understanding of all the ways in which these forgeries are assembled. Humanists don't have to take their own magnifying glass to the programmer's language, but they will have to cooperate with those who do have the right lens to examine irregularities in the digital traces.

Each time a discussion unfolded an aspect of the digital world, cautions were expressed about sticking too closely to the familiar territory of postmodern theory. Imperceptibly, the reader was being urged to reconsider the relationship between the humanities and the sciences. The flood of technological innovation and the power of companies collecting information was an unexpected development in the humanities, at a time when the humanities finally thought it had won a battle against the hard sciences of the eighteenth and nineteenth centuries. Humanists cannot afford to play the Luddites and have to pause to consider where the impact of these technologies begins and where it ends; the interests of the humanist lie somewhere between their beginning and their end. As this narrative draws to a close, the corollary consequences of the digital revolution have to be placed in the widest and broadest framework possible.

As the digital age intensifies, active cooperation with scientific partners will become more frequent, and one can expect to see more names of scientists and humanists next to each other. The complexity of statistical analysis, the writing of sophisticated programming code and similar tasks, cannot be effectively performed by a single person. The interdisciplinarity will become a function of teamwork rather than of a single author's multidisciplinary ambition. This may sound more like an engineering project, but it indicates how the digital age does more than introduce time-saving tools. This assertion has a precedent in the library sciences, another word pair with transformative implications. The cooperation implied in the training of librarians, humanists par excellence, already moves in that direction.

The prevailing winds are pulling the humanities in the direction of the sciences, though the sails have long been set to do otherwise. In some circles, this has been treated as an existential crisis in which the humanists will become the oarsmen while the technocrats captain the ship. The danger is real, but only if humanists react to it in the wrong way. The first step is to look forward with the eyes of those who can build on the conclusions of postmodernism while recognizing their limitations in a technological world. In the 1980s, overcoming postmodernism meant rejecting it in all its aspects. Thirty years later, it is possible to recognize its accomplishments without having to continually repeat its platitudes. As the academic community and society in general move deeper into the digital age, they cannot afford to forget these accomplishments.

When one looks back at these achievements, one should not do so with a fixed stare. Poststructuralism of the 1960s will neither fend off technology nor advance its interests. We do not want to find ourselves in a situation where conceptual thinkers in Paris start debating the disappearance of an *hors digitale*. Humanists have to find that ground of common concern and work together with technologists, programmers, and scientists to advance the interests of the humanities. Flexibility might be the key term, and flexibility will require adding a drop of logic here and a dose of objectivity there. Humanists do not have to accept this as a fait accompli, since they have the skills and training to debate anything, but they simply cannot afford to sweep these terms off the table.

Frequently, technological advancements within the humanities fall under the umbrella heading of the Digital Humanities, a term sparsely used in the preceding pages. Because the movement is so new, advocates have often struggled to define it. Its lack of a concrete definition has become a mantra for its innovative capacities—how could a forever changing movement be straightjacketed with a simple definition? Commentators have proposed their own versions of the Digital Humanities with their particular lists of constitutive characteristics. A postmodernist and an analytic philosopher necessarily read the expression in different ways—one with a more cautious, even frightened mien, the other with open arms. These efforts are admirable, but they obscure the fact that defining the humanities is no less difficult than defining the Digital Humanities; they make it appear as if the adjective, not the noun, is the source of confusion. In the current unsettled state of affairs, defining or exploring what is meant by the humanities is no less important. On the one hand, authors such as Johanna Drucker give the false impression that to be a humanist is to be a postmodernist.[1] The assumption that humanism is postmodernism could not be further from the truth. An author who seeks absolute beauty in nature is no less a humanist, though traveling along what to a postmodernist is a hopeless path.

On the other hand, the position of postmodernism has tended to overlook the functional and technological components of humanism that have never disappeared. Scores of humanists should have no problem with the addition of the adjective *digital*. The adjective incorporates methods that are not identical to past experience but have longstanding family resemblances. The corollary to an equation that places postmodernism on one side and humanism on the other is a convenient ignorance of technical and mathematical components that imbue many humanist works. Arthur Danto, whose works have been richly referenced throughout, never shied away from introducing a logical equation, even in his most artistic writing. Like so many analytic philosophers of his generation, a generation that came of age with continental postmodernism, he was trained in logic. This continued a tradition that included mathematically inclined philosophers such as Ludwig Wittgenstein. These thinkers flirted with or lightly embraced postmodernism, but the rule-based mathematics never went away. Analytic philosophers were not strictly bound to their equations, but a significant portion of their intellectual apparatus used them as guides. If these philosophers felt comfortable sprinkling their writings with equations, why shouldn't the modern humanist do the same with algorithmic language? The use and understanding of algorithms does not have to be much different. Algorithms may be a threat to postmodernism insofar as the logic and decision-making processes embody procedures foreign to it, but they do no more than continue a long tradition of humanist writing, firmly embedded in what was for a long time the center of humanist thought.

Philosophy and philosophers are not the only candidates. Cliometricians found brief mention with their historical analyses, though a doubter may choose to situate them in the social sciences. More traditional historians, as seen, dealt with numbers and data to chart social transformations in cities such as Rochester, New York. They integrated these quantitative analyses with textual stories to interpret a historical situation. Both the quantitative and qualitative interpretive efforts in the study on Rochester form part of age-old humanist methodologies.

One does have an alternative choice, which would be to settle upon a narrow and exclusive definition of the humanities. For example, one could exclude any whiff of logic or attempt that proposes a geometric representation. The humanities will then become a narrow pursuit with the self-serving purpose of promoting a specific worldview, that of the postmodernist, rather than exploring humanity with as expansive a vision as possible. This attitude would end up excluding almost all digital technologies and the concrete humanistic applications that have appeared along the way in this volume.

188 *Conclusion*

In practice, an openness to the digital world is already common. Scores of humanists have recognized the digital potential, and Arts and Science colleges now have full-time positions in areas of digital study. The bulk of the energy, however, is devoted to functional issues, and the methodological consequences do not get sufficient attention. In fact, the functional approach to the digital world mirrors the ambitions of the scientific community and goes too far in that direction; the functional approach is a concession. As an antidote, this narrative has continually tried to push methodological issues in different directions. The pluralism of the discussions, for time and algorithms do not follow linearly from each other, respects the postmodernist desire for diversity. Data visuals, time, and algorithms are interesting to the humanist, but all in their own way. Each vista shores up the confidence of the humanist in a technological world as long as the humanist gazes into the distance with methodological intent.

Hopefully, this is precisely what all the previous chapters have done. In the limited space of a single volume, they have sought to identify aspects of digital culture that are ripe for evaluation and thus ready for re-evaluation within the context of standard procedures. It was not possible, however, to identify every detail on the horizon. Therefore, the secondary aspiration of this work is to encourage further methodological investigation that reveals the true potential of the digital age for the humanist. The only condition placed on this search is that it respects the development of a new identity, one that neighbors the technical world but is neither steered nor defined by it. New worlds remain to be discovered with the same enthusiasm of Chinese explorers who set out on the Indian Ocean centuries ago.

The humanist will never be reduced to bits and bytes and does not yet have to worry about a society reduced to robots. The inner core of human emotions and individual quirks will not go away, and as long as they remain, the humanist will have plenty to explore. To retain their position at the hub of human experience, humanists must never lose sight of those hues, tones, smells, emotions, and all the other constituent pieces of our species. While holding on to this core, they must also delve into the rich world of digital technologies and understand the story that is woven when the two worlds intersect.

The humanist of the 1860s is not the humanist of the 1960s and the humanist of the 1960s is not the humanist of the 2060s. It is hard to imagine what the technological landscape will look like a generation from now, much like scholars in the 1960s had no preparation for the digital world. Yet we have to anticipate the future and what it might hold. The future will contain all sorts of unexpected surprises, and a crystal ball won't remove the fog that surrounds any predictions. Anticipation, however, is not an act of fortune telling but an act of preparation. This preparation is precisely what generates new ideas and directions to influence the future. Our aspirations as humanists should be clear: to live in a world of rapidly advancing technologies, to have an effective understanding of them, and to work together with appropriate technologies to capture the spirit and essence of a species that has continually transformed itself over thousands and thousands of years on a remarkably resilient planet.

Note

1. Drucker, "Humanistic Theory and Digital Scholarship," 88.

Bibliography

Anderson, Chris. "The End of Theory: The Data Deluge Makes the Scientific Method Obsolete." *WIRED*. Accessed April 24, 2018. www.wired.com/2008/06/pb-theory/.

Arnheim, Rudolf. "On Duplication." In *The Forger's Art: Forgery and the Philosophy of Art*, edited by Denis Dutton. Berkeley: University of California Press, 1983.

Barthes, Roland. *La chambre claire: Note sur la photographie*. Paris: Cahiers du cinéma, 1980.

Beard, Charles A. "That Noble Dream." *The American Historical Review* 41, no. 1 (October 1935): 74–87.

Beardsley, Monroe C. "Notes on Forgery." In *The Forger's Art: Forgery and the Philosophy of Art*, edited by Denis Dutton. Berkeley: University of California Press, 1983.

Benjamin, Walter. "Das Kunstwerk im Zeitalter seiner technischen Reproduzierbarkeit." In *Illuminationen: Ausgewählte Schriften 1*. Frankfurt a. M: Suhrkamp Verlag, 1977.

———. *Moskauer Tagebuch*. Erstausgabe. Frankfurt am Main: Suhrkamp, 1980.

———. *The Writer of Modern Life: Essays on Charles Baudelaire*. Cambridge, MA: Harvard University Press, 2006.

Berger, John. *Ways of Seeing*. London: British Broadcasting Corp.; New York: Penguin Books, 1972.

Bergson, Henri. *Duration and Simultaneity: With Reference to Einstein's Theory*. Indianapolis: Bobbs-Merrill, 1965.

Berkowitz, Peter. *Nietzsche: The Ethics of an Immoralist*. Cambridge, MA: Harvard University Press, 1996.

Berlin, Isaiah. *Historical Inevitability*. Auguste Comte Memorial Trust Lecture 1. London: Oxford University Press, 1954.

Bernstein, Leonard. *Leonard Bernstein at Harvard: "The Unanswered Question," Norton Lectures 1973*. Videorecording. Kultur, 1992.

Bertin, Jacques. *Sémiologie graphique: Les diagrammes, les réseaux, les cartes*. Paris: Gauthier-Villars, 1967.

Bloch, Matthew, and Wilson Andrews. "How Every New York City Neighborhood Voted in the Republican Primary." Accessed April 4, 2018. www.nytimes.com/interactive/2016/04/19/us/elections/new-york-city-republican-primary-results.html.

Bloom, Allan. *The Closing of the American Mind*. New York: Simon and Schuster, 1988.

Bodenhamer, David J. "The Spatial Humanities: Space, Time and Place in the New Digital Age." In *History in the Digital Age*, edited by Toni Weller. London and New York: Routledge, 2013.

Bodenhamer, David J., John Corrigan, and Trevor M. Harris, eds. *The Spatial Humanities: GIS and the Future of Humanities Scholarship*. Spatial Humanities. Bloomington: Indiana University Press, 2010.

Borges, Jorge Luis. "Pierre Menard, Author of the Quixote." In *Collected Fictions*. New York, NY: Viking, 1998.

Bosker, Story by Bianca. "Why Everything Is Getting Louder." *The Atlantic*, November 2019. www.theatlantic.com/magazine/archive/2019/11/the-end-of-silence/598366/.

Boswell, Thomas. *Why Time Begins on Opening Day*. New York, NY: Penguin Books, 1987.

Bronner, Stephen Eric. *A Rumor about the Jews: Antisemitism, Conspiracy, and the Protocols of Zion*. Oxford and New York: Oxford University Press, 2003.

Burke, Peter. *Eyewitnessing: The Uses of Images as Historical Evidence*. Picturing History Series. Ithaca, NY: Cornell University Press, 2001.

Burns, William E. *The Scientific Revolution in Global Perspective*. New York: Oxford University Press, 2016.

Butler, Judith. "Introduction." In *Of Grammatology*, edited by Jacques Derrida, translated by Gayatri Chakravorty Spivak. Baltimore: Johns Hopkins University Press, 2016.

Carnap, Rudolf. *The Logical Structure of the World*. Translated by Rolf A. George. Berkeley, CA: University of California Press, 1967.

Carr, Edward Hallett. *What Is History?* 1961. New York: Vintage Books, 1961.

Chakrabarty, Dipesh. *Provincializing Europe: Postcolonial Thought and Historical Difference*. Princeton, NJ: Princeton University Press, 2000.

Cheshire, James, and Oliver Uberti. *Where the Animals Go: Tracking Wildlife with Technology Technology in 50 Maps and Graphics*. New York: W. W. Norton & Company, 2017.

Chun, Wendy Hui Kyong. *Programmed Visions: Software and Memory*. Cambridge, MA: MIT Press, 2011.

Clark, Maudemarie. *Nietzsche on Truth and Philosophy*. Modern European Philosophy. Cambridge: Cambridge University Press, 1990.

Collins, Patricia Hill. "Learning from the Outsider Within: The Sociological Significance of Black Feminist Thought." *Social Problems* 33, no. 6 (1986): S14–32. https://doi.org/10.2307/800672.

Comrie, Bernard. "Causative Verb Formation and Other Verb-Deriving Morphology." In *Grammatical Categories and the Lexicon*, edited by Timothy Shopen, III: 309–48. Language Typology and Syntactic Description. Cambridge: Cambridge University Press, 1985.

Comte, Auguste. *The Positive Philosophy of Auguste Comte*. Translated by Harriet Martineau. Vol. I. London: G. Bell and Sons, 1896.

———. *The Positive Philosophy of Auguste Comte*. Translated by Harriet Martineau. Vol. II. London: G. Bell and Sons, 1896.

Conant, James Bryant. *On Understanding Science: An Historical Approach*. New Haven: Yale University Press; London: G. Cumberlege, Oxford University Press, 1947.

Conrad, Alfred H., and John Robert Meyer. *The Economics of Slavery, and Other Studies in Econometric History*. Chicago: Aldine Pub. Co, 1964.

Bibliography

Corbin, Alain. *Village Bells: Sound and Meaning in the 19th-Century French Countryside*. European Perspectives. New York: Columbia University Press, 1998.

Danto, Arthur C. *After the End of Art: Contemporary Art and the Pale of History*. The A.W. Mellon Lectures in the Fine Arts 1995. Princeton, NJ: Princeton University Press, 1997.

———. *Analytical Philosophy of History*. Cambridge: Cambridge University Press, 1965.

———. *Nietzsche as Philosopher*. New York: Columbia University Press, 2005.

———. *The Transfiguration of the Commonplace: A Philosophy of Art*. Cambridge, MA: Harvard University Press, 1981.

Davidson, Donald. "Indeterminism and Antirealism." In *Subjective, Intersubjective, Objective*, 69–84. Oxford : New York: Oxford University Press, 2001.

De Kruif, Paul. *Microbe Hunters*. San Diego: Harcourt, Inc, 1996.

Deleuze, Gilles. "Postscript on the Societies of Control." *October 59* (1992): 3–7.

Derrida, Jacques. *Limited Inc*. Evanston, IL: Northwestern University Press, 1988.

———. *Margins of Philosophy*. Translated by Alan Bass. Chicago: University of Chicago Press, 1982.

———. *Of Grammatology*. Translated by Gayatri Chakravorty Spivak. Baltimore: Johns Hopkins University Press, 2016.

Dilthey, Wilhelm. *Introduction to the Human Sciences*. Vol. 1. Princeton, NJ: Princeton University Press, 1989.

Domingos, Pedro. *The Master Algorithm: How the Quest for the Ultimate Learning Machine Will Remake Our World*. New York, NY: Basic Books, 2015.

Doyle, Arthur Conan. *The Sign of Four*. New York: Quality Paperback Book Club, 1994.

———. "Speckled Band." In *Sherlock Holmes: The Major Stories with Contemporary Critical Essays*, edited by John A. Hodgson, 152–73. Boston: Bedford Books of St. Martin Press, 1994.

Drucker, Johanna. "Humanistic Theory and Digital Scholarship." In *Debates in the Digital Humanities*. Minneapolis: University of Minnesota Press, 2012.

Dutton, Denis, ed. *The Forger's Art: Forgery and the Philosophy of Art*. Berkeley: University of California Press, 1983.

Elgammal, Ahmed. "Computer Science Can Only Help—Not Hurt—Art Historians." *The Conversation*, December 4, 2014. https://theconversation.com/computer-science-can-only-help-not-hurt-art-historians-33780.

———. "Which Paintings Were the Most Creative of Their Time? An Algorithm May Hold the Answers." *The Conversation*, July 30, 2015. https://theconversation.com/which-paintings-were-the-most-creative-of-their-time-an-algorithm-may-hold-the-answers-43157.

Elias, Norbert. *Time: An Essay*. Oxford: B. Blackwell, 1992.

Ellenberg, Jordan. "Opinion: How Computers Turned Gerrymandering into a Science." *The New York Times*, October 6, 2017, sec. Opinion. www.nytimes.com/2017/10/06/opinion/sunday/computers-gerrymandering-wisconsin.html.

Erwig, Martin. *Once upon an Algorithm: How Stories Explain Computing*. Cambridge, MA: The MIT Press, 2017.

Finn, Ed. *What Algorithms Want: Imagination in the Age of Computing*. Cambridge, MA: MIT Press, 2017.

Fogel, Robert William, and Geoffrey Rudolph Elton. *Which Road to the Past? Two Views of History*. New Haven: Yale University Press, 1983.

Foucault, Michel. *The Birth of the Clinic: An Archaeology of Medical Perception.* New York: Pantheon Books, 1973.

———. *Les mots et les choses: Une archéologie des sciences humaines.* Paris: Gallimard, 1990.

———. "Nietzsche, Genealogy, History." In *The Foucault Reader*, edited by Paul Rabinow. 1st ed. New York: Pantheon Books, 1984.

———. *The Order of Things: An Archaeology of the Human Sciences.* New York: Vintage Books, 1970.

Foucault, Michel, and Colin Gordon. *Power/Knowledge: Selected Interviews and Other Writings, 1972–1977.* 1st American ed. New York: Pantheon Books, 1980.

Francesco, Grete de. *The Power of the Charlatan.* Translated by Miriam Beard. New Haven: Yale University Press, 1939.

Frege, Gottlob. *The Foundations of Arithmetic: A Logico-Mathematical Enquiry into the Concept of Number.* New York: Philosophical Library, 1950.

Frith, Clifford B. *Charles Darwin's Life with Birds: His Complete Ornithology.* New York, NY: Oxford University Press, 2016.

Fukuyama, Francis. *The End of History and the Last Man.* New York: Free Press, 1992.

Fung, Brian. "If You Search Google Maps for the N-Word, It Gives You the White House." *Washington Post*, May 19, 2015. www.washingtonpost.com/news/the-switch/wp/2015/05/19/if-you-search-google-maps-for-the-n-word-it-gives-you-the-white-house/.

Gaddis, John Lewis. *The Landscape of History: How Historians Map the Past.* New York: Oxford University Press, 2002.

Galka, Max. "Here's Everyone Who's Immigrated to the U.S. Since 1820." *Metrocosm* (blog), May 3, 2016. http://metrocosm.com/animated-immigration-map/.

Galton, Francis. *Hereditary Genius: An Inquiry into Its Laws and Consequences.* London: Macmillan and Co, 1869.

Gane, Mike. *Auguste Comte.* Key Sociologists. London and New York: Routledge, 2006.

Gauger, Hans-Martin, and Herbert Heckmann. *Wir sprechen anders: Warum Computer nicht sprechen können: Eine Publikation der Deutschen Akademie für Sprache und Dichtung.* Frankfurt am Main: Fischer, 1988.

Geertz, Clifford. *Available Light: Anthropological Reflections on Philosophical Topics.* Princeton, NJ: Princeton University Press, 2000.

———. "Thick Description: Toward an Interpretive Theory of Culture." In *The Interpretation of Cultures: Selected Essays.* 3rd ed. New York: Basic Books, 2017.

Gillespie, Tarleton. "The Relevance of Algorithms." In *Media Technologies: Essays on Communication, Materiality, and Society*, edited by Tarleton Gillespie, Pablo J. Boczkowski, and Kirsten A. Foot. Cambridge, MA: The MIT Press, 2014.

Ginzburg, Carlo. "Clues: Roots of an Evidential Paradigm." In *Clues, Myths, and the Historical Method.* Baltimore: Johns Hopkins University Press, 1989.

Gold, Matthew K., ed. *Debates in the Digital Humanities.* Minneapolis: University of Minnesota Press, 2012.

Gold, Matthew K., and Lauren F. Klein, eds. *Debates in the Digital Humanities 2016.* Minneapolis and London: University of Minnesota Press, 2016.

Goodman, Nelson. "Art and Authenticity." In *The Forger's Art: Forgery and the Philosophy of Art*, edited by Denis Dutton. Berkeley: University of California Press, 1983.

Grallert, Till. "Mapping Ottoman Damascus through News Reports: A Practical Approach." In *The Digital Humanities and Islamic & Middle East Studies*, 175–98. Berlin and Boston: De Gruyter, 2016.

Gregory, Ian. "Time in Historical GIS Databases." In *Historical GIS: Technologies, Methodologies, and Scholarship*, edited by Ian Gregory and Paul S. Ell, 119–44. Cambridge Studies in Historical Geography 39. Cambridge and New York: Cambridge University Press, 2007.

Grimmelmann, James. "The Google Dilemma." *New York Law School Law Review* 53 (September 2008): 939–50.

Guenther, Rebecca, and Leslie Myrick. "Archiving Web Sites for Preservation and Access: MODS, METS, and MINERVA." In *Archives and the Digital Library*, edited by William E. Landis and Robin L. Chandler, 141–66. Binghamton, NY: Haworth Information Press, 2006.

Hacking, Ian. *The Emergence of Probability: A Philosophical Study of Early Ideas about Probability, Induction and Statistical Inference*. 2nd ed. Cambridge and New York: Cambridge University Press, 2006.

Hamer, Bent. *Kitchen Stories*, 2003.

Hanson, Stephen E. *Time and Revolution: Marxism and the Design of Soviet Institutions*. Chapel Hill, NC: University of North Carolina Press, 1997.

Hardin, C. L. *Color for Philosophers: Unweaving the Rainbow*. Indianapolis: Hackett Pub. Co, 1988.

Hayles, Katherine. *My Mother Was a Computer: Digital Subjects and Literary Texts*. Chicago: University of Chicago Press, 2005.

Heidegger, Martin. *Being and Time*. Translated by John Macquarrie and Edward Robinson. London: SCM Press, 1962.

———. "Der Weg zur Sprache." In *Unterwegs zur Sprache*. Frankfurt am Main: Vittorio Klostermann, 1985.

———. "Die Sprache." In *Unterwegs zur Sprache*. Frankfurt am Main: Vittorio Klostermann, 1985.

———. *Holzwege*. Frankfurt am Main: V. Klostermann, 1950.

———. "Nietzsches Wort 'Gott ist tot.'" In *Holzwege*. Frankfurt am Main: V. Klostermann, 1950.

———. *Off the Beaten Track*. Edited by Julian Young and Kenneth Haynes. Cambridge and New York: Cambridge University Press, 2002.

———. "Science and Reflection." In *The Question Concerning Technology and Other Essays*, translated by William Lovitt. New York: Harper Perennial, 2013.

———. *Was heisst Denken?* Frankfurt am Main: Vittorio Klostermann, 2002.

Herbst, Ludolf. *Hitlers Charisma: Die Erfindung eines deutschen Messias*. Frankfurt am Main: S. Fischer, 2010.

Herder, Johann Gottfried. *Abhandlung über den Ursprung der Sprache*. Stuttgart: Reclam, 1969.

Hewitt, Kenneth. "Excluded Perspectives in the Social Construction of Disaster." In *What Is a Disaster? Perspectives on the Question*, edited by E. L. Quarantelli, 75–92. London and New York: Routledge, 1998.

Hill Collins, Patricia. *Black Feminist Thought: Knowledge, Consciousness, and the Politics of Empowerment*. New York: Routledge, 2000.

Hvistendahl, Mara. "In China, a Three-Digit Score Could Dictate Your Place in Society." *WIRED*. Accessed July 2, 2018. www.wired.com/story/age-of-social-credit/.

Iggers, Georg G. *The German Conception of History: The National Tradition of Historical Thought from Herder to the Present*. Middletown, CT: Wesleyan University Press, 1983.

Jackson, Kenneth T. *Crabgrass Frontier: The Suburbanization of the United States*. New York: Oxford University Press, 1985.

Jay, Martin. *Downcast Eyes: The Denigration of Vision in Twentieth-Century French Thought*. Berkeley: University of California Press, 1993.

———. "In the Realm of the Senses: An Introduction." *The American Historical Review* 116, no. 2 (2011): 307–15.

Jenner, Mark S. R. "Follow Your Nose? Smell, Smelling, and Their Histories." *The American Historical Review* 116, no. 2 (April 2011): 335–51.

Johnson, Paul E. *A Shopkeeper's Millennium: Society and Revivals in Rochester, New York, 1815–1837*. American Century Series. New York: Hill and Wang, 1978.

Jones, Michael N., ed. *Big Data in Cognitive Science*. New York, NY: Routledge, 2017.

Kennan, George. *Tent Life in Siberia*. Salt Lake City: Peregrine Smith Books, 1986.

Komlos, John. *The Habsburg Monarchy as a Customs Union: Economic Development in Austria-Hungary in the Nineteenth Century*. Princeton, NJ: Princeton University Press, 1983.

Kotkin, Stephen. *Magnetic Mountain: Stalinism as a Civilization*. Berkeley: University of California Press, 1995.

Krischke, Wolfgang. "Sprachwissenschaft: Altbewährtes frischgemacht." *Frankfurter Allgemeine*. May 10, 2018. www.faz.net/aktuell/feuilleton/hoch-schule/digital-humanities-eine-bilanz-1-6-sprachwissenschaft-15579104.html.

Kuhn, Thomas S. "The Function of Measurement in Modern Physical Science." *Isis* 52, no. 2 (June 1961): 161–93.

———. *The Structure of Scientific Revolutions*. Chicago: University of Chicago Press, 1962.

LaCapra, Dominick. *History and Reading: Tocqueville, Foucault, French Studies*. Toronto and Buffalo: University of Toronto Press, 2000.

Lacey, Alan Robert. *Bergson*. London and New York: Routledge, 1989.

Lemov, Rebecca M. *Database of Dreams: The Lost Quest to Catalog Humanity*. New Haven and London: Yale University Press, 2015.

Lenain, Thierry. *Art Forgery: The History of a Modern Obsession*. London: Reaktion Books, 2011.

Lindenbaum, Shirley, and Margaret M. Lock, eds. *Knowledge, Power, and Practice: The Anthropology of Medicine and Everyday Life*. Comparative Studies of Health Systems and Medical Care. Berkeley: University of California Press, 1993.

Lock, Gary. "Representations of Space and Place in the Humanities." In *The Spatial Humanities: GIS and the Future of Humanities Scholarship*, edited by

Bibliography

David J. Bodenhamer, John Corrigan, and Trevor M. Harris, 89–108. Spatial Humanities. Bloomington: Indiana University Press, 2010.

Markoff, John. "Time Split to the Nanosecond Is Precisely What Wall Street Wants." Accessed July 2, 2018. www.nytimes.com/2018/06/29/technology/computer-networks-speed-nasdaq.html.

Megill, Allan. *Prophets of Extremity: Nietzsche, Heidegger, Foucault, Derrida*. Berkeley: University of California Press, 1985.

Metz, Christian. *Language and Cinema*. Vol. 26. The Hague: Mouton, 1974.

Milligan, Ian. *History in the Age of Abundance? How the Web Is Transforming Historical Research*. Montreal; Kingston: McGill-Queen's University Press, 2019.

Monmonier, Mark S. *How to Lie with Maps*. Chicago: University of Chicago Press, 1991.

Moretti, Franco. *Distant Reading*. London: Verso, 2013.

Muhanna, Elias. "Islamic and Middle East Studies and the Digital Turn." In *The Digital Humanities and Islamic & Middle East Studies*. Berlin and Boston: De Gruyter, 2016.

Navickas, Katrina. *Protest and the Politics of Space and Place 1789–1848*. Manchester: Manchester University Press, 2016.

Newman, William. "A Preliminary Reassessment of Newton's Alchemy." In *Cambridge Companion to Newton*. Cambridge: Cambridge University Press, 2016.

Ng, Kwong Bor, Jason Kucsma, and Metropolitan New York Library Council, eds. *Digitization in the Real World: Lessons Learned from Small and Medium-Sized Digitization Projects*. New York: Metropolitan New York Library Council, 2010.

Nietzsche, Friedrich. "Die Philosophie im tragischen Zeitalter der Griechen." In *Werke in drei Bänden*. Vol. 3. München: Carl Hanser, 1966.

———. "Götzendämmerung." In *Werke in drei Bänden*. Vol. II. München: Hanser Verlag, 1966.

———. "Zur Genealogie der Moral." In *Werke in drei Bänden*. Vol. II. München: Hanser Verlag, 1966.

Noble, Safiya Umoja. *Algorithms of Oppression: How Search Engines Reinforce Racism*. New York: New York University Press, 2018.

Novick, Peter. *That Noble Dream: The "Objectivity Question" and the American Historical Profession*. Cambridge: Cambridge University Press, 1988.

Oliveira, Arlindo L. *The Digital Mind: How Science Is Redefining Humanity*. Cambridge, MA: The MIT Press, 2017.

Pasquale, Frank. *The Black Box Society: The Secret Algorithms that Control Money and Information*. Cambridge, MA and London: Harvard University Press, 2015.

Paul, Gerhard, and Ralph Schock, eds. *Sound der Zeit: Geräusche, Töne, Stimmen: 1889 bis heute*. Göttingen: Wallstein, 2014.

Pinker, Steven. *The Stuff of Thought: Language as a Window into Human Nature*. New York: Viking, 2007.

Prost, Antoine. *Republican Identities in War and Peace: Representations of France in the Nineteenth and Twentieth Centuries*. The Legacy of the Great War. Oxford and New York: Berg, 2002.

Proust, Marcel. *Du côté de chez Swann*. Paris: Gallimard, 1987.

———. *Le Temps retrouvé*. Paris: Gallimard, 1992.

Putnam, Lara. "The Transnational and the Text-Searchable: Digitized Sources and the Shadows They Cast." *American Historical Review* 121 (April 2016): 377–402.

Quine, Willard Van Orman. *Word and Object*. Cambridge: Technology Press of the Massachusetts Institute of Technology, 1960.

Ranke, Leopold von. "On the Character of Historical Science (A Manuscript of the 1830's)." In *The Theory and Practice of History*, edited by Georg G. Iggers, 8–16. London and New York: Routledge, 2011.

———. "On Progress in History (From the First Lecture to King Maximilian II of Bavaria 'On the Epochs of Modern History,' 1854)." In *The Theory and Practice of History*, edited by Georg G. Iggers, 20–23. London and New York: Routledge, 2011.

———. "Pitfalls of a Philosophy of History (Introduction to a Lecture on Universal History; a Manuscript of the 1840's)." In *The Theory and Practice of History*, edited by Georg G. Iggers, 17–19. London and New York: Routledge, 2011.

Rich, Motoko, Amanda Cox, and Matthew Bloch. "Money, Race and Success: How Your School District Compares." Accessed April 4, 2018. www.nytimes.com/interactive/2016/04/29/upshot/money-race-and-success-how-your-school-district-compares.html.

Riskin, Jessica. *Science in the Age of Sensibility: The Sentimental Empiricists of the French Enlightenment*. Chicago: University of Chicago Press, 2002.

Rorty, Richard. *Eine Kultur ohne Zentrum : Vier philosophische Essays und ein Vorwort*. Stuttgart: Reclam, 1993.

———. *The Linguistic Turn: Recent Essays in Philosophical Method*. Chicago: University of Chicago Press, 1967.

———. *Philosophy and the Mirror of Nature*. Princeton, NJ: Princeton University Press, 1980.

Rorty, Richard, Jerome B. Schneewind, and Quentin Skinner, eds. *Philosophy in History: Essays on the Historiography of Philosophy*. Cambridge [Cambridgeshire] and New York: Cambridge University Press, 1984.

Rosenthal, Nicolas G. *Reimagining Indian Country: Native American Migration & Identity in Twentieth-Century Los Angeles*. First Peoples: New Directions in Indigenous Studies. Chapel Hill: University of North Carolina Press, 2012.

Rosenzweig, Roy. *Clio Wired: The Future of the Past in the Digital Age*. New York: Columbia University Press, 2011.

Ruwedel, Mark. *Westward: The Course of Empire*. New Haven, CT: Yale University Art Gallery: Distributed by Yale University Press, 2008.

Sahlins, Marshall. *Islands of History*. Chicago: University of Chicago Press, 1985.

Schafer, R. Murray. *Voices of Tyranny, Temples of Silence*. Arcana Editions, 1993.

Schivelbusch, Wolfgang. *Disenchanted Night: The Industrialization of Light in the Nineteenth Century*. Berkeley: University of California Press, 1995.

Schuessler, Jennifer. "Reading by the Numbers: When Big Data Meets Literature." Accessed April 5, 2018. www.nytimes.com/2017/10/30/arts/franco-moretti-stanford-literary-lab-big-data.html.

Schwartz, Claudia. "Der Mythos von Hitlers Charisma | NZZ." *Neue Zürcher Zeitung*, August 10, 2018. www.nzz.ch/feuilleton/der-mythos-von-hitlers-charisma-ld.1409935.

Searle, John R. "Minds, Brains, and Programs." *Behavioral and Brain Sciences* 3, no. 3 (1980): 417–57.

Selb, Peter, and Simon Munzert. "Examining a Most Likely Case for Strong Campaign Effects: Hitler's Speeches and the Rise of the Nazi Party, 1927–1933." *American Political Science Review* 112, no. 4 (2018): 1050–1066.

Shapin, Steven, and Simon Schaffer. *Leviathan and the Air-Pump: Hobbes, Boyle, and the Experimental Life*. Princeton, NJ: Princeton University Press, 1989.

Sheppard, Eric. "Knowledge Production through Critical GIS: Genealogy and Prospects." *Cartographica* 40, no. 4 (2005): 5–21.

Skinner, Quentin, ed. *The Return of Grand Theory in the Human Sciences*. Cambridge and New York: Cambridge University Press, 1990.

Skloot, Rebecca. *The Immortal Life of Henrietta Lacks*. New York: Crown Publishers, 2010.

Sobieszek, Robert A. *Ghost in the Shell: Photography and the Human Soul, 1850–2000: Essays on Camera Portraiture*. Los Angeles: Los Angeles County Museum of Art; Cambridge, MA: MIT Press, 1999.

Sokal, Alan D., ed. *The Sokal Hoax: The Sham that Shook the Academy*. Lincoln: University of Nebraska Press, 2000.

Spiegel, Gabrielle M. "History, Historicism, and the Social Logic of the Text." In *The Past as Text: The Theory and Practice of Medieval Historiography*. Parallax. Baltimore: Johns Hopkins University Press, 1997.

———. *The Past as Text: The Theory and Practice of Medieval Historiography*. Parallax. Baltimore: Johns Hopkins University Press, 1997.

Spivak, Gayatri Chakravorty. "Afterword." In *Of Grammatology*, edited by Jacques Derrida. Baltimore: Johns Hopkins University Press, 2016.

———. "Can the Subaltern Speak?" In *Can the Subaltern Speak? Reflections on the History of an Idea*, edited by Rosalind C. Morris. New York: Columbia University Press, 2010.

———. "Can the Subaltern Speak?" In *Marxism and the Interpretation of Culture*, edited by Cary Nelson and Lawrence Grossberg, 279–313. Urbana: University of Illinois Press, 1988.

Staten, Henry. *Wittgenstein and Derrida*. Lincoln and London: University of Nebraska Press, 1984.

Svensson, Patrik, and David Theo Goldberg, eds. *Between Humanities and the Digital*. Cambridge, MA: The MIT Press, 2015.

TechCrunch. "Eric Schmidt: Every 2 Days We Create as Much Information as We Did Up to 2003." Accessed September 25, 2019. http://social.techcrunch.com/2010/08/04/schmidt-data/.

Tufte, Edward R. *Beautiful Evidence*. Cheshire, CT: Graphics Press, 2006.

———. *The Visual Display of Quantitative Information*. 2nd ed. Cheshire, CT: Graphics Press, 2001.

———. *Visual Explanations: Images and Quantities, Evidence and Narrative*. Cheshire, CT: Graphics Press, 1997.

Virgil. *The Aeneid*. Translated by C. Day Lewis. London: Hogarth Press, 1961.

———. *Aeneid 5: Text, Translation and Commentary*. Edited by Lee Fratantuono and R. Alden Smith. Mnemosyne. Supplements; Monographs on Greek and Latin Language and Literature, volume 386. Leiden and Boston: Brill, 2015.

Whaley, John H., Jr. "Digitizing History." *The American Archivist* 57, no. 4 (Fall 1994): 660–72.

White, Hayden V. *Metahistory: The Historical Imagination in Nineteenth-Century Europe*. Baltimore: Johns Hopkins University Press, 1973.
Wiesenfeldt, Christiane. "Zu viele Noten?" *Frankfurter Allgemeine*, May 17, 2018. www.faz.net/aktuell/feuilleton/hoch-schule/digital-humanities-eine-bilanz-2-6-musikwissenschaft-15579191.html.
Wilkerson, Isabel. *The Warmth of Other Suns: The Epic Story of America's Great Migration*. New York: Random House, 2010.
Williams, Lucy, and Barry Godfrey. "Bringing the Prisoner into View: English and Welsh Census Data and the Victorian Prison Population." *Australian Historical Studies* 47, no. 3 (September 2016): 398–413.
Wittgenstein, Ludwig. *Philosophical Investigations*. Edited by G. E. M. Anscombe. 3rd ed. Oxford and Malden, MA: Blackwell, 2001.
———. *Tractatus Logico-philosophicus*. London and New York: Routledge & Paul, 1961.
Yuan, May. "Mapping Text." In *The Spatial Humanities: GIS and the Future of Humanities Scholarship*, edited by David J. Bodenhamer, John Corrigan, and Trevor M. Harris, 89–108. Spatial Humanities. Bloomington: Indiana University Press, 2010.

Index

abstraction 10, 71–74, 76–77, 81–83, 179
abstract models 71
abstract theories 10–11, 78, 81, 83
academic environment 1
acoustic space 54–55
Aeneid (Virgil) 137–38, 183
aesthetic representation/charm 157–58
African artistic production 5
After Walker Evans (Levine) 162
"agent-specific" approach 33
air-pump 6, 32
alchemists 32–33, 112
alchemy, revival of 32–33
algorithmic decision-making 11, 86, 92
algorithmic machinations 122
algorithmic oppression 91
algorithmic reading 90
algorithmic techniques 93, 114
algorithms 4, 9, 11–12, 20, 38, 65, 70–71, 83–87, 92, 99, 119, 122, 132, 153, 155–56, 168–69, 177–78, 180–81, 183–84, 187–88; adapting to presence of 90–91; aesthetic and emotional judgments 107; ambiguities 93–94; binary decision-making 92–94; black box metaphor 91–92, 96, 106; brevity risks 92; claims about neutrality of 94; *vs.* classification 103–5; computations executed by 93; data input and social output of 91; data processing 12, 107; Erwig's strategy for 89–90, 95–96; factors influencing success of 99; feedback loop 12, 94–95; flow chart 94; as formula *vs.* cliometrics 102–3; gendered discourse 11–12; Google's automated ranking system 91; humanistic stories with mechanics of 89–90, 106; identification of trope 101; influence of 105; language 12, 90, 97, 98, 99, 178, 180; linguistic qualities 12; logic of 89–90; methodological analysis of 92; pedagogical requirement for 105–6; racist qualities of 91; reduced to language 90; repetitive nature of 101–2; self-referentiality 95; story on 89–90; translation 96–99; visual recognition 104
Algorithms of Oppression (Noble) 11
alphabetization 94
ambiguities 93, 96, 105
American Historical Review 63
American mind, closing of 1, 6
America's Most Wanted (Komar and Melamid) 151
analytic philosophers 7, 47, 52, 55, 57, 79, 173, 186–87
analytic philosophy 43, 52
Anderson, Chris 70; end of theory 9
anti-gay legislation 24
antirealism 70
antirealist postmodern theories 79, 83, 86
aphorisms 55, 77
approximation 115, 154, 156–57
archives 112, 117
Arnheim, Rudolf 19, 161–62
arts 2, 19, 50–51, 59, 75, 139–40, 147–48, 156, 158, 162–63, 168, 172; of collection and analysis 51; connoisseur 164–66; forgeries 5; philosophy of 49, 147; visual 166
artwork 6, 49–50
ascription 99

attitude 13, 17, 29, 33–34, 37, 50, 78, 82, 86, 106, 113, 122–24, 177, 180, 187
aural environment 54, 56
Austin, John 43
authenticity 19, 139, 162–65, 167–69
Axé Bahia exhibition 151–52

Bacon, Francis 35
ball throwing 56
Barthes, Roland 81
bathroom politics 38
Battle Between Carnival and Lent (Brueghel) 54
Beard, Charles 74
beauty 30, 104, 137, 151–52, 157–58, 161, 172
behavior 35, 38, 54, 61, 73, 92, 94
Benjamin, Walter 16, 136, 138–39, 167–68
Berger, John 59, 61
Bergson, Henri 15, 131–33
Berlin, Isaiah 71
Bernstein, Leonard 6, 49–50, 52, 56
Bertin, Jacques 154
Big Data 3–4, 12–15, 51, 53, 70–72, 74, 83, 108, 110–13, 118–24, 131, 151, 180–84, 181–82; ancestry 110–11; asocial component of 182; Carr's example for 120–21; definitions 13; digital layer beneath 120; and digital time 137; facticity of 13–14; graphic expression of data 17–18; institutional and local data 122–24, 126; interaction with Little Data 127; vs. Little Data 121–24, 182–83; in ocular mode 148; positivism ties with 72; on real-world activities 119; as seductive force 121; spaceless decisions 119; spaces of 111; in terms of time 141; time encapsulated in 134; traditional sources and 121; and visual imagery 148, 149
binaries 20, 36–38, 103, 173; decision-making 11, 92, 100, 181; operations 11; search tree 94
binary oppositions 36–38, 45–46, 94; attack on 38; bathroom politics 38; dichotomous oppositional difference 36; European revolutions 37; othering and 37; transgender rights 37, 38; weaknesses 38

bios praktikos 80, 81
bios theoretikos 80, 81
birth 118–19
black box metaphor 12, 91–92, 96, 106
Black Box Society (Pasquale) 91
Black feminist thought 36
board game (Wittgenstein) 56
Bodenhamer, David J. 3, 112–13
Bolsheviks 37, 51; *see also* Speaking Bolshevik (expression)
Borges, Jorge Luis 163
Boswell, Thomas 144
Boyle, Robert 57
Brahe, Tycho 74
British science 32
Brueghel, Peter 54
Butler, Judith 82

Caesar 120–21
calendric time 134
capillary power 125, 126
capitalism, and imperialism 29
capitalist advertising 61
car-driving database 119
Carnap, Rudolf 98
Carr, E.H. 120
Carte Figurative (Minard) 148
cartography 127
catastrophe 138
censorship laws 2
Chakrabarty, Dipesh 28, 35
Chambre claire, La (Barthes) 17
Chekhov, Anton 75
chemistry 73
chess game 56
Chomsky, Noam 23, 43, 49
chronometric surveillance system 142
church bells 140–42, 144
Clark, Maudemarie 79
classical music 29
classification 93, 103–5
classifier 103–4, 107
"Clatter of Wheels, The" (*Stuchit!*) (Turgenev) 54
cliometrics 93, 102–3, 107
Clock, The (Marclay) 130
code, programming 12, 185
cognitive linguistics 50–52, 64
cognitive linguists 7, 51–52, 97, 101
Collingwood, R.G. 62
Collins, Patricia Hill 36
colors 5, 18, 60–61, 150–51, 154, 156
commitment 80, 103, 106

computational methods 64
computer surveillance 152
Comtean system 75
Comte, Auguste 10, 70–75, 77, 82, 83, 90, 170, 179
Conant, James 6, 31
conception 86, 111, 131, 184
conceptualization 72, 75, 83, 100, 111, 137, 142, 147, 153, 166, 169, 178, 182, 184
connoisseur 107, 164–66, 168, 171, 173
consciousness 15, 55, 132–34, 141
construction, social 2, 7–8, 49, 124–25, 182, 184
contemplation 80
contemporary politics 74
contemporary world 81
context: historical 27, 152; social 31, 43, 50, 52, 101, 167
conventions 143, 162, 166–67, 169–70, 172–74
Corbin, Alain 140
counterfeiting 161
Crabgrass Frontier (Jackson) 150
crafts (term) 5
craftsperson 122
cubism 75
cultural achievements 5, 6
cultural authority, of humanities 3
cultural construction 2
cultures 5–6, 8, 27–28, 106, 121
Culture Without a Center, A (Rorty) 27
curiosity 63, 80, 142, 161
"cybernetic and infometrics revolution" 3–4

Danto, Arthur 49–50, 52, 78, 147
Darwin, Charles 110
data: accumulation 13; collection 85; processors 9; production 12, 14; set 75, 151, 162, 164–65; world 85, 112, 120, 178–80, 184
databases 7, 10, 12–14, 16–17, 65, 83–86, 93, 113–16, 119–20, 124, 127, 131, 135–41, 148, 168, 183, 185; car-driving 119; computational methods and 64; digital 114, 118, 126; of dreams 110–11; fragments 120; humanist theories and 86; inductive nature of 83; as intermediary 85; limitations 85; museum 115; prison 111, 114, 115; search of object in 115; search word 84; socially unacceptable results 83–84; structural change tracking 65; time elements 135; veracity of 83
data visuals 3, 16, 62, 123, 149–51, 156–59, 177–78, 180, 184–85, 188; Bertin's work 154; Big Data and visual imagery 149; conceptualization of 149, 153–54; French anti-ocular tradition 152; graphs/graphics 149, 151–54; inherent complexities 18; migration visuals 151–52; names on 9/11 memorial 155; Napoleon, Minard's representation of invasion 148, 150, 157–58; oscilloscopes 153; photographs 155; qualitative and quantitative emphasis 155–56; qualities of 153; training 159; Tufte's analysis 150, 157; zoning practices 150; *see also* visuals
Debates in the Digital Humanities (Gold) 3
decentralization 27, 33
decision-making process 89
deconstruction 81
deductive process 83
deracination, practice of 78
Derridaean tradition 82
Derrida, Jacques 1, 3, 7–8, 12, 23, 36, 43–46, 52, 56, 58, 64, 71, 81, 84, 95, 102, 179; on empirical investigation 81; notion of trace 12; recursive trace 95
dichotomous oppositional difference 36
digital age 3, 5, 9, 11, 13, 15, 40, 50, 61, 71, 83, 85, 93, 113, 124, 126, 131, 140, 147–48, 161, 183, 185–86, 188
digital correspondence 171
digital decision-making process 95
digital environment 3–4, 6, 19, 25, 84, 111, 133, 140, 172, 182, 184
digital experience 134, 180
digital facts 13–14, 118
digital film 133
digital forgery 4–5, 18–20, 19, 161, 166, 167, 185; comparative perspective 170; connoisseur in 164–65, 168; digital record 171; fake news 172; fingerprint 163–64; formats 163; identification process 19–20, 168–69, 171–74; Thorpian work 164–65, 167, 171
digital fragmentation of time 130, 132
digital grid 135–36

Digital Humanities 3, 14, 20, 92, 186
digital knowledge 14, 116, 182
digital laboratory 8
digital language techniques 64
digital layer 20, 120, 180
digitally born materials 111, 118–19
digital maneuverings 125
digital manipulations *vs.* forgery 161
digital mapping 124, 126–27
Digital Panopticon project 111, 113–14, 126–27
digital phenomena 72
digital research 3
digital scan 171
digital scholarship 51
digital space 13, 126, 181–82; Digital Panopticon project 111, 113–14; museum 114–15; Wayback Machine 116–19, 127
digital techniques 176
digital technologies 2, 14, 44, 49, 53, 64, 110, 131, 133–34, 139, 162, 176–77, 187–88
digital time 14–16, 130–45, 156, 168, 178, 180, 183–84; Big Data and 137; complexity 132; Corbin's work 140–41; cultural assessment of 144–45; Einsteinian concept 133, 136; empirical nature 143–44; Heideggerian critique 14–15; humanism in 145; literary examples 136–39; measurement 133–34; positivism and 144; tag for data components 135, 136
digital tools 3, 64, 127, 178
digital traces 95, 165, 185
digital transmission, of snapshots 62
digital universe 38, 44, 57, 130, 133, 149, 170–71
digital world 2–4, 11, 13, 15–16, 38–40, 44, 49, 64, 70, 83, 85–86, 106–7, 111, 118, 120, 126–27, 131–32, 136, 141, 162–63, 166–73, 177–80, 182–85, 188
digital zoom 166
digitization 3, 40, 72, 111, 130, 135, 139, 140
Dilthey, Wilhelm 10, 71, 75–77
discourse 2, 6–7, 43, 47, 48, 96, 100, 115, 158, 162; of power 1, 44–45; senses presented as 53; theory 12, 57
discursive analyses 50
distant reading 8, 14, 51, 111, 122

Domingos, Pedro 90
drafting 82
Drucker, Johanna 3, 39–40
Duchenne, Guillaume-Benjamin 104

ears 38, 50, 54–55
earthquake measurement 33–34
echo 63
Egyptian creation myth 55
Einstein, Albert 123, 131, 133, 136, 143–44, 176
Einsteinian relativism 126
Elias, Norbert 15, 131–33, 141
emotions 5, 32, 52, 100, 104, 188
English translation 98
Enlightenment 1, 25, 27–32, 37–39, 59–60, 72, 103
Erwig, Martin 89–90, 92, 93–96, 95, 101
eternal return, concept of 102
Eurocentric medical researchers 35
European settlement of American continent 38
exactitude 51, 74, 143, 153, 157
exactness 73–74
existentialism 77
extralinguistic reality 52
eyewitnessing 116

facial expressions 104
facticity 14, 43, 111, 115, 121, 184
facts: and abstract contemplation 77; as social constructs 23
factual objectification 79
fake news 18, 172
fakes *see* digital forgery; forgery
fashion photography 158
feedback 94–95, 142
feedback loops 12, 93–94, 103
financial industry 91
fingerprint 85, 163–64
Finn, Ed 90
flâneurs 136, 138
flow chart 94
foggy writing 39
forged digital imagery 168; *see also* digital forgery
forgery 4–5, 18–20, 161, 185; conspiratorial text 163; evidence 162; paintings 162–63; of writing 163; *see also* digital forgery
Foucauldian archaeology 58
Foucault, Michel 1, 6, 13, 17, 23, 25, 31–32, 35, 43–47, 52, 57, 78, 81, 113

fragmentation 16, 115–16, 119, 140, 183
France 27
Frege, Gottlob 43
French anti-ocular tradition 152
French church bells 63
French Revolution 37
Freud, Sigmund 75

Gaddis, John 124–25
Galileo Galilei 56, 58
Galton, Francis 110
Garmin device 141–42
gay pride parade 24
gaze 2, 17, 35–36, 148
Geertz, Clifford 27, 140
gender 5, 37–38, 103, 123
genealogy 71, 77–78
Genealogy of Morals ((Nietzsche) 77
generalizations 73, 76, 85
Geographic Information Systems 112–13, 122–23, 125, 127, 182
German, Aleksei Sr. 63
gerrymandering 105
Gillespie, Tarleton 91
Ginzburg, Carlo 164
GIS *see* Geographic Information Systems
Goodman, Nelson 166, 167
Google: algorithms 11; search 84–85, 91
Google Maps 39, 83, 85, 125, 179
Google Translate 9, 39, 97–98, 99, 107
grammar 47, 49–50, 52, 81, 92–93, 95–96, 99–101, 177–78
grammatical fictions 77
graphical mode of representation 17
graphic artists 158
graphic design 149, 153–55
graphics 148–50, 152–55, 157–58, 161, 164–66, 170, 172–73
graphs 17–18, 139, 148–49, 151–52, 154–55, 161, 166
Greek concept of theory 79–80
Grimmelmann, James 91
guilt, concept of 78
Gutenberg printing press 176

Habermas, Jürgen 43
Habsburg Monarchy as a Customs Union, The (Komlos) 149
Hamer, Bent 26
hand-assembled database of terms 135–36

Handel, Georg Friedrich 29
hand-picked data, analytic impact of ignoring 122–23
Han van Meegeren forgery 161, 163–64
hard sciences 71
Hegelian dialectic 95
Heideggerian nostalgia 20
Heidegger, Martin 11, 12, 15, 20, 38, 43, 45, 58, 71–72, 79–80, 89–90, 101, 106, 122, 140, 142
Herder, Johann Gottfried 43
heterosexual discourse 47
heuristic devices 90, 124, 133, 162
Hewitt, Kenneth 33
hierarchical relationships 36
historians 6–7, 9, 12, 17, 23, 26, 31, 33, 38–39, 45–46, 48, 50–51, 57–58, 59, 62–63, 74–76, 78, 84, 93, 101, 105–6, 112, 117–18, 120, 124, 140, 147–48, 150, 155, 169, 183
historical and literary documents 51–52
historical epochs, boundaries between 33
historical idealism 62
historical laws 75
historical research, scientific component of 75
history 74–75
Hitler, election results of 150
Hobbes, Thomas 57
Hobsbawm, Erik 118
Holzwege (Heidegger) 89–90, 101
home languages 52, 98–99
homonyms 93
homosexual discourse 47
homosexuality 24, 37
human experience 58, 76, 107, 131, 134, 143, 188
humanism 145, 186–87; concerns 39; and database 86; methods 96; research 20; study 64; theories 3
humanists 2, 4, 7, 10–11, 13–14, 17, 20, 27, 50–51, 53, 56, 64, 80, 83, 90–92, 94–96, 99, 102–3, 105–7, 110, 116–17, 120–22, 124, 126, 148–49, 153–55, 164, 176, 180–88
humanities, incompatibility of 39
humanity, history of 72
human life 6
human movement 151–52

identity 5
Iggers, Georg 77

illustration 61
images/pictures *see* visuals
Immortal Life of Henrietta Lacks, The (Skloot) 35
imperialism 28–29
impressionism 75
incommensurability 39, 44, 57, 65
India, women's position in 28–29
Indic phonemes 46
inexact language, effectiveness of 157
information 2, 14, 16, 18, 59, 74–75, 83, 85–86, 94, 104–5, 111–12, 114–15, 117–20, 140, 148–50, 154, 157–58, 178, 182, 184–85; access 112; digital 19, 133, 166, 182; sorting 104; storing 115, 117–18, 127, 182; visualization 39
internal ambiguity 94
Internet Archive 2
island metaphor 27
Islands of History (Sahlins) 27
itemization 119

Jackson, Kenneth T. 150
Jay, Martin 52, 56, 177
Johnson, Paul E. 149–50

kaleidoscope 166
Kantian aesthetic, denunciation of 30
Kennan, George 61
Keynes, John Maynard 32
Kitchen Stories (Hamer) 26
knowledge 1, 13, 16–18, 25, 27–28, 30, 44–45, 47, 74, 83, 95, 103, 111, 113, 121–23, 172, 180; acquisition 27, 35, 46; network 27; and power 35–36, 91–92; primary factor in formation of 7; production 122, 182; as social construction 7
Koraks, Siberia 61
Koselleck, Reinhart 43
Kotkin, Stephen 51
Kuhn, Thomas 31–32

labour, colonial practices associated with 51
LaCapra, Dominick 46
Lacks, Henrietta 34
landscape 8, 90, 112, 123–25, 124–25
language 2, 4, 6–9, 15, 25, 45, 77, 84, 90, 93, 95–100, 105, 107, 115, 120, 126, 156–58, 163, 177–78, 181; algorithmic 96, 99, 156, 178, 180, 187; control 7, 47–48;

debates about 55; evolutionary revelations of 65; expression of time in 51; games 8, 44, 48, 52, 56–58, 65; grammatical expressions 50; home, changes in 52; layers of 12; linguistic qualities 12; pattern shifts 135; philosophy of 6–7, 43, 45, 58, 177; relativist claims of 48; role in social setting 47; senses and 52; and song 49; structure 53–55; thoughts and 62–63
large data sets 110, 178
Las Meninas (Velazquez) 17
laws 2, 10, 24, 61, 72–75, 82–83, 105, 114, 144, 165, 179
layering 180
Lemov, Rebecca 110
Lenain, Thierry 162
Lenin, Vladimir 29
Levine, Sherrie 162
Lévi-Strauss, Claude 27
light 15–16, 23, 57, 59–61, 70, 168
linguistics: analysis 8, 43, 46–47, 58, 61, 64, 178; boundaries 46; change 48, 65; construction 93; control 47; incommensurability 3, 9; limitations 178; philosophy of postmodernists 46; power 65; reduction 60; situation 50; terms, relationship between 45; usage 7
linguistic turn 4, 6–9, 7, 8, 12, 18–19, 40, 72, 95–96, 162, 177–78, 181; applications of 48; assumptions about 57; centripetal force of 45; christening 43; defense of 53; Derrida and Foucault's work 44–45; development and parameters of 44; dynamic elements of 8; fragilities of 57; impact in scientific writing 95; as interdisciplinary phenomenon 48; limits of 52; maximalist projection of 47–48; maximal understanding of 45; minimalist projection of 48–49; plea to end 9; power of 49; problems 44; pure enthusiasm for 47; shifting word usage 48; theoretical work 48; *see also* language
Linnaeus, Carl 103
listening 19, 30, 54, 56, 59, 99
Little Data 14, 121–24, 126–28, 182–83
local histories 28
local knowledge 31, 123–24

206 *Index*

Lockean empiricism 16
Lock, Gary 125
Logical Positivism 78–79

machine translator 98
madeleine 60
magnifying glass 19, 162, 165–66, 185
malapropism 107
male hegemony 1
mapping 98, 111, 113, 124, 127, 182
maps 49, 117, 122, 134–36, 149–51, 154, 157, 185; digital time and 135; of England 124, 125; GIS 125, 126; institutional and local data 122–24, 126; of New York City 151; representation 124; of Rochester 149–50; spatial relations in 134; urban environment 124
Marclay, Christian 130
marginalization, of African women 36
Master Algorithm 90
materiality 111–12, 116, 118, 121
material practices, impact of phenomenon on 111–12
maximalist approach 45
medical practice 34
Meegeren, Han van 19, 163–64, 169–70
Megill, Allan 79
Menard, Pierre, fictional story of 163, 167
Mercalli scale 33–34
Metahistory (White) 48
metalanguage 43, 98
metaphors 27, 43, 55, 58, 90, 92, 95–96, 100–101, 107, 113, 130, 181; casual references to 100; in programming language 100–101
metaphysical rationality 112
methodological diversity 177
Metz, Christian 6, 158
migration visuals 151–52
Minard, Charles Joseph 148
mirroring function 119
models 59, 142, 163
modern imperialism 1
morality 77–78
Moretti, Franco 8
mouth 55
moveable type press 176
museum 5, 115–16, 118, 130, 142; database 114–15, 127; objects 111, 127, 182

music 6, 29–30, 38, 49–50, 53, 56, 93; and digital world, structural parallels between 49; grammatical components of language in 49; grammatical structure to 53; study with digital technologies 49; as universal language 49
musical-grammatical competence, innate 49
musical phrase 49
music listening habits, shifting 29–30

Napoleon, Minard's representation of invasion 18, 148, 150, 157–58
narratives of heroes, individuating 120–21
narrative structures 39
natural disasters 33
natural languages 107, 132, 181; grammars of 95; time expression 96; translation 96–97
Navickas, Katrina 134
neologism 48
neopositivism 86
Newman, William 32
Newtonian conception of time 15
Newton, Isaac 32
New York Subway 158
Nietzsche, Friedrich 5, 25, 55, 64, 71, 75–76, 76–79, 81, 102, 144
Nietzsche, Genealogy, History (Foucault) 78
Noble, Safiya Umoja 11–12, 91
non-European artistic creation 5
non-linguistic phenomena 56
non-listening 54
Nose, The (Gogol) 63
nose, visual depictions of 63
numerical indexing system 135

obituary 24–25
object and observation, boundaries between 79
objections 25, 46, 107, 157
objective biological facts 37
objective fact 120
objective knowledge 36
objective science *vs.* subjectivity and relativism 31
objectivity 1, 5–6, 16, 45, 74, 131, 156, 186; objections to 25; religious beliefs and 31; and truth, link between 59

Index 207

observation 16, 73–74, 76, 77, 79, 84, 125
ocularization 59
Of Grammatology (Derrida) 81
Om 55
Once Upon an Algorithm (Erwig) 89
"On Duplication" (Arnheim) 161
Order of Things, The (Foucault) 17, 25, 35, 46
oscilloscopes 153
othering 37
outhouses 38

pain (grammatical word) 37, 49, 56
paintings 16, 19, 29, 59, 107, 148, 150–51, 181, 184; abounded with sounds 54–55; forgery of 162–66, 168–70
Paley, William 144
panopticon 13, 35, 80, 111, 113–14, 126, 143
Pasquale, Frank 91
patriarchy and development 29
personalities 104, 114, 155, 163
persuasive argument 74
Philosophical Investigations (Wittgenstein) 52, 55–57, 96, 184
philosophy 6, 9, 49, 54, 62, 74, 181, 187; alternative views from 78; analytic 43, 52; digital 86; of language 6–7, 43; linguistic 46; political 23; position shift within academy 26
photographs 16–17, 116, 139, 148, 153, 155–57, 162, 164, 171–72, 178, 184–85
photoshopping 161
Picasso 5
Pierre Menard, fictional story of 163, 167
Pinker, Steven 50, 51
pluralism 38, 115, 120, 126, 167–68, 173, 188
pluralist discourse 36
polemical approach to theory 70
positive philosophy 73
positivism 10–11, 46, 76, 84, 103, 113, 120, 143–44, 178–79; close ties to 85; exactness 73–74; observation and general law 73; opposition to 71, 76; relation to theory 71; sociological precision 73–74; ties with Big Data 72
positivist methods 74
positivist theorizing 80

postmodern achievement 24; attack on universalism of Enlightenment 27; binary opposition 36–37; condemnations of imperialism 28–29; decentralization of knowledge 27–28; demotion of rationality 25–26; Drucker's assertions 40; Kuhn's work 31; local histories and 28; medical ethics 34–35; Mercalli scale 33–34; philosophy (academic discipline) 26–27; pluralist discourse 36–37; power–knowledge connection 35–36; refreshing look at science 31; revival of alchemy 32–33; shifting music listening habits 29–30; social change and academic theories 30–31; Sokal hoax 33, 34; universality 25; voice to local culture 27–28; works on madness 26
postmodernism 1–2, 1–6, 11, 16, 18, 49, 52, 64–65, 71–72, 78, 84, 86, 92, 100–102, 106–8, 111, 115–16, 126–27, 143, 149, 162, 176–77, 179, 180–81, 184, 186–87; adoption 24; anti-ocularism 18; blurring of lines between historical fact and fiction 7; discursive techniques 28; 'frame of reference' 123; homosexuality and 24; intellectual aging process 38–39; language 6–7, 11; model of trace 94; opposition to 23–24; pluralism 126; postwar discontent as 31; relativism 77, 115–16; technological critiques 20; and theory, association between 86; vitality 24
postmodern theory 2–4, 10, 24, 71, 72, 79–82, 105, 185
poststructuralism 6
power 1, 7, 11, 25, 35–36, 44–45, 47, 49, 52, 58, 65, 81, 83, 90–92, 107, 125, 151–52, 181, 185; capillary 125–26; capillary affects of 36; epistemological 125; metaphorical 113; raw 35, 47, 125–26; relations 47, 125–26
power–knowledge connection 35–36, 47
precision 74, 89, 93, 95
prediction models 33
programming code *see* language
programming language 95–98, 100–101, 107, 168; grammar rules 95; and

208 Index

metalanguage 98; metaphors in 100–101; time expression 96; translation 96–97
propositions 79
Protocols of the Elders of Zion 163
Proust, Marcel 16, 20, 60, 136
Provincializing Europe (Chakrabarty) 28
psychological uncertainties 75
punishment 78
Putnam, Lara 112

QGIS 134
quantum gravity 33
Quine, W.V.O. 43

racism 83
Rankean system 75
Ranke, Leopold von 70, 74–75, 155
rationality 1, 23, 25–26, 32, 44, 65
rational subject, Cartesian view of 25
raw power 125, 126
reading and visual accompaniment 61–62
real phenomena 73
recursion 94–95
reenactment societies 62
"Regime of Computation" 90
relational mapping 124
relationship 8, 13, 15, 45, 65, 78, 115–17, 124, 133, 148, 173, 176, 178, 180, 182–83, 185
relativism 1, 6–7, 23, 31, 33, 65, 77, 102, 118, 120, 124–25, 179
relativist model 76
relativist theory 77
religious beliefs and objectivity 31
repetition 15, 55, 64, 85–86, 102, 126, 167–68, 170, 173, 179
"Return of Grand Theory" (Skinner) 10–11
Richter scale 33
Robespierre, Maximilien 37
Rorty, Richard 26–27, 43
Rosenzweig, Roy 110
rule-based game 56

Sahlins, Marshall 27
sati *see* wife-burning, ban on ritual practice
Schafer, R. Murray 53, 177
Schaffer, Simon 32
science 1, 8, 11, 29, 32–33, 35, 75, 77, 80, 93, 103, 106, 126, 132, 177, 185–86; abstract pursuit of 73; British 32; changes in study of 5–6, 31; discovery 25, 31–32, 77, 180; end of theory 70; error 33; forces and humanists 10; prominence gained by 79; revolution 58; socially constructed 2; theories 32, 70; theory-making 9
search word 84
Searle, John 23, 43
seeing 59
seismologists 33
self-referentiality 81, 95
sensations 63
senses 9, 16, 53–54, 58, 60, 79, 96, 177, 179; digital impact on 63–64; emphasis on 64; and language 52; proponents 63
"sensory turn" 58
sequential grid 82
shades 59–61, 150
Shapin, Steven 32
Sheppard, Eric 122
Shopkeeper's Millennium, A (Johnson) 149–50
shopping database 119
signpost 97
silence 53–55
"Silent Night" (*Stille Nacht*) 53
singularity 82
Skloot, Rebecca 34
smells 44, 58, 62, 121, 188
Smith, Adam 36
social behaviors and light 61
social change and academic theories 30–31
social classes 38
social construction 2, 7–8, 49, 124–25, 182, 184
social context 31
social discourse, debates about 55
socially constructed event/tradition 2
social problems, solution to 107
social relationship 15
social sciences 75
social standing, of scientists and scientific theories 32
social theories 81
society 17, 27, 29–30, 47, 73, 75, 82, 114, 121, 131, 182, 186, 188
socio-historical reality, totality of 76–77
sociological precision 73–74
software 13, 90, 100, 115–16, 134, 165, 169–70

Sokal, Alan 33
Sokal hoax 33, 34, 39
sounds 5, 9, 53–56, 58–59, 62–64, 121, 125, 138, 177, 185
space 4, 11, 13–14, 28, 54, 80, 101, 110–15, 118–19, 121, 123–28, 130, 132, 134–35, 141, 153, 182
spacelessness 117–18, 126, 131, 166, 182–83
spatial architectural project 114
spatial dimension 116
spatial experience 123–25
spatial oddities 13
spatial problems of digital age 124–25
Speaking Bolshevik (expression) 51, 52, 59, 91
Spiegel, Gabrielle 45–46, 65
spirituality 9
Spivak, Gayatri Chakravorty 3, 28–29, 34, 83
Sportsman's Sketches (Turgenev) 54
standardization 38
statistical collections 71
stillness 43
street lighting 61
Structure of Scientific Revolutions, The (Kuhn) 31
subaltern women 29
subjectivity 6, 15, 23, 31, 48, 75
"subjugated knowledge" 36
surveillance device 35
synoptic tables 104

tastes 58, 60, 62–63, 102
technological pessimism of postmodernists 20
technological revolution 3
technology as mediator 112–13
temporal linguistic change 65
textual analysis 8
textual environments 61
theoretical abstraction 74, 76, 82–83
theory in digital world 83
theory in humanities 77; abstract component to 81; apotheosis of 72; definition of 72, 81; end of 71; Foucault's version of 81; negating existence of *hors texte* 81; polemical approach to 70; positivism 70; theoretical 70; to undermine facts 70; vociferous positions 70
theory in sciences *see* science
theory wars 9–10
thinking powers of humans 62

Thorp, Jer 155, 164–65
thoughts: controlling 47; and language 62–63
time 8, 14–15, 24–25, 33–34, 36, 39, 43, 46, 50–51, 55, 58, 60, 74, 76, 80, 82, 84, 94–96, 99, 101, 103, 115, 117–19, 122–23, 130, 149–50, 152, 157, 168, 172, 185, 188; component 14, 136, 138; digital age impact on 131–32; digitization of 130–31; duration 15, 131–34, 136, 140, 183; duration concept 132, 133; dynamic representation of 134–35; expression in language 51; grid 130, 141–42, 183; muse fascinated by 131; passage in consciousness 132; slicing up, into segments 130; synchronization and segmentation 132; tags 16, 135–36, 142
timekeeping 142, 178
Time Regained (Proust) 60
time tags of digital grid 16
timing system 15
totalitarian states 7
traces 12, 19, 46, 72, 80, 82, 89, 94–95, 99, 102, 125, 138, 164–65, 168
traditional forgeries 19
transcendental thought structure 63
Transfiguration of the Commonplace (Danto) 49–50
transgender rights, push for 37–38
translation 62, 65, 82, 85, 120, 148, 153, 156, 158, 178, 181; problematic 82; technology revolutionizing 82
translation, algorithms 96–99; algorithmic phrase 96–97, 99; impact on linguistic usage 99; indeterminacy of 97; machine translator 98; paradoxes 100; pattern recognition 98–100; success of 99; unidirectional 97; *see also* Google Translate
tropes 101
Tufte, Edward 17–18, 148–50, 155, 157
Turgenev, Ivan 54
Twilight of the Idols (Nietzsche) 79

universal human nature 25
universalism, of Enlightenment 31
universal rationality, of Enlightenment 27–28
Unterwegs zur Sprache (Heidegger) 58

urban environment, spatial conception within 124
urban museums 61
urban worldview 61

value-neutral approach 74
values 6, 24, 28–29, 39, 70, 78, 84, 94, 103–4, 106, 134, 157, 172
Vermeer, Johannes, forged paintings of 19, 161, 169–170
videos 64, 147, 152, 155, 161
Vienna Circle 43, 53
vision 2, 9, 16, 35–36, 58–59, 73, 79, 123, 133, 152–53, 162, 179, 187
visual education 148
visual experience 112, 158
visual footage 61
visuality, models of 59
visual landscape, changes in 17
visually processed information 62
visual materials 18, 147–49, 157, 158
visual media 16–17
visual pessimism 17
visual recognition 104
visual representations 17–18, 148–49, 153, 156, 158, 165, 173
visual revolution 17, 62, 147, 185
visuals 32, 147, 149–51, 153–54, 157–58, 185; discursive definitions of 17; extent of 62; inherent complexities 18; preference for 17; as representations of knowledge 18; *see also* data visuals
visual stimulus 62, 148, 152, 169, 185
visual tendencies 61

Warmth of Other Suns, The (Wilkerson) 36
Wayback Machine 13, 111, 116–19, 127, 182
Ways of Seeing (Berger) 59
web data 2
websites 13–14, 18, 112–13, 116–18, 172, 182
well-ordered facts 11
Western society, protest movements in 30–31
Western standard 23
Western value system 1
Where the Animals Go (Cheshire and Uberti) 107
White, Hayden 7, 38–39, 48
white oppression of African Americans 36
wife-burning, ban on ritual practice 28
Wilkerson, Isabel 36
Wittgenstein, Ludwig 7, 8–9, 43–44, 46, 48, 52–58, 53, 61, 63, 73, 96, 98, 147, 157, 177
women 2, 26, 28–29, 37–38, 123
wonder, Greek concept of 80
words 76, 78
World Wide Web 3

Yahoo! Personals 171

zoning practices 150
zoological databases 110
zoom/zooming function 19, 125, 156, 162, 166

Ingram Content Group UK Ltd.
Milton Keynes UK
UKHW022111040523
421267UK00006B/37